THE LORD IS SAVIOR:
FAITH IN NATIONAL CRISIS

INTERNATIONAL THEOLOGICAL COMMENTARY

Fredrick Carlson Holmgren and George A. F. Knight
General Editors

Volumes now available

Genesis 1–11: From Eden to Babel
  by Donald E. Gowan

Joshua: Inheriting the Land
  by E. John Hamlin

Ezra and Nehemiah: Israel Alive Again
  by Fredrick Carlson Holmgren

Song of Songs and Jonah: Revelation of God
  by George A. F. Knight
  and Friedemann W. Golka

Isaiah 1–39: The Lord Is Savior: Faith in National Crisis
  by S. H. Widyapranawa

Isaiah 40–55: Servant Theology
  by George A. F. Knight

Isaiah 56–66: The New Israel
  by George A. F. Knight

Jeremiah 1–25: To Pluck Up, To Tear Down
  by Walter Brueggemann

Daniel: Signs and Wonders
  by Robert A. Anderson

Hosea: Grace Abounding
  by H. D. Beeby

Joel and Malachi: A Promise of Hope, A Call to Obedience
  by Graham S. Ogden
  and Richard R. Deutsch

Amos and Lamentations: God's People in Crisis
  by Robert Martin-Achard
  and S. Paul Re'emi

Micah: Justice and Loyalty
  by Juan I. Alfaro

Nahum, Obadiah, and Esther: Israel among the Nations
  by Richard J. Coggins
  and S. Paul Re'emi

Habakkuk and Zephaniah: Wrath and Mercy
  by Mária Eszenyei Széles

Haggai and Zechariah: Rebuilding with Hope
  by Carroll Stuhlmueller, C.P.

Forthcoming in 1990

Judges: At Risk in the Promised Land
  by E. John Hamlin

1 Kings: Nations under God
  by Gene Rice

THE LORD IS SAVIOR: FAITH IN NATIONAL CRISIS

A Commentary on the Book of

Isaiah 1–39

S. H. WIDYAPRANAWA

WM. B. EERDMANS PUBLISHING CO., GRAND RAPIDS

THE HANDSEL PRESS, LTD, EDINBURGH

First published 1990 by Wm. B. Eerdmans Publishing Company,
255 Jefferson Ave. S.E., Grand Rapids, Mich. 49503
and
The Handsel Press Limited
139 Leith Walk, Edinburgh EH6 8NS

Printed in the United States of America

Library of Congress Cataloging-in-Publication Data

Widyapranawa, S. H., 1926–
The Lord is Savior: faith in national crisis: a commentary on the
Book of Isaiah 1–39 / S. H. Widyapranawa.
p.   cm.   —(International theological commentary)
Includes bibliographical references.
ISBN 0-8028-0338-5
1. Bible. O.T. Isaiah I-XXXIX—Commentaries.   I. Title.   II. Series.
BS1515.3.W53   1990
224′.107—dc20   89-28137
                                    CIP

Handsel ISBN   1 871828 02 3

CONTENTS

CONTENTS

ABBREVIATIONS

BH	*Biblia Hebraica;* ed. R. Kittel and P. Kahle
DSS	The Dead Sea Scrolls
IB	*The Interpreter's Bible*
JB	The Jerusalem Bible
KJV	King James (or Authorized) Version
LXX	The Septuagint
MT	Masoretic Text
NEB	The New English Bible
NIV	New International Version
Peake	*Peake's Commentary on the Bible*
RSV	Revised Standard Version
Torch	*Torch Bible Commentaries*

EDITORS' PREFACE

The Old Testament alive in the Church: this is the goal of the *International Theological Commentary*. Arising out of changing, unsettled times, this Scripture speaks with an authentic voice to our own troubled world. It witnesses to God's ongoing purpose and to his caring presence in the universe without ignoring those experiences of life that cause one to question his existence and love. This commentary series is written by front-rank scholars who treasure the life of faith.

Addressed to ministers and Christian educators, the *International Theological Commentary* moves beyond the usual critical-historical approach to the Bible and offers a *theological* interpretation of the Hebrew text. Thus, engaging larger textual units of the biblical writings, the authors of these volumes assist the reader in the appreciation of the theology underlying the text as well as its place in the thought of the Hebrew Scriptures. But more, since the Bible is the book of the believing community, its text has acquired ever more meaning through an ongoing interpretation. This growth of interpretation may be found both within the Bible itself and in the continuing scholarship of the Church.

Contributors to the *International Theological Commentary* are Christians—persons who affirm the witness of the New Testament concerning Jesus Christ. For Christians, the Bible is *one* scripture containing the Old and New Testaments. For this reason, a commentary on the Old Testament may not ignore the second part of the canon, namely, the New Testament.

Since its beginning, the Church has recognized a special relationship between the two Testaments. But the precise character of this bond has been difficult to define. Thousands of books and articles have discussed the issue. The diversity of views represented in these publications makes us aware that the Church is not of one mind in expressing the "how" of this relationship. The authors of this commentary share a developing consensus that any serious explanation of the Old Testament's relationship to the New will uphold the integrity of the Old Testament. Even though Christianity is rooted in the soil of the Hebrew Scriptures, the biblical interpreter must take care lest he or she "christianize" these Scriptures.

Authors writing in this commentary will, no doubt, hold varied views concerning *how* the Old Testament relates to the New. No attempt has been made to dictate one viewpoint in this matter. With the whole Church, we are convinced that the relationship between the two Testaments is real and substantial. But we recognize also the diversity of opinions among Christian scholars when they attempt to articulate fully the nature of this relationship.

In addition to the Christian Church, there exists another people for whom the Old Testament is important, namely, the Jewish community. Both Jews and Christians claim the Hebrew Bible as Scripture. Jews believe that the basic teachings of this Scripture point toward, and are developed by, the Talmud, which assumed its present form about A.D. 500. On the other hand, Christians hold that the Old Testament finds its fulfillment in the New Testament. The Hebrew Bible, therefore, belongs to both the Church and the Synagogue.

Recent studies have demonstrated how profoundly early Christianity reflects a Jewish character. This fact is not surprising because the Christian movement arose out of the context of first-century Judaism. Further, Jesus himself was Jewish, as were the first Christians. It is to be expected, therefore, that Jewish and Christian interpretations of the Hebrew Bible will reveal similarities *and* disparities. Such is the case. The authors of the *International Theological Commentary* will refer to the various Jewish traditions that they consider important for an appreciation of the Old Testament text. Such references will enrich our understanding of certain biblical passages and, as an extra gift, offer us insight into the relationship of Judaism to early Christianity.

An important second aspect of the present series is its *international* character. In the past, Western church leaders were considered to be *the* leaders of the Church—at least by those living in the West! The theology and biblical exegesis done by these scholars dominated the thinking of the Church. Most commentaries were produced in the Western world and reflected the lifestyle, needs, and thoughts of its civilization. But the Christian Church is a worldwide community. People who belong to this universal Church reflect differing thoughts, needs, and lifestyles.

Today the fastest growing churches in the world are to be found, not in the West, but in Africa, Indonesia, South America, Korea, Taiwan, and elsewhere. By the end of this century, Christians in these areas will outnumber those who live in the West. In our age, especially, a commentary on the Bible must transcend the parochialism of Western civilization and be sensitive to issues that are the special problems of persons who live outside of the "Christian" West, issues such as race relations, personal survival and fulfillment, liberation, revolution, famine, tyranny, disease, war, the poor, religion and state. Inspired of God, the authors of the Old Testament knew what life is like on the edge of existence. They addressed themselves to everyday people who often faced more than everyday problems. Refusing to limit God to the "spiritual," they portrayed him as one who heard and knew the cries of people in pain (see Exod. 3:7-8). The contributors to the *International Theological Commentary* are persons who prize the writings of these biblical authors as a word of life to our world today. They read the Hebrew Scriptures in the twin contexts of ancient Israel and our modern day.

The scholars selected as contributors underscore the international aspect of the series. Representing very different geographical, ideological, and ecclesiastical backgrounds, they come from more than seventeen countries. Besides scholars from such traditional countries as England, Scotland, France, Italy, Switzerland, Canada, New Zealand, Australia, South Africa, and the United States, contributors from the following places are included: Israel, Indonesia, India, Thailand, Singapore, Taiwan, and countries of Eastern Europe. Such diversity makes for richness of thought. Christian scholars living in Buddhist, Muslim, or Socialist lands may be able to offer the World Church insights into the biblical message—insights to which the scholarship of the West could be blind.

The proclamation of the biblical message is the focal concern of the *International Theological Commentary*. Generally speaking, the authors of these commentaries value the historical-critical studies of past scholars, but they are convinced that these studies by themselves are not enough. The Bible is more than an object of critical study; it is the revelation of God. In the written Word, God has disclosed himself and his will to humankind. Our authors see themselves as servants of the Word which, when rightly received, brings *shalom* to both the individual and the community.

—George A. F. Knight
—Fredrick Carlson Holmgren

AUTHOR'S PREFACE

To write a theological commentary on the first thirty-nine chapters of the book of Isaiah in a brief and clear way has not been an easy task for the author. This is due to the composite structure of the book, the historical and chronological problems involved, the various types of prophecies in the Isaianic collection, the specific theological outlook of Isaiah, and last but not least the limited scope and space available to deal with the problems exhaustively. Yet it has been a real pleasure to work on this part of the book of Isaiah. In the course of painstaking study of the texts, the author became increasingly impressed by the eminence of the living Word, by the amazing work of salvation of the LORD, and by the beauty of the Isaianic literature. From page to page the book reveals the unfathomable wealth of God's wisdom, the tremendous knowledge of God, and the living truths of faiths which are still valid and relevant in our lives today.

The author does not aim at presenting a purely academical study of Isaiah 1-39. Rather, he seeks to share a theological interpretation which could serve as study material for pastors, preachers, theological students, and the Christian community in general.

The author would like to express his deep gratitude to his former professor and the co-editor of this commentary series, the Very Rev. Prof. George A. F. Knight, for his guidance and encouragements. The author's thanks go also to his colleague at Duta Wacana Theological College Yogyakarta (Indonesia), Prof. Tjaard Hommes, and to Mrs. Anne Hommes for their kind attention in reading parts of the manuscript and providing some linguistic advice, as well as to other colleagues who showed kind interest in this writing project. Last but not least, the author is grateful to his wife, Trees, for her patience and understanding, without which it would have been impossible to have this work completed in due time. Finally, the author humbly presents this book to the esteemed readers with the hope that it might be of use and value for a deeper understanding of the theology of Isaiah.

Yogyakarta   S. H. Widyapranawa
March 1985

INTRODUCTION

The activities of the prophet Isaiah took place mainly in the second half of the 8th cent. B.C., covering a period of at least forty years. It was a time of crucial importance for both the northern kingdom (Israel) and the southern kingdom (Judah). It was a time of crisis and troubles, a time of changes and challenges in political as well as in cultural life. It was a time of severe tensions where human faith was put to a severe test. In such a situation both kingdoms were called to adopt a firm stand without compromise.

Precisely at this time of national and international crisis the prophet Isaiah was called to proclaim the word of judgment, hope, and salvation. He made the prophetic message truly relevant to the actual circumstances and problems being faced by all layers of society: the authorities, the spiritual leaders, the common people (esp. the poor), the oppressed farmers, and civilians.

PART I

THE KINGDOM OF THE NATIONS AND THE KINGDOM OF GOD

Isaiah 1:1–12:6

PROPHECIES CONCERNING JUDAH AND ZION

1:1–5:30

THE TITLE OF THE BOOK (1:1)

The importance of this opening verse has been recognized as suggestive not only for the date and origin of the prophecies, but also for the character and reliability of the material to follow. In fact, ch. 1 as a whole forms an introduction to the entire book. It is a kind of summary of the situation that Isaiah must deal with over his active years, so that succeeding chapters actually stem from here (cf. 2:1).

Two keywords may be considered of special importance, "vision" and "he saw." They stem from the Hebrew root *hazah,* usually meaning "see" in the sense of having insight. Seeing is not just a physical, ocular function. Rather it is a spiritual, inward function which can see things more sharply and convincingly. Seeing precedes speaking. For the ancient Eastern peoples there was no contradiction between hearing and seeing. They were both aspects of the one totality. To the prophet the words of God had become vivid, concrete, close, and real. The actual and living relationship between God and his people, of which the prophet was to be the mouthpiece, is expressed straightaway after the opening verse.

THE LORD'S COMPLAINT ABOUT HIS UNFAITHFUL PEOPLE (1:2-9)

This passage presents us with a vivid picture of the actual relationship that obtained between Israel and their God within the bonds of the Covenant that God had bestowed upon his people at Sinai (Exod. 19:5-6). In this covenant Israel is called to be "a kingdom of priests and a holy nation." We are in the atmosphere of a law

3

court, only—unlike the ordering of a human court—Yahweh
speaks as simultaneously both Prosecutor and Judge.

1:2-3   The heavens and the earth are called upon to witness to
the apostasy of Israel. These must necessarily pay attention simply
because the LORD had spoken, and he had created them to be the
instruments of his purposes. The word "apostasy" is like that for
rebellion *(pasha**ʿ)*, the verbal root of which is generally employed
for the breaking of the covenant agreement.

The father-son relationship is the basis of God's dealing with
Israel. Israel has been reared and brought up by God's loving-kindness. The people of Israel were God's "sons," not by nature but by
grace (Exod. 4:22; Deut. 14:1, 2; 32:6b, 18; Hos. 11:1-4). The
individual responsibility of each man, woman, and child is emphasized by the employment of the plural "sons," or "children."

The comparison between this rebellious people on the one hand
and the ox and the ass on the other produces a striking anticlimax.
Isaiah uses the verb *yada**ʿ*, "to know," to describe the relationship
of God and people. This verb (see its use at Gen. 4:1) indicates a
relationship of fellowship and affection, while the following verb,
bin, usually "to understand," may be rendered "to emphathize
with." Instead of allowing the nations to see the wonder of their
relationship to the Almighty, the Creator of the heavens and the
earth, Israel valued that relationship less than did the ox and the ass
their dependence upon their owners. "They have rebelled *(pasha**ʿ)*
against me," says God, and he uses the verb employed for breaking the Mosaic covenant.

1:4   Isaiah continues his indictment with the harsh-sounding
phrase, *hoi goi hote,* "Ah, sinful nation," which must have struck his
hearers with devastating effect. (1) Normally in the OT the people
of God are known as God's *ʿam.* But it seems that now they have
turned themselves into a mere gentile people, a *goi.* (2) The call *hoi*
was used by the town crier as he announced a death in the city. (3)
The OT employs many words for sin and sinners. The word used
here, *hote,* accepts the fact of humanity's free will to choose between good and evil. Thus Isaiah was declaring that Israel had
deliberately aimed at the wrong target. Israel, the prophet implied,
was no longer "sons of God" (v. 2); they were now "sons of evil-

4

doers" (v. 4), "sons who deal corruptly." This is a very strong word in the Hebrew, used of those who are deliberately destructive in their behavior.

Then Isaiah says, "They have despised the Holy One of Israel." This is Isaiah's own chosen title for the LORD. The structure of this title is striking. As holy, God is utterly other than Israel in his majesty and glory, whereas Israel is that human people which is described here in such piercing language. Yet this title of God is in reality one word in the original: The-Holy-One-of Israel. What a juxtaposition of grace and disgrace!

1:5-6   Two contrasting aspects stand out: the stubbornness of Israel and God's continuing commitment to Israel that never gives up. The LORD'S cry of despair at v. 2 reveals his constant concern for Israel. Now, however, is added the harrowing statement, "The more you are smitten, the more rebellious you have become." Since Israel does not "know" God, obviously the people do not appreciate that his chastisement is for their peace, and that his judgment upon Israel is made in order to win the people back to himself. Israel had been called to be "a holy nation" (Exod. 19:6); to individuals within the covenant people God had constantly declared "You shall be holy, even as I am holy." Now however, so far from being "holy," Israel appeared as a sickly, whipped slave, standing naked in the slave market, all covered with bruises, sores, and bleeding wounds. Nor was there anyone present to bind up Israel's wounds. On the other hand where Israel was really standing was before the court that comprised the heavens and the earth (Isa. 1:2)!

1:7-9   God's judgment is directed also toward the land, which had now become desolate at the hands of aliens. Even Zion, the city of God, is to be besieged and to become lonely and humbled, like a booth in a vineyard or a lodge in a cucumber field. What a terrible contrast with the former splendor and glory of the city of God.

Only God's grace holds Israel back from suffering the fate of Sodom and Gomorrah, for he had left Israel "a few survivors." To call the rulers of his people "rulers of Sodom" (v. 10) is to accuse them of having plumbed the depths of degradation to which any city can descend, even today. What we have here incidentally is that, as God himself declares, hypocrisy is possibly the greatest of all sins. Yet by use of the word "survivors" Isaiah is declaring that there is still hope of salvation. Verse 9 thus serves as a link with the following passage, which proclaims forgiveness and then later on makes a call to repentance.

GOD'S CALL TO TRUE RELIGION (1:10-20)

The hypocrisy of "Sodom" is shown in Israel's case to be a self-centered glorification as the people find gratification in their performance of "religion," while caring nothing for their Father's love (v. 2). It must have sounded shocking when the prophet denounced their meticulous keeping of all the sacrifices and feasts. "My soul hates your feasts," says God. "I have had enough. I have no delight in the blood of bulls." "Abomination" *(to'ebah)* is a very strong term (v. 13). Obviously, however, it was not sacrifice as such that God had rejected, but rather its misuse. It was the sinful and wrong motivations behind all these practices that was abhorrent to the LORD.

Those who have never taken the Bible seriously cannot recognize why the biblical faith is not to be identified with "religion." There are secularists who denounce all religions equally as enemies of the progress of mankind. They may not have noticed, however, that here God himself denounces the "religious" practices of Israel. We proceed therefore to discover what God looks for in place of "religion."

Clearly regular temple attendance, when it is only a form, is virtually meaningless and is rejected by the LORD (cf. Jer. 7:11; Mark 11:15-17). To appear before the LORD must be understood in terms of fearing him and of full obedience to his commands. Nowhere in the Bible is there any stronger and more terrible criticism of the cult than what is written in Isa. 1:13-15. The holy God cannot be deceived, nor can he be bribed by vain offerings or by multitudes of feasts and assemblies. All these had indeed been tolerated by God in the past; but now he has become weary under this heavy "burden." So the time might well come when God would no longer hear Israel's prayers because of their "bloody hands" (Ps. 66:18; Isa. 1:15, 21) and will reject all religious ostentation. So we are shown the unique nature of the God of Isaiah, in comparison

6

with all the gods of the nations; for in the Torah there is a continuing emphasis on the ethical, on what we today call "religion." And so, just because of that, there is still hope. The command, "Cease to do evil, learn to do good," which accompanies his indictment of Israel's pretentiousness, expresses God's loving concern for his people.

How true and necessary this serious warning against such religious practices is, even within the Christian Church. God and the world rightly claim faithful Christian practices, paired with humility, cross-bearing, forbearance, and understanding towards persons of non-Christian religions. Haughtiness and evidence of superiority by Christians can only harm the Christian witness and the maintenance of peaceful relations with other religions. Such can only create tensions and mutual suspicions, especially within the pluralistic societies of the Third World. Conversely, Christian people can often learn much from the faithful Muslim, the pious Buddhist, the sincere Hindu, and the meditative Javanese mystic.

1:16-17   In a positive way then the people of Israel are summoned to wash and cleanse themselves. Clearly the physical washing required by the ritual laws is to be regarded as a symbol of the moral cleansing that God requires. Thus, Israel is to "wash their hands." But they are to cleanse themselves by ethical deeds as well. This was not an attempt to seek through repentance or good deeds the salvation of their individual souls. What God desires is that his people, as a whole, offer justice and show a compassionate concern for the poor and the weak. In truly prophetic exaggerated terms he declares that Israel's sins are scarlet, bloody, in that they are the actions of totally self-centered, greedy, and compassionless people—as might be said of the Church throughout the centuries. Simple folk suffer at their hands (v. 15). This appeal for justice, compassion, and love towards the poor and the weak (together with Amos 5:24; Mic. 6:6-8; Ps. 85:8-13, etc.) becomes one of the most important emphases the Church can make for the world in its needs for today. Such Christian motivations, commitment, and initiatives will surely bring blessings in the various dialogues now proceeding between North and South, East and West, between industrialized, capitalistic, and developing nations. If these same people were to discover that the heart of "religion" is love, then they would find that they could live in harmony—not only with their fellow human beings, but also with the natural world. If they were to refuse to let God forgive and renew them, then they would learn that he who takes the sword will perish by the sword.

1:18-20 To "reason together" implies the background of the court of appeal mentioned at Isa. 1:2. God appeals to Israel with the hope that they are still reasonable beings who can discuss matters without prejudice. The very nature of forgiveness is of grace alone. It is *sola gratia,* radical but also conditional—radical because it is complete and perfect, conditional because it requires an honest response from Israel. There are only two alternatives for Israel: either to be willing and obey, resulting in new life and in eating the good of the land—and this includes the promise of the renewal of the land (v. 7); or to refuse and rebel, resulting in total destruction by the sword of the Assyrians. This is indeed the essence of the gospel message (cf. John 3:16, 18). Between life and death there is no compromise!

THE TERRIBLE JUDGMENT RESTING ON JERUSALEM
(1:21-31)

This is a lament on Jerusalem's fate, with reference to its former splendor and to its present wretchedness, presented by Isaiah in the form of a funeral elegy.

Jerusalem stands here for the covenant people. That city is described as the once "faithful" city (v. 21), full of justice (i.e., moved by a compassionate concern for all its inhabitants, rich and poor alike), the faithful wife who loyally followed her divine Husband in the Wilderness (Jer. 2:2; Hos. 2:18-20). But now, in Hezekiah's day, Jerusalem's wretchedness is described as that of a harlot, the "scarlet" woman (Isa. 1:18), unfaithful to her husband and seeking fulfillment in other liaisons. Isaiah then continues with strong terms to show what Jerusalem has become—dross, wine mixed with water, rebels and thieves, corrupted by bribes, and hardened to the cry for compassion. That is to say injustice had corrupted the whole of Jerusalem's social life. This is what happens to a people that ceases to be obedient to a God of love. In all we are given a most realistic picture. In contrast, it is fascinating to learn how the LORD insists upon defending the cause of the poor and the weak, the fatherless and the widow. This is one of the most important emphases of the OT, and it has many implications for modern social ethics. It is not a person's private sins that God loathes, but his or her lack of love. The solidarity of Yahweh with the poor and the weak makes the biblical message so very much alive in today's world.

1:24-26 The LORD now solemnly announces his purifying wrath and judgment on Israel. In v. 24, which begins this divine speech, it is clear that God's ultimate goal is the rehabilitation of Jerusalem so as to become again "the city of righteousness, the faithful city" (v. 26). This act of purification can be brought about when one separates the dross from the pure metal, as has been known since earliest times. It requires the application of intense heat to the impure metal. Later in this book (e.g., 33:14) we learn that the heat required to smelt away the dross is the intense heat of God's creative love. The three characterizations of the LORD in the opening speech depict God as Leader and King of Israel, as the Almighty in heaven and earth, and as the holy God of Israel who does not tolerate any uncleanness.

Clearly the rehabilitation of Jerusalem is not within the capability of mankind. It can result only from an act of God, and that through a process of purification which will necessarily entail suffering. In the meantime, however, Israel is to "cease to do evil, learn to do good; seek justice, correct oppression" (1:16-17). In other words, Israel is to *shub*, "turn around," "return," and so "repent."

1:27-28 Thus it is only here, for the first time, that Isaiah mentions the redemption of Zion. Let us note that this does not mean here Judah-Jerusalem, for "Zion" is not limited in meaning to the geographical city known as Jerusalem. Zion is that city's theological name, and so it encompasses both the city and its inhabitants as the people of God. But at what price is this redemption to take place? By *mishpat* ("justice") and by *tsedeq* ("righteousness"). The LORD passes judgment, but with righteousness. After Zion has endured the judgment with repentance and regret, then Zion will be redeemed from all uncleanness, so that the initial covenant relationship will be restored.

9

Justice and righteousness are the two pillars on which the restoration will rest. This is also true of the national development of the developing countries, which cannot rely merely upon well designed programs and huge capital investments. A program is "just" only if it is based on the justice of God who loves mankind; it is only "right" if it serves the well-being of the whole nation in all aspects of its life, its harmony of life in relation to God, to society, and to surrounding Nature.

But the reverse is also true. Those who persevere in their sins, ignoring the LORD, will be consumed by his judgment. The message of redemption and salvation is never complete without this converse. The Word of the LORD is like a two-edged sword, both condemning and saving at once. This message pervades the whole Bible.

THE MISLEADING NATURE OF THE CANAANITE FERTILITY CULT (1:29-31)

This is actually the background to Israel's sin of rebellion. Gardens were favorite places for such "worship" (65:4; 66:17a; cf. Deut. 12:2; 1 Kgs. 14:23; 2 Kgs. 16:4; 17:10; Jer. 2:20; 3:6, 13). The cult seems to have been a continuing threat for Israel (Deut. 16:21-22). "An oak whose leaf withers" describes a deciduous tree that appeared to die when its leaves dropped. To provide an example to all other plants and particularly to food crops, the Canaanite people anxiously sought to ensure that it would flourish again. But first the divinities of fertility, Baal and Ashtoreth, now down below the ground in the "dead" season, had to be induced to copulate themselves. The Canaanites sought to bring this about by what we today call "imitative magic." They themselves gathered in these gardens to "worship" the gods by copulating together in order to encourage Baal and Ashtoreth to do likewise.

It is clear from this chapter that what the LORD utterly rejects is the sinful practice of any cult, syncretistic or otherwise, since such practice will necessarily be bound up with social injustice. The LORD demands that his people be personally responsible to him, in faithfulness and in true worship, and thus involved in the struggle for social justice and righteousness. His basic demand therefore is for repentance (cf. Matt. 25:41 and frequently in post-biblical Jewish literature).

10

ZION AS CENTER OF THE KINGDOM OF PEACE (2:1-5)

Before entering into detailed interpretation it might be helpful to consider Isa. 2:1–4:6 as a unity. This lengthy passage describes (1) the situation of Jerusalem at the time of the prophet, and (2) the future of Jerusalem in an eschatological perspective. Both descriptions reveal a sharp contrast, both terrifying and consoling. Those parts which give an eschatological perspective to the redeemed Zion (Jerusalem) probably originated about the end of the 8th cent. B.C. or even from a later period, such as the 6th century. To this section and period then belongs 2:1-5.

Since this oracle is to be found also at Mic. 1–3, it may be a "floating" poem known already to both Isaiah and Micah. It was thus quoted by each of them with deep conviction about its reality. Or perhaps the final editor of the book of Isaiah included it because it fit well with the prophet's view.

Zion as the seat of the temple is described as the highest of all mountains. According to the ancient mythologies of the Near East, high mountains were considered to be sacred because they were the dwelling place of the gods "in the midst of the stones of fire" (Ezek. 28:14; cf. Ps. 48:1-2). Since Zion is the highest mountain in the world, all nations will go up it to worship the Lord, the God of Jacob, "that he may teach us his ways and that we may walk in his paths" (Isa. 2:3). In other words, Zion will attract all those everywhere who seek to obey the law of the one true God. It was quite common in those mythologies to regard the dwelling place of the god as the center of the universe, and so this place became the royal seat of the king, since he was the representative of the god. Such is the case, for example, with the royal names attributed to a Javanese king, such as he who upholds the earth or "he who is the nail of the universe."

This then is the background of the prophet's proclamation, and accordingly must not be applied literally to any centralized church government or authority in the world. The unity of the Church and of all believers is centered on the risen Lord who is no longer earthbound.

The passage offers a fascinating picture of what eschatological peace in Zion will entail. Certain aspects of that picture are to be found in several parts of the OT. Thus Zion is the loftiest of all mountains (Ezek. 40:2; Zech. 14:10); the nations go up to Zion

11

to worship the LORD (Zech. 8:20-23; 14:16; Isa. 66:20); there the
nations seek the "instruction" of the LORD (Isa. 42:4); all weapons
of war are destroyed (Hos. 2:18), and so on. Thus altogether the
passage implies the "conversion" of the whole of creation.

The vision is followed by an urgent call to the "house of Jacob,"
meaning Judah in particular, to come to the LORD and to walk in
his ways. It is spoken in the first person, with the prophet urging
his own people to be first to respond to the universal invitation
given in the poem. Thereafter the other nations will "flow,"
"stream" to join Israel. Such a "flow" is the reverse of the scatter-
ing of the nations at Babylon in Gen. 11:8. On the other hand, not
all peoples will come to Zion, only *many*.

THE DAY OF THE LORD (2:6-22)

This is a long passage dealing with God's judgment upon a haughty
people. Its composition gives the impression of its being a unity
compiled from two originally independent passages, one bearing
the theme "the haughty shall be brought low," the other "how
terrible is the day of the LORD." The order of verses, however, is
rather confused; there are indications of repetition (Isa. 2:9, 11,
17) and of parallelism (vv. 10-11; 12-17; 18-19; 20-22). It might
be helpful to subdivide this passage into three parts, vv. 6-11, 12-
19, 20-22.

2:6-11   The poem in 2:2-4 seems to reveal that some people in
Israel, and our prophet in particular, were sure that God, like the
father of the Prodigal Son, would welcome his children home to
live in *shalom,* in fellowship and peace with him. Yet these same persons seem to be aware how far they have strayed from God's
covenant love. They had strayed so far indeed that God had necessarily to deal with them the hard way, by withdrawing himself from
them to the extent that Isaiah could declare in horror and despair,
"thou hast rejected thy people" (v. 6). This rejection is based on
three reasons: (1) the acceptance of foreign and heathen super-
stitious practices which induce them to forsake the LORD; (2) their
love for and reliance upon material wealth and power (e.g.,
chariots); (3) idolatry which makes them proud and haughty,

losing all sense of righteousness, justice, and humanity towards their fellows (cf. 1:17, 23).

Israel's trading with such as the Philistines, who ran at least one great slave market for the Near East, resulted in material wealth. In this way they strengthened their capability for war, purchasing from the Philistines chariots, horses, and all kinds of weapons (31:1). Actually, in Uzziah's day and in that of Jotham (i.e., in the middle of the 8th cent. B.C.) there was a period of peaceful co-existence in Palestine, and so commerce was flourishing and increasing. Yet it entailed various threats to the purity of Israel's religion. In 2 Chr. 26:16 it is said of Uzziah, "But when he was strong he grew proud, to his destruction." For with all this silver and gold and other treasures at their command, the people had been fashioning idols which they then worshipped. Isaiah calls them *elilim,* "wee gods," in contrast with the word *elohim,* the name of Israel's God. So he could call these gods "the work of their hands, what their own fingers have made" (Isa. 2:8; cf. 40:19-20; 41:7; 44:10-20). Isaiah recognized that human beings could thus regard themselves as gods, since they were able to create their own idols. So humankind is humbled, and individual people *(ish)* are brought low. Indeed, the latter will not be allowed to escape responsibility in the mass. In fact, the idol makers will be destroyed by their works, so that their fall will be total and they will never again be raised up.

The last line of 2:9, "forgive them not!" finds no parallel in vv. 11 and 17, and so it seems to be quite out of place at this point. Could it be merely a nasty remark by a "pious" scribe in later centuries?

There will be no taking refuge from the terror of the LORD, neither in caves nor in the dust, that is, in holes in the ground (v. 10). People shall reap whatever they have sown! In the glory of his majesty the LORD cannot be deceived by sinful mankind. The LORD is implacably against mankind's egotistical self-worship. And so v. 11 emphasizes what Isaiah has seen in his inaugural vision (6:3), that the glory of the LORD is all in all.

2:12-19 The LORD of hosts will be exalted above all who are lofty and haughty. This is one of the features of the *day* of the LORD. In a masterly way all this loftiness is contrasted with trees, mountains, towers, and ships of Tarshish. These all represent the pride of mankind.

The cedars of Lebanon and the oaks of Bashan are very highly regarded trees. For example, the cedar is "lofty and lifted up," and so is the symbol of natural strength and glory (Ezek. 31:3ff.). It was considered as the most important of all trees, having been planted by God himself (cf. Judg. 9:15). The oaks of Bashan were big, beautiful, strong, and shady trees. They were much admired and used as places for Baal worship and for cult gatherings (cf. Deut. 12:2; Ezek. 6:13; Isa. 1:29-31; 57:5). Their wood was used for the manufacture of images and idols. Therefore these trees too were to be humbled and deprived of their glory.

Even the high mountains with their impressive peaks, magnificent and proud and considered to be the dwelling-places of the gods, would be debased. Towers and fortified walls were symbols of human-crafted places of security and safety, but also symbols of pride in a nation's military strength. The "ships of Tarshish" were big strong "liners" that carried not only passengers but also the crafts and treasures from the gold and copper mines of the western Mediterranean. Thus these ships were symbols of material wealth and the luxury on which people had come to rely.

The passage ends with the recurring refrain which proclaims judgment on all pride and haughtiness, and the vanity of all idols that are the creation of human hands (2:10-11).

2:20-22   The vanity of idols and the panic that strikes people are described further. In an ironic way Israel's idols made of silver and gold, once precious objects of trust and worship, now prove to be totally worthless. No one has any longer a desire to keep them in his home, since it is now recognized that they are the source of all disasters and terror from the LORD. In this situation of panic the people cast their idols to the moles and bats that live in those desolate caves or holes in the ground where human beings have taken refuge (v. 19). So the fate of both the idols and their worshippers will be one and the same.

Verse 22 is lacking in the LXX. It seems to have been added as a word of consolation and for teaching purposes. People might be able to "create" gods, yet they are to be aware that their lives are fragile and completely dependent upon the true and living God.

But the verse also forms a link with what comes after. The OT always draws a sharp dividing line between God and his creature mankind. Yet also throughout the OT God never ceases to show his loving-kindness to mankind as he relentlessly pursues his purpose of seeking mankind's salvation and in offering to humans his own fullness of life (Amos 5:4-6).

In the growing process of modernization and industrialization in developing countries, many people have been tempted to put their trust mainly in human and material resources as well as in various "cults"; these ultimately lead to frustration. In this situation the gospel can be a real blessing for the people (cf. Matt. 6:19-34; Luke 12:13-21; 16:19-31). The widening gap between the rich and the poor, the privileged and the underprivileged, can only be bridged by love.

AGAINST THOSE LEADERS WHO LEAD PEOPLE ASTRAY (3:1-15)

This passage can be subdivided into two parts, vv. 1-12 and vv. 13-15.

Verses 1-12 speak of anarchical confusion in Jerusalem's society. This will take place when the LORD takes away from Jerusalem and Judah "stay and staff." These two words refer to the twin pillars on which society rests. They serve as symbols, summarized as follows: (1) "Water" and "bread" are primary vital needs for human life (v. 1). The famine of these might be caused by either war or drought. Thus the fertility cult proves to be in vain. The idea of famine includes natural disasters, for these also can create hunger and anguish. (2) Then come military leaders (cf. vv. 7b and 12), those who hold authority in the nation. Their authority, however, is based upon force that they impose upon the ordinary people. After the words "the captain of fifty" the Hebrew reads "with their faces lifted up," meaning that they were haughty, proud, and despotic. (3) Then there were prophets, diviners, and elders; these were supposed to be the people's spiritual leaders, charged with upholding righteousness and justice. However, they have failed badly in their calling (cf. Mic. 3:5, 11; 7:3; Amos 5:12; Jer. 6:13; Ezek. 22:12). They evidently did not have the fortitude to stand out against the stream of opinion, even when they knew that they were being disobedient to God. (4) There follow the counselor, the magician, and the "expert in charms." These are closely connected with the preceding group, who are wholly corrupt. These latter thus represent the world of superstition as well as those who ever seek for private gain.

There is as yet no satisfactory explanation as to why the king and the priest are not mentioned in the list of "stay and staff." It has been suggested that the judgment of the LORD is not against the office of king and priest as such, but rather against the practice of those who are dominated by the need to resort to soothsayers and depend on other forms of superstition.

3:4-7   When all "stay and staff" have been taken away, anarchy emerges. People look for a leader, but none is available. This chaotic situation finds its expression in government officials ("boys" and "babes," v. 4) who have no authority at all, but who are only louts and hoodlums. So there follows social disorder paired with oppression, slander, and all kinds of brutish behavior. Gone is any sense of decency or mutual appreciation of one's neighbors. "The youth will be insolent to the elder, and the base fellow to the honorable" (v. 5).

However, there are still some sincerely motivated people who are concerned to improve the situation. Yet no one feels able or has the courage to be a leader in this situation. As we say today, no one wants to get involved. In this spirit of defeatism Judah is quite unable to restore itself. Personal good intentions do not help much. It is clear that this calamitous situation has not happened by chance, but through a judgmental act of God. Relief can therefore come only from the LORD of hosts himself; he may use the surface efforts of young people who want to change the world through their idealism and despair of the present state of society. Yet it is Yahweh who is the LORD of history and of the nations as well! In such a situation what really matters is spiritual enlightenment and repentance (cf. Jonah 3–4). Obedience and devotion must have a high priority, and all social and political systems must be based on that truth. The upbuilding of a country and of a society—including the life of the world today, even with all the developmental programs that are now available—depends upon taking this passage seriously. Material welfare does not automatically mean well-being for mankind; on the contrary, in fact, it can be disastrous.

3:8-9   The basic cause of the fall of Judah and Jerusalem is that they have defied the LORD in both words and deeds, and are yet quite without shame.

The word "partiality" in v. 9 could also be translated, on the basis of the Hebrew text, "the expression of their faces." Such is the KJV translation. It means that the people's faces express their deep-rooted sins; they are no longer sensitive towards their sin, and so they act it out shamelessly. The haughty and proud look on their faces gives evidence of this demoralized attitude. No wonder their sins are compared with those of Sodom and Gomorrah. Woe to them who have degenerated and fallen into such a state of sinfulness.

3:10-12   These verses offer a practical conclusion and provide a lesson similar to those found in the Wisdom Literature or in some of the Didactic Psalms such as Ps. 1. The theme is very familiar in this literature: a blessed reward for the righteous and woe to the wicked. Considering the line of thought in this passage, however, these two verses are rather out of context. Therefore it has been suggested that they were inserted in a later period.

Again, all this chaos and sodomic sinfulness are clearly related to the unqualified and corrupt leadership in the country, where "children" and "women" are ruling (cf. Isa. 3:4). This disarray is the deepest possible tragedy that can befall "my people," the covenant people of God himself. It is also the shocking new message of the 8th cent. prophets, a message despised by Israel and Judah. Self-satisfaction and self-pride in a traditional slumbering church can be a fatal danger and a tragedy.

3:13-15   So the LORD enters into judgment. He has occupied his judgment seat (1 Sam. 24:15; Isa. 41:1) to pass judgment on his people. The LORD is the righteous Judge of the nations, but of his own people as well. He will also judge the leaders of the people. Leadership and responsibility always go together.

According to the old tradition that Judah had inherited, the people were divided into tribes. These were represented by elders who are called here "princes" *(sarim)*. These princes include also the officials and the army generals. Together they are responsible for the welfare of the people; but actually they do the reverse:

- *They have devoured the vineyard,* the latter being a symbol of the people of Israel (cf. Isa. 5:7; Hos. 10:1; Jer. 12:10).
- They have stored in their own homes spoil taken from the poor.

In this way the elders and princes have misused their position and their authority by enriching themselves at the expense of the poor, who have been deprived of their rights.

The fate of the poor is described as like grapes in a winepress— squeezed, crushed, ground—even though they are called "my people" (Isa. 3:15), the holy covenant people, the elect of the LORD. It might be worth noticing that young leaders, whether men or women, should not be blamed if they reveal a corrupt leadership in a chaotic situation. It is the sinfulness and foolishness of their hearts that is to be blamed! Oppression of the poor and the underprivileged seems to be deeply rooted in human societies of all varieties, both ancient and modern.

AGAINST THE WANTON DAUGHTERS OF ZION (3:16–4:1)

This passage is closely connected with Isa. 2:7, 15-17, where Isaiah deals with the haughty and proud in Jerusalem who rely on their silver and gold, their towers, chariots, and horses. In this passage the prophet now turns to deal with the women, "daughters of Zion"—in particular that class in society which can afford to live a luxurious and frivolous life (cf. Amos 4:1-3). It seems that Isaiah also sees a close connection between Jerusalem's social evils (Isa. 3:13-15) and the women's behavior and lifestyle, whereby they induce their husbands in turn to act corruptly and unjustly.

The way these haughty daughters of Zion behave themselves is described vividly in v. 16. It reveals their low morality and lustful sexual desires. In consequence the LORD will "smite with a scab" (a pox) their beautifully attired heads, and "lay bare" (in what terrible circumstances?) "their *secret* (or 'private') parts." It is there that their scabs will be made public.

The last two verses of ch. 3 are marked by a significant shift in the description. It concerns the destruction of the city itself and the fall of "your mighty men," the husbands of the daughters of Jerusalem. The city gate can only lament and mourn. The "stay and staff" (v. 1) of the city have collapsed; the city is ravaged and debased, like a woman sitting on the ground, mourning, desolate, and helpless. Great will be the fall of Jerusalem and its inhabitants.

Yet the aftermath of the city's fall will be even worse for the women. Men become relatively scarce when there is war. The seven women mentioned in 4:1 are most likely widows who needed a security and protection. In ancient times the fate of widows was tragic; they were exposed to all kinds of maltreatment and became helpless victims of oppression. To be "called by the name" of a man does not necessarily mean to become his wife; adopted sisters or even slaves may be the reference here.

Nevertheless, at the moment there is still a chance of repentance and of fleeing from the terrible judgment of the LORD.

NEW HOPE FOR A PURIFIED ZION (4:2-6)

God's judgment is not given for the sake of destruction but for the sake of purification, rehabilitation, and renewal. Assuming that this prophecy dates from the end of the 8th cent. B.C., it is much in line with those of the prophet Amos, which also include eschatological features.

Who is meant by "the branch of the LORD"? The word "branch" occurs also at Jer. 23:5; 33:15; Zech. 3:8; 6:12. But the sudden appearance of any idea of Messiah is out of context here, as the real object of this oracle is the glorious situation of the land and of its people after the purification. So it is more likely that the reference is to the remnant of Israel, now redeemed and purified. It is described as a branch sprouting forth from a stump of a tree that has been cut down. This sapling or branch now grows beautifully and gloriously, showing that it is rooted in the grace of the LORD.

There will be new growth in nature, new fertility from the LORD, so that the land will bring forth "the fruit of the land" as the "pride and glory" of the survivors of Jerusalem. These survivors "will be called holy" and their names "recorded for life in Jerusalem." This conception of the "Book of Life," known since early times long before the Exile (cf. Exod. 32:32, 33; Ps. 69:28), is now related to the eschatological future (cf. Dan. 12:1; Rev. 20:12). The filth and bloodstains of Jerusalem referred to at Isa. 1:15-16 (where Israel was to "wash your*selves*") God will wash away "by a spirit of judgment and by a spirit of burning." The Hebrew word *ruah,* meaning "spirit," "breath," or "wind," is often associated with judgment (cf. Jer. 4:11, 12; 51:1; Isa. 30:28), but it is also at times related to renewal and to new life (Ps. 104:30). However, the term can involve both meanings at once. So God's judgment will result in total purification and sanctification through his Spirit.

As we have noted already, Isaiah is the prophet who makes continued emphasis upon the holiness of God. But now the "survivors of Israel" themselves will actually be called holy. That is to say, they will be holy even as God himself is holy! First they will have to wash themselves and make themselves clean (Isa. 1:16). Thereupon, by the grace and love of God these survivors will be "recorded for life"—so as to live even as lives the living God. Till now they have been "dead" in their rebelliousness against any sense of loyalty to the Covenant, and thus heading for the "death" that overtook Sodom and Gomorrah (1:10). So what God is promising here is no less than life from the dead, and this will be life in Jerusalem, the chosen abode of the people of God, that spot on earth where the fellowship of God is most truly to be found.

4:5-6 Moreover, Mt. Zion will experience what will be no less than a new creation. God will *bara'* (the word used for "create" at Gen. 1:1, that verb which has only God as its subject). In other words, God creates new "life" out of "death." The first creation of the people of God saw them possessing the glory of God as it hovered over the tabernacle in their wilderness wanderings. But God will now create a cloud by day and a flaming fire by night over the people as well, gathered as they will be in their "assemblies." So the people too will experience the presence of the living God. As the Deus Absconditus (the God who hides himself) he will be present in his hiddenness in the cloud, unseen by the human eye; as the passionate God of love he will be the shining of a flaming fire. The glory of God which Isaiah "saw" in 6:3 will reveal his love, for it will be a shade by day from the heat of God's own righteous wrath against the powers of evil, and a shelter from the storm and rain of the vicissitudes of human life upon this earth that is subject to earthquakes, storms, and diseases of body and soul.

Such an eschatological hope permeates the whole Bible. But the purging heat of the fires of God keep on "creating" the new people of God at all times. The word "eschatology" does not limit God's activity to some period beyond the life of this world. God's re-creating presence is always in our midst. For God is Immanuel (as we shall learn later from Isaiah), who is *with* us here and now. This means that such an eschatological hope as Isaiah expresses here is available at all times and in all places, since the eternal world is always present at all points in time and space. This is not the thinking of the Greek philosophers, to whom we of the modern world are so indebted for our awareness of the scientific spirit. We must therefore never read into the Bible that which is alien to it, namely the "Greek" conception of the separation of heaven and earth, the present and future, body and soul, the ideal and the actual, and so on. Rather, Isaiah gives us a view of God's workings that are in full accord with the truth about the Word that we find demonstrated in the first chapter of the Fourth Gospel.

THE SONG OF THE VINEYARD (5:1-7)

It would seem that Isaiah sings this song on the occasion of the autumn vintage festival, usually a time of joy and mirth (Lev. 23:34; Deut. 16:13-15). He begins first, however, by informing his hearers whose fertile vineyard it is they are standing on, that it belongs to a great friend of his and he is singing this song about it on this friend's behalf.

This vineyard was in a good position and was well cared for. It had a protecting wall around it. The owner had high hopes for it and great expectations that his work on it and his expertise in viticulture would produce grapes that would make good wine. Moreover he himself had "chosen" the stock he had planted in it. How disappointed Isaiah's friend must have been then when the vineyard yielded only "wild" grapes. Of course, the owner of the vineyard could not be blamed for this.

So the owner invites "the inhabitants of Jerusalem and men of Judah" to adjudicate in the situation. This call for judgment, however, is merely rhetorical. The owner knows exactly what he will have to do with his own vineyard. The hearers can only testify to and confirm the validity of his actions to follow.

Up to this point the peasants who had been entertained by this song must have listened open-mouthed to hear what the judgment was to be upon this particular vineyard. "And now I will tell you what I will do to my vineyard." They were all ears! "I will remove its hedge, and it shall be devoured; I will break down its wall, and it shall be trampled down." "All very just," the peasant audience would agree. The result is that this fine cultivated area would resort to bearing only briars and thorns. "Yes, that is what would surely happen," they would nod their heads. But Isaiah goes on: "I will also command the clouds that they rain no rain upon it." What an extraordinary thing for any vinedresser to say! And only then did the audience understand who Isaiah's "friend" must be. For it is only God who can withhold the rain, not mankind. Thus, like Nathan's parable to David which ends with the words "You are the man. . ." (2 Sam. 12:1-7), Isaiah brings home the judgment of God to his "chosen" vine, Israel (Amos 3:1, 2; Ps. 80:14-15; Hos. 10:1), to the "men of Judah" who are "his pleasant planting." By forsaking the LORD they had yielded only wild grapes.

The last two lines of Isa. 5:7, in the Hebrew, sound both harsh and sorrowful. "He looked for *mishpat* ('justice'), but behold, *mispah* ('bloodshed'; with a gutteral "h," not soundless as in English); for *tsedaqah* ('righteousness'), but behold, *tse'aqah* ('a cry')!" This is a brilliant and effective poem. The NT takes up its theme at Mark 12:1-9, while at John 15:1-8 Jesus is called the "true vine" who gives new life and abundant fruit to all the branches of the vine (cf. also Isa. 27:2ff.; Jer. 2:21; Ps. 80:8).

THE "WOE ORACLES" (5:8-24)

The length of these six woe oracles varies. The second (vv. 11-17) is the longest. It is interesting to note that the second and the sixth (vv. 7, 22-24) oracles both deal with drunkenness occasioned by imbibing strong liquor, a habit as persistent today as in ancient Israel. The general impression left us, however, is that these oracles have not been well edited.

22

5:8-10   *The first woe* is aimed at those who accumulate wealth and enrich themselves in a cruel and oppressive way. Pictured here are poor farmers forced to sell their lands because of their accumulated debts. By means of blackmail they have become poorer and poorer until the rich landowners have gained full possession of the poor farmers' lands (cf. 1 Kgs. 21; Mic. 2:1-2, 8-9). But the LORD, says Isaiah, has noticed what has happened and has "sworn in my hearing"— surely a fascinating comment on Isaiah's part. Their spacious houses, their acres of vineyards all become desolate (cf. Amos 3:15; Isa. 5:13).

Consequently the vineyard becomes desolate. Ten acres (an area that ten yoke of oxen can plow in a working day) of vines produce only one *bath* (equivalent to about 22.5 litres), and one *homer* of seed (equivalent to some 220 litres) produce only one tenth of that amount, or one *aphah* (equivalent to 22 litres). Such results of their hard work would prove devastating to any farmer.

The anger of the LORD is therefore connected with the misuse of the land, for the land is considered as Israel's holy inheritance from the LORD through their forefathers (Deut. 6:10). In the final analysis land is considered to be the possession of the LORD himself (cf. Ps. 24:1; Lev. 25:23). Therefore it should be distributed amongst the tribes in proportion to their needs (cf. Num. 33:53-54), and it is illegal to sell it (cf. Lev. 25:23-24). Oppression of the poor too is illegal (Lev. 25:35-43). These agricultural and social laws are clearly fundamental for securing social justice. So Israel will be "made to dwell alone," that is, without God and his law, in *his* land!

5:11-13   The second woe is directed towards those wealthy people (most likely the rich landowners) who enjoy themselves by holding parties, feasting, and getting drunk from early in the morning till late at night (cf. Isa. 22:12-14; 28:7-8; Amos 4:1-3). Once they are in such a state they cannot discern the acts of God nor recognize his control over events (cf. Amos 6:4-6; Dan. 5). Assyria, which will soon be used as God's instrument to express his judgment (Isa. 10:5-6), was even then emerging as a serious threat against Judah. The LORD would punish his people by letting the Assyrians take them into exile, where they would be deprived of all the privileges and blessings of an ordered life (cf. Hos. 4:6). The honored men (and the women too) as well as the multitude of ordinary folk would equally suffer from hunger. All this has been caused by the fact that there is no "knowledge" of the LORD, which means no fellowship with and true worship of the living God.

5:14-17   The total destruction of Jerusalem is described as if the city and its people were devoured by Sheol. Sheol is the netherworld where all deceased persons dwell in a ghostly state far below the ground (Isa. 38:18); there they are no longer able to have fellowship with God. Sheol is represented here as a colossal monster with its throat and mouth open "beyond measure," ready to devour Jerusalem and its inhabitants—feasts, pride, treasures, and all. So Judah will indeed be "bowed down"; those who noisily "exult in her" will enter the terrible silence of Sheol. This vital humiliation of the haughty and proud cannot be separated from what follows in 5:16, where Isaiah speaks of the exaltation of the holy God in justice and righteousness. This vindication of the kingdom of God is thus the total goal to be achieved.

The word "righteousness" (v. 16) needs examination. In Hebrew the word has two forms, one masculine *(tsedeq)* and one feminine *(tsedaqah)*. It is the feminine *tsedaqah* that occurs here. The verbal root of this term means something like "to be in the right," and so "to be in a right relationship" with God. The transitive form of the verb, the hiphil, thus means "to put in a right relationship"; it is used of God's action when through sheer grace he declares a sinner to be in a right relationship with himself. Out of love he creates a new situation. God does so by accepting the sinner as he is (and not because of anything that he does), forgiving him totally so that he is now virtually a new person in a new situation. This act of God is known as his act of *tsedeq.*

It is Isaiah who first draws a distinction between *tsedeq* and *tsedaqah*. He is followed later by the authors of both Deutero-Isaiah and Trito-Isaiah, and then by writers of the Psalms. (See discussion of this issue in George A. F. Knight's volumes on Isaiah 40–55 and 56–66 in the *International Theological Commentary* series.)

The theological distinction between the two terms for "righteousness" is clarified at 45:8, where both are used in picture form. There we see how the gracious "righteousness" of God *(tsedeq)* comes showering down from God, "putting people right with

24

himself" through grace. The result of God's action is the human response of *tsedaqah*. Just as the rain coming down from above puts the soil in a right state to let wheat and barley grow *up*, so does *tsedaqah* spring up out of the heart of mankind. They do not do this themselves: "I the LORD have *created* it," using the verb *bara'* that is used of the first creation in Gen. 1:1. So it is that, once God has "justified" (to use the NT translation of *tsedeq*) the sinner, God himself created in his heart a similar compassionate love for his fellow humans.

Returning to Isa. 5:16 we see then that it means: "The LORD of hosts is exalted *by creating justice on this earth;* and the Holy ('utterly other') God *displays his divinity by creating love in the hearts of men and women.*" What a depth of insight Isaiah gives us here!

Verse 17, which seems to be rather out of place, can be considered as a continuation of v. 13. It describes Jerusalem in its desolation as a city now good for only lambs, fatlings, and kids to roam, as they graze amongst its ruins.

5:18-19   The third woe is against those who are enslaved by sin. It would be helpful to see v. 18a and b in parallel. In the OT one way of regarding sin is to see it as a heavy burden pressing upon people's shoulders (Jer. 9:6). But strangely, in daily life people do not distance themselves from sin; rather they cling all the more to it. Humanity is like a slave of sin; they are like the ox, and sin is like the cart. So they must "draw sin as with cart ropes." Thus the "cart ropes" here has a meaning in parallel with "cords of falsehood" (Isa. 5:18a). Because human beings are slaves of sin and falsehood, their work can only be iniquity. But that is not the whole story.

It is interesting to note then that in the OT mankind is pictured as an active slave of sin and evil. They are fully responsible for the iniquity they do; they must then *want* to return to the LORD. On the one hand, they are incapable of freeing themselves from sin; on the other hand, the LORD is present with them in the Covenant to help them change. Thus they do not remain *victims* of sin and evil, the commonly held belief in many Eastern popular religions (e.g., in "the Javanese religion" and in Buddhism).

Verse 19 thus describes Israel's ironical attitude towards both sin and the LORD. People like to live in and enjoy sin, and in their foolishness they becomes ironical, even challenging God's plans. They say, "Let him make haste . . . that we may see it." (That is, "The LORD should not tarry to execute his plans and decisions!") Thus they despise the judgment of the LORD, because there is no knowledge of the LORD (cf. v. 13). This is not atheism in the modern sense; it is just the view that God is too remote to be interested in the life of mankind (cf. Jer. 5:12).

Human nature does not change. It is the same today as in OT times. Men and women still regard God not as a living Person but as an obscure abstraction. On the other hand, mankind's capacity and rational ability is taken for granted to be the finally decisive factor for the future and for the salvation of human life and of the universe (cf. Isa. 28:15; 29:14).

5:20 The fourth woe is directed at those who twist the truth. Such persons reverse God's revealed norms of good and evil. In consequence they reject the revelation God has made through Moses, in fact they even turn the Ten Commandments upside down. It was God who created both "light" and "darkness" (Gen. 1:1-5), not they. These two words always referred symbolically to good and evil, to salvation and destruction, to blessings and punishment. "Sweet" and "bitter" were terms employed to represent joy (happiness) and anguish (suffering). In all these matters these citizens had rejected the Word of the LORD. They actually considered it to be a burden, a hindrance, a nuisance.

5:21 The fifth woe is thus closely connected with the previous one. It concerns people who are completely self-sufficient, who depend on their own reason, their own deliberations, and their own native wisdom, meanwhile rejecting all divine claims. In doing so they consider themselves to be wiser than God, "wise in their own eyes," in not accepting that God had made a separation between light and darkness (Gen. 1:4). Their life had now become completely rationalized and secularized.

5:22-24 The sixth woe concerns two kinds of sin which are closely connected with one another and with mankind's rejection of revelation: first, the sin of drunkenness, and second, the sin of distorting justice and righteousness. Isaiah portrays such persons as "great guys" in their drinking habits, heroes at mixing their drinks to make them ever more potent (Isa. 5:11, 12). Drunkenness dulls and insensitizes the human mind against any demand for justice and righteousness, for drunkenness is an expression of the drinker's absorption in himself. Moreover, such drinking bouts absorb so much money that the drinkers may become susceptible to bribes and other such corrupt practices, even as are drug addicts in our day (cf. Amos 4). Those guilty of such egotistical practices were actually the judges, the leaders—even the priests and prophets (cf. Isa. 28:7).

Isa. 5:24 proclaims God's punishment for all this; it can be considered as a continuation of vv. 13, 14 which also commence with "therefore. . . ." God's punishment is terrible indeed: it is pictured as "stubble" devoured in a flame of fire or "dry grass" thrown into an oven.

This punishment will occur because of Israel's sin of rejecting the LORD of hosts and despising the word of the Holy One of Israel. Special notice should be made of the full connotation of the phrase, "the Holy One of Israel." Such is the LORD the people have to reckon with!

AN ARMY FROM AFAR (5:25-30)

This chapter has some difficulties with the order and location of some of its verses. It has often been suggested that this section should be related to 9:8–10:4 in that it does not seem to follow from 5:22-24; moreover, it carries the same refrain "For all this his anger is not turned away and his hand is stretched out still" (v. 25). This refrain occurs frequently in 9:8–10:4. The MT, however, adds this passage as a climax to the six oracles of woe against Judah.

5:25 The prophet reminds his people of the terrible earthquake that has newly happened (cf. Amos 1:1; Zech. 14:5). It was so terrible that for a long time afterwards people continued to remember it: "and the mountains quaked." Many people died, and their corpses were as refuse scattered "in the midst of the streets."

This closing refrain therefore points to the tremendous wrath of the LORD seen as his outstretched hand, yet also to God's forbearing grace, if only Judah would understand and repent.

5:26   To execute the dreadful blow of punishment the LORD will call "a nation afar off." The LORD is like a mighty general who commands his troops from afar, ordering them to assemble immediately. Banners are planted on a high mountain, marking the place where the army is to assemble. At his "whistle" they come speedily from a long way off.

Who is this nation? It is the mighty emerging kingdom of Assyria whose troops have already reached Syria and are even now becoming a serious threat to both Israel and Judah (cf. Isa. 7:17-19; 8:5-10).

5:27-28   How mighty and well-equipped these Assyrian troops are! Their physical and mental condition is excellent. They are very strong, well trained, and ever ready for battle. Their war equipment also is superb, namely their arrows, bows, horses, and chariots. They are coming like a "whirlwind," irresistible and overwhelming!

5:29   The Assyrians' mighty attacks are terrible, and they growl like roaring lions seizing their prey. There is no escape possible from their advance. Yet however mighty and glorious they may be, in fact they are merely tools in God's hand. They are merely what Isaiah calls elsewhere "the rod of my anger" (Isa. 10:5).

5:30   This verse is not clearly related to the preceding one. It is rather similar to 8:22. It may have been placed here because of its use of the verb "growl" found in 5:29. Yet both the picture and the subject are different. Here the subject is the LORD himself, in line with 8:11–9:1 (and not the plural "they" of the RSV), who will act through the Assyrians. The picture is even more terrible than that in 5:29. This will be a day of darkness and anguish for the whole land, because the LORD has hidden his face (which is "light") from the house of Jacob (cf. 8:17). This verse thus confirms the truth of the preceding passage, 5:26-29.

It is most interesting to note how frequently Isaiah describes the LORD'S superior power and glory over mighty kings and nations. He does so by employing them as his agents—such as the Assyrians, "the rod of my anger" (10:5)—to execute his judgments against his own people. The LORD indeed acts in history through the nations. Therefore the Church today must seek for theological significance in the historical events of our time. It must do so in the light of the universal lordship of Christ if it is to understand its calling to be "the Church in the midst" of national and international events. The Church dare not avoid the problems relating to God's interference in history, simply because it is called to be present in those very events as his agent of faith. The future of the younger churches in the Third World, humanly speaking, will be determined by their dynamic presence and involvement in an inclusive manner.

ISAIAH'S CALLING AND COMMISSION

6:1-13

Unlike the preceding chapters, this section of the book (along with Isa. 8:1-8, 11-18) contains an autobiographical record from the hand of the prophet himself. The importance of this chapter lies in the fact that the experience he underwent as recorded here made an impact upon Isaiah's whole theological position. In his vision he sees the glory and the holiness of God, surrounded by strange inhuman creatures. This experience produces such a deep impression on Isaiah's mind and soul that it always remains fresh and vivid in his memory. In consequence, as a prophet Isaiah is always conscious that he is living and working in the presence of the holy God, who is surrounded by his glory, splendor, and majesty, high and lifted up (cf. 2:10). It is most likely that this vision was seen in an atmosphere of worship at the temple.

Initially 6:1-8:18 was probably one long passage, one collection of prophetic material—the prophecies of Isaiah during his first period, from his calling on down to the Syro-Ephraimite War in 734-733 B.C.

6:1-2 The opening verse sheds some light on the historical background of when Isaiah was called to be a prophet. During the reign of Uzziah (783-742) Judah enjoyed a relatively stable government, and so a degree of peace and material welfare. After Uzziah's death in 736, the political and social situation changed rapidly; his death thus forms a turning point in the history of Judah, and roots Isaiah's call firmly into history. It was at that moment, then, that Isaiah was called, just a few years before the war broke out.

While attending a cultic ceremony and while watching the priests offering up the burnt offerings, the incense filling the temple with a cloudy veil of smoke, Isaiah felt himself to have been

30

placed in the holiest part of the temple. Here he was surrounded
by the glory and holiness of God who was sitting upon a throne
high and lifted up—not as the human king "down below." Isaiah
of course did not "see" God in the literal sense of the word. What
he saw were just aspects of the presence and nature of God in a
symbolic manner. For no one can see God and remain alive (Exod.
33:20-23). Consequently Isaiah has given us no description of the
exact form and appearance of Yahweh; what he did was to describe
the throne and the train (the skirts of the royal robe) that filled the
temple. The throne, high and lifted up, signifies that the glory of
the LORD fills both the heavens and the earth; it declares as well
that the LORD is King.

In later centuries the seraphim were regarded as fire-spirits and
the cherubim (not mentioned here) as air-spirits. Then they gradually became names for the chief angels. In Isaiah's day, however, a
seraph was an effigy of a foreign god, something like the Sphinx
that can be seen today in Egypt. In shape it was part human and
part animal; also it had six wings and so was unlike any bird that
we know. In Isaiah's day Judah was not an entirely independent
country. Just as small kingdoms could continue to exist provided
they paid regular tribute to the ruling power of the day, so Uzziah
had evidently compromised with the Assyrian king of kings.
Uzziah apparently had agreed, doubtless under duress, to set up in
the temple courts several of these seraphim; they were there to remind him just who was the real overlord of heaven and earth!
Though with his human eye Isaiah now saw (and of course had
often seen before) these ugly monstrosities, with his eye of devotion he perceived them to be "around" the throne (following the
LXX, rather than "above" it, as the MT and RSV). In other words,
Isaiah became aware that the LORD of hosts was LORD even over
the gods, and that the monstrous idols of humans actually served
the living God. What he recognized at that moment was that the
LORD could make even the wrath of mankind to praise him.

Awed by being in the presence of the Holy One, each seraph
covered its face with two of its wings, its "private parts" with
another two, and with the remaining two it flew.

6:3   The trishagion sung by the seraphim left a deep impression
on the mind of the prophet. The threefold "holy" indicates that the

holiness of the LORD is total and is the absolute essence of God. He is holy in both heaven and on earth, so that the hosts of the LORD comprise both the hosts of heavenly beings—perhaps even including the stars—and the army of the living God on earth (Exod. 12:41), God's covenant people. Holiness covers several areas of understanding. God is absolutely transcendent over all his creatures and the whole universe. He is without sin, so that he cannot tolerate sin in his creature mankind. Yet as Isaiah is about to discover, the holy God is also the savior of his people. Thus while his holiness on the one hand creates distance between him and mankind, on the other hand his holiness creates a renewing fellowship between God and mankind. Holiness and glory *(kabod)* are closely connected with each other. Glory is the external manifestation of the divine essence which is holiness. In his vision therefore Isaiah beholds the glory of Yahweh even as it was at the primal age of creation and as it shall be at the future eschatological climax (cf. Isa. 66:18).

6:4 Such is the dynamic force of God's holiness and glory that the foundation of the threshold of the temple shook at the divine voice (cf. Ps. 18:7-8; 97:2-5; Exod. 19:18). The smoke that fills the whole place keeps the divine hidden from the eye of mortals, like the cloud at other such manifestations of the divine presence. The earthly temple has been virtually transformed into the heavenly pavilion that is the dwelling place of God.

6:5 Suddenly Isaiah realizes his own uncleanness and that of his people in the presence of the divine holiness. Feeling himself one with his own people, he cannot see any trace of holiness in either himself or in them. Clearly, as we noted at 1:2-11, he has not exaggerated their uncleanness, for such is the real nature of mankind.

6:6-8 The symbolic act of purification is carried out by one of the seraphim. Evidently God is able to use human religions and people's religious ideas to convey his will to his people. When the "fiery" seraph touches Isaiah's mouth with the burning coal from off the altar, the very heart of God, we are given a potent image of the forgiveness of the God who is himself "fire" (33:14). Clearly its heat was too intense for even a seraph to touch; so he had to use tongs to transfer the burning coal to the lips of this sinful human being. The seraph then accompanies the act of sacrifice with a "preaching of the word." The passive tense used in the two verbs "is taken away" and "is forgiven" is a device to reveal that it is God alone who can effect this total forgiveness. Isaiah's lips, through which there issued the thoughts of his heart, had now been "cauterized," by which means his "iniquity" or "guilt" had been taken away and his sin "covered over" or "expiated." It seems that the whole of Isaiah's being—his body as well as his "soul"— had to experience the heat of God's wrath. There was nothing that Isaiah himself could or did do to be thus renewed. All that was asked of him was acceptance and obedience.

Now that his uncleanness has been removed, Isaiah is to be permitted to partake in God's service and worship. In consequence he feels ever more eager to proclaim God's message to his own people without any fear. Without this cleansing of the heart and ears, people's hearing and understanding are "heavy," "fat," and "shut" (v. 10) towards the word of God.

The prophetic calling was not conveyed to Isaiah in the form of a demand, but was expressed as an offer and a challenge. It required a personal response and a willingness to obey. His was a straightforward answer given without any preceding bargaining, questioning, or argument. Rather, the renewed Isaiah's answer revealed his wholehearted willingness to dedicate himself fully to the prophetic task.

6:9-13 The task set before Isaiah is a terrible one, and one seemingly impossible to carry out. As evidence that even thoughtful believers cannot at times grasp the fiery nature of the all-consuming love of God, we note what happens when this chapter is selected as "the OT lesson." Usually the reader reads no farther than v. 8. And v. 8 ends on an introverted note: "Here am *I! Send me.*" So the reader thinks: "It is as if the heart of Israel will surely change if I but preach the word to them." It is only too easy for a prophet then or now to make the assumption that he is called of God to a grand messianic task.

Since mankind is by nature sinful (Gen. 6:5-7)—including even "covenantal" mankind, the people of Israel with whom God had entered into a special relationship—the preaching of the word may actually "make the heart of this people fat," instead of converting them and bringing them back home to God. Mankind's inborn egotism and natural self-satisfaction, such as Isaiah has described in the previous chapter, makes them rebel against a demand such as Isaiah is called upon to pronounce. Deuteronomy 6:4-5 sums up the essence of what Isaiah has to proclaim: You *shall* (by necessity) love the LORD your God, totally. What Isa. 1–5 had described of Israel's behavior revealed a perverse refusal to receive God's one, central, basic demand. And now Isaiah was to see the situation worsen still further. The more he preached, he was told, the more Israel would bring upon themselves the judgment of God. This would take the form of the Assyrian invasion with its attendant "total war" *(shemamah),* when cities would lie waste without inhabitants, houses without people, and the LORD (not merely the Assyrians) would remove the population *(ha-adam)* into exile.

What can most offend our natural egotism are God's words to Isaiah: "Lest they see with their eyes . . . and turn and be healed" (6:10). In fact some scholars have sought to wriggle out of the plain meaning of the word "lest" and render it "in order that" or such like. But here Isaiah is given to see two realities. First, as the NT puts it, "And this is the judgment, that the light has come into the world, and men loved darkness rather than light, because their deeds were evil. For every one who does evil hates the light" (John 3:19-20; cf. 9:39). Second, a superficial, humanly inspired repentance—a decision to live a moral life—is far from what God demands of mankind. A person cannot save himself by turning over a new leaf. His salvation depends utterly upon God. For only the burning, consuming love of God can reach down into the depths of our egotistical human heart. In consequence the "old person" has to be totally destroyed and become desolation *(shemamah,* Isa. 6:11) before God can bring new life out of the ruins of the old. The radical wickedness of mankind can be dealt with only by the radical love of the living God.

Some commentators believe that this difficult sermon (vv. 9-13) is not contemporary with Isaiah's call. They do so on the ground that only a century later such prophets as Jeremiah, Joel, and Zephaniah took the view that humanity was totally depraved. Yet, in view of Isaiah's general condemnation of the sinful state of all mankind (e.g., 3:6ff.) there seems no reason why his conviction

34

about this should not follow naturally from his experience of the holiness of God recorded in 6:1-8.

We should note here that the view of the prophets on the sinful nature of mankind is similar to, but also dissimilar from, that of Paul in the NT. The OT generally makes no emphasis upon, nor does it even refer to, the fall of mankind in Gen. 3. Paul deals with sin as a cosmic power in its relation to mankind, thus depending more upon Gen. 6:1-4 than upon v. 5. Isaiah speaks of sin as rebellion against the Covenant, that is, as what people *do* in their relationship with God.

The absolute nature of the judgment of God rests upon those who use power and religion for their own purposes, while sincere, God-loving folk are oppressed by the greedy and the violent. However, what is implied is that since mankind is one the simple poor must suffer along with the wicked in this unified world.

We see a forest fire sweeping through a stand of trees, yet leaving an area of a tenth of the forest untouched by the flames. But then the wind changes, and the flames sweep round and devour all of the remaining stand of trees. All that is then left of the forest— those great sturdy trees, terebinths and oaks (2:13)—is their stumps, as when those trees have been felled by an axe.

We should note carefully that (1) all of this terrible sermon which Isaiah is to preach has come from the mouth of God himself; and (2) Jesus quotes it at Mark 4:12 and in the related Synoptic Gospels, thereby showing his agreement with its tenor.

But the sermon is not finished yet. There is a final line: "The holy seed is its stump." Whether or not this line was original or added later (for it is not found in the LXX) is of little account. For it is in full accord with Isaiah's main theme that God's forgiveness and renewal and even life itself comes out of death and desolation. The real remnant are not just the sincere God-fearers we have newly mentioned. The "holy seed" are those, both good and evil, who have emerged from the fire by grace alone.

Just as the root out of dry ground pictured by Deutero-Isaiah at Isa. 53:2 was a fresh shoot miraculously emerging from the underground root of the "dead" tree (cf. 11:1), so here the sermon ends with a theological declaration expressed in parabolic language. The loving purpose and creative plan of God to renew mankind through Israel will not be thwarted even by Israel's hardness of heart and consequent judgment. We saw at 4:3-4 that the remnant, the "survivors of Israel," "will be called holy . . . when the LORD shall have . . . cleansed the bloodstains of Jerusalem . . . by a spirit of burning." So the stump here, left from that forest fire, would actually be the holy seed of a forgiven and renewed covenant people whom God would continue to use in days to come. "Unless a grain of wheat (a seed) falls into the earth and dies, it remains alone; but if it dies, it bears much fruit" (John 12:24). And to produce this end God employs the human lips of an Isaiah who must proclaim a message that is even beyond the grasp of his own human understanding.

THE BRITTLE KINGDOMS OF
THE NATIONS
AND THE SUBSTANTIAL
KINGDOM OF GOD

7:1–12:6

This important section of the first book of Isaiah dates from the first part of Isaiah's prophetic activities, during the reign of Ahaz in the period of the Syro-Ephraimite War (734-733 B.C.).

During this period of political crisis and turbulence among the nations we observe one strong and mighty nation after the other emerging and disappearing in shame. But behind all this turbulence the prophet points to the reality of the kingdom of God which is eternal and solid, and to the reality of him whose name is Immanuel. A remnant of Israel will survive, as Isaiah had learned at his call, and will be redeemed not for its own sake but for the glory of the LORD. The theme of this section reveals a contrast between the turbulent and brittle nature of the secular kingdoms of Isaiah's day and the solidity of the kingdom of God. And so it reveals a contrast between the ambitions of the earthly kingdoms and God's plan that is working out in history.

The section falls into five subdivisions:

I	7:1–9:7	Confrontation with secular politics; the sign of Immanuel
II	9:8–10:4	God's anger against Ephraim
III	10:5-34	Proud Assyria will be humbled; comfort will be given to Zion
IV	11:1-16	The "messianic" kingdom which is solid and peaceful
V	12:1-6	A song of thanksgiving to the LORD

CONFRONTATION WITH SECULAR POLITICS;
THE SIGN OF IMMANUEL (7:1–9:7)

The Sign of Shear-Jashub (7:1-9)

7:1-2   According to 2 Kgs. 16 and 2 Chr. 28, Ahaz had forsaken God: "He did not do what was right in the eyes of the LORD." (2 Chr. 28:1). He worshipped Baal, sacrificed his own son in the valley of Hinnom, introduced foreign religious ideas from Damascus, and desecrated the temple. Therefore the LORD delivered him into the hands of Pekah king of Israel and Rezin king of Damascus, when many of his men were killed in battle (2 Chr. 28:5, 6). After those defeats Pekah and Rezin invited him to join a military treaty against Assyria. After his refusal Pekah and Rezin came to besiege Jerusalem, but they were unsuccessful and did not conquer the city. Their failure was possibly due to the Assyrian army coming to offer help to Ahaz. But Isaiah pointed to another cause which Ahaz could not see.

"When the house of David was told . . ." (Isa. 7:2) is an expression peculiar to Isaiah. By it the prophet sought to show that the Assyrian threat was in fact directed against the kingdom and throne of David (v. 6). The house of David was in former days famous for its courage, but now the heart of Ahaz and of his people "shook as the trees of the forest shake before the wind." What a dramatic contrast! This was happening, declared Isaiah when he deliberately waylaid the king, because the people had lost their confidence in the LORD and were depending on their own resources and strength instead.

7:3-4   Isaiah is sent to meet Ahaz. It is interesting to note the location of the place of meeting. Most likely "the conduit of the upper pool" took its source from the well of Gihon, which lay at the southeastern corner of Jerusalem just outside the city wall. This place was of vital importance because it contained pools on which the water supply of Jerusalem depended. Probably Ahaz was there supervising the defense works because of the Assyrian or Ephraimite threats. Here Isaiah met with Ahaz in an attempt to strengthen the king's faith. This was exactly the very meeting place where Rabshakeh, the envoy of the Assyrian king, sought to persuade Hezekiah to surrender some thirty years later (cf. 36:2ff.).

The name of Isaiah's son, Shear-jashub (meaning "a remnant shall return"), expresses the central message of Isaiah's prophecies. We have seen how Isaiah learned its meaning at his call. The name implies both punishment and salvation, threat and comfort, the LORD'S anger and the LORD'S grace (see 10:20-23). Throughout the years lying ahead, even after Isaiah's death, his son would continue to be a living witness to and proof of the validity of the divine promise. Ahaz himself has therefore to make his choice between these two alternatives, not knowing however that they were one and the same.

The word of God that Isaiah was to pass on to Ahaz admonished him to be faithful and to trust in God. He had to remain quiet and wait for the saving acts of the LORD. Such trust would give him the necessary strength and help (cf. also 30:15-17). Ahaz need not be frightened, because these two enemies were actually merely "two smoldering stumps of firebrands." That is, they were already almost burnt out and were now producing only smoke; there was no danger of fire left in them anymore.

The annotation "the son of Remaliah" for Pekah is an allusion to his being the descendant of the illegitimate king of Ephraim (2 Kgs. 15:25).

7:5-6   Syria and Ephraim had planned to dethrone Ahaz and set up someone else of their own choice, namely, a son of Tabeel. The name Tabeel is rather obscure; it means "the bad one," but the LXX reads it as meaning "the LORD is good" (cf. Ezra 4:7). It is uncertain whether he is a Syrian or an Israelite. According to the results of recent excavations there apparently was a place called Beth Tab'el, located in the northern area of Trans-Jordan.

It has now become clear that "the house of David" and the throne of David are in danger.

7:7-9   But the God of Israel is the LORD both of history and of the nations. The wicked plans of the two kingdoms will be frustrated. According to human and political calculations Judah would never be able to withstand the allied forces of Syria and Ephraim. But the word of God that Isaiah was to pass on to the king was this: "It shall not come to pass."

Isaiah is here looking back through the history of his people. He recognizes how God, again and again, has fought *for* his people.

Moses had shown him to be the "warrior God" (Exod. 15; Deut. 32:35-36, 39-42; Pss. 105, 124, 136). Consequently, Isaiah points out, it would be a sign of faithlessness for Israel to join in a pact with Assyria and have Assyria come to their rescue. God's people are to be utterly content to leave their fate in the hands of their warrior God. In this, then, Isaiah is not in agreement with the "holy war" concept found in Deut. 20.

It would be helpful if we read Isa. 7:8, 9 in the following order: vv. 8a, 9a, 8b, 9b. Israel's enemies were: Rezin (Syria-Damascus) and Remaliah (Ephraim-Samaria); it was God's purpose that the enemies' rule should be limited to their own domains, apart from the fact that their power was even now actually crumbling.

Instead of reading the number "sixty-five years," a figure that makes no sense here, we should probably read: "In six, even five years time Ephraim . . ." In v. 9 Isaiah makes a basic statement of faith more trenchant than any prophet who has preceded him. The word "to believe" derives from the root *aman,* meaning "confirm" or "(make) sure and steadfast." By saying "Amen" we affirm our total agreement with the words of a prayer. As seen in both the ancient Song of Moses (Deut. 32:31) and the Song of David (2 Sam. 22:32), among others, the faithfulness of Israel's God had long been depicted under the figure of Rock. Thus to believe, while it included an act of human decision such as placing one's feet upon a rock, became credible and meaningful only because God, in the first place, was himself *aman,* totally reliable. So what Isaiah is saying to his king is that national security is attainable only when one is securely reliant upon the faithfulness of God.

Today we categorize Isaiah as the prophet of faith par excellence. Isaiah 36–39 shows us that faith in action, as Isaiah inspires Hezekiah to live it out in a historical situation. But Ahaz and his officials were still hesitant, because by now they had devised their own plans, expecting help from Assyria.

The Sign of Immanuel (7:10-17)

7:10-12   Ahaz was permitted to ask for a sign: "Let it be deep as Sheol or high as heaven," meaning that God was giving him immensely wide choice. In this offer we see the wonderful love and forbearance of God to convince one offspring of David. It is "the LORD your God," who still remembers Ahaz.

Ahaz's refusal is a refusal of the way of faith. But still he uses a scriptural pretense, saying, "I will not put the LORD to the test," meaning that there was no need for a test since he firmly believed in God. In fact, the issue is not the test at all because the LORD himself had graciously offered one. Rather, it is a matter of unbelief in Ahaz's heart, a matter of the hardening of heart. This is, in fact, a most decisive moment for the fate of Judah, but Ahaz now rejects the LORD deliberately (cf. 6:9-10).

7:13   Isaiah still addresses Ahaz as "house of David"; this means Ahaz is not a mere individual but is a member of the royal house of David, with which the LORD had made an everlasting covenant. Isaiah reproaches him for his past attitude, which was "to weary men," to exhaust their patience. Ahaz had always despised the word of God as it had been proclaimed by the prophets. But now it is even worse, adds Isaiah: "that you weary *my* God also," and so exhaust his patience too. The prophet puts emphasis on *"my* God," the God whom Ahaz opposes. We note that Isaiah does not say *"your* God," because Ahaz had now forsaken his God! In the eyes of the prophet the king is moving farther and farther away from God, the God of Israel, the God of the Covenant.

7:14-16   "The LORD himself will give you a sign," says Isaiah. A sign *(ot)* is a physical happening, a material event in the world of physical phenomena that in itself represents an eschatological reality, or the incursion of eternity into time. For example, the *ot* that God promised Moses at Exod. 3:12 turned out to be a fact of history. "You shall serve God upon this mountain," God had said; and Israel did in fact do just that after escaping from Pharaoh. Thus the sign that Ahaz was to be given would be a concrete event in history which he himself would see and learn from.

The Hebrew word *'almah* stands for an ordinary young woman, as at Gen. 24:43; Exod. 2:8; Ps. 68:26. The Hebrew word for a virgin is usually *bethulah*. The quotation of Isa. 7:14 in Matt. 1:23 is probably based on the LXX, which uses the word *parthenos* to translate Heb. *'almah,* and it is this word which means "virgin" in Greek. Now since a sign in the biblical sense should be concrete

41

and actual, it is not clear who this young woman is. She would have to be someone familiar to both Ahaz and Isaiah. Note the definite article "*ha*" with the noun, to emphasize *the, that,* young woman. Is she someone belonging to the family of Ahaz? This finds support in the LXX; but the MT says that the woman herself (not Ahaz!) would give the child its name.

The word *Immanuel* means "God is with us." God's *ot* to Moses had been accompanied by the words "I will be with you" (Exod. 3:12). That had been Israel's glorious awareness ever since; God is faithful (cf. Isa. 7:9) and does not go back on his promises. Consequently the name could be interpreted as a symbol of God's delivering power which makes itself apparent even in human weakness. There is even a slight possibility that "Immanuel" is meant as an ironical symbol of the hypocritical attitude of Ahaz and Judah, which is now being criticized so strongly by the prophet. Anyway, the name Immanuel, meaning "God is with us" is Isaiah's central message to a people living in disloyalty to God.

The significance of a "sign" was something "wonderful," that is, belonging to eternity (cf. Gen. 17:7-14; 18:1-15). "Is anything too *hard* for the LORD"? asks the LORD himself in the guise of a visitor when he promised the aged Sarah a baby (Gen. 18:14). It is the word *pele'* that occurs there; this word in its various forms is confined in its usage to the strange, understandable acts of the living God when he invades the human consciousness by acting in person in the human scene. No wonder Matt. 1:23 regards this promise made at Isa. 7:14 as a pointer to the birth of Christ, for Matthew emphasizes that the wonder, the *pele',* does not depend on the nature of the birth but upon the astonishing revelation that the living God was "with" that human baby.

Nevertheless here we are dealing with the imminent birth of a baby boy, whose birth and "growing up" would underline the reality that God's presence in Israel's history would be proved when Syria and Ephraim were made desolate, followed by the terrible domination of Assyria. "Curds and honey" are delicate foods such as were enjoyed by the people's forefathers during the wilderness wanderings (cf. Gen. 18:8; Judg. 5:25). This means that the child would be brought up according to the ancient traditions of true Yahwism. Therefore this child would open a new way and initiate a new people based on "Immanuel," choosing the good and refusing evil. The LORD would preserve the people in a wonderful way!

The significance of this sign can be summarized as follows:

1. A fulfillment and confirmation of the LORD'S promises in Isa. 7:7. Shortly afterwards Assyria defeated the two kingdoms.

2. A judgment against Ahaz and his followers. Eventually Assyria would appear to be an instrument in God's hand expressing God's wrath.

3. A sign that provides new life and comfort for "a shoot from the stump of Jesse" (11:1). It is therefore related to the sign of Shear-jashub (7:3).

4. A contradiction between Ahaz, who relied on his own political strategy and power, and the LORD, who devised a new nation based on faith and obedience to God.

5. A viewpoint of the whole history of salvation. It provides an important messianic perspective.

7:17   The closing words, "the king of Assyria," are probably an additional clarification for the reader (cf. v. 20; 8:7). Assyria, on whom Ahaz had initially put his trust, will be the new oppressor of Judah. Increasingly heavy tributes would then have to be paid, especially during the reign of Hezekiah, Ahaz's successor.

The Lord's Punishment on Judah (7:18-25)

This series of punishments consists of four parts: 7:18-19, 20, 21-22, 23-25. The first two deal with the invasion of enemies, while the last two deal with the situation of the land after the invasions.

7:18-19   Judah will be oppressed continually by its two great neighboring states, Assyria and Egypt. The LORD will only have to whistle, as a shepherd to his dog, and he will have all these foreign nations under his control. These nations are pictured as "flies" from Egypt and "bees" from Assyria. These terrible insects are at times found abundantly in Judah: in the forests, hills, plains, and rocks. The enemies will come, one surge after the other, in enormous great numbers, occupying the whole country—even the steep ravines, the clefts of the rocks, thornbushes, and all pastures (cf. 5:5-6). Judah will then be completely overrun.

7:20 The LORD will use Assyria as a hired "razor" to shave Judah. As such Assyria would serve God's purpose only temporarily, for Assyria was certainly not the "possession" of God; it can be employed only as a "hired" instrument! These mercenaries will arrive brandishing their swords, which will then act as razors that will shave off the hair on the people's heads. It will also shave their "private parts" (for which "feet" is a euphemism), and "will sweep away the beard also"—the ultimate ignominy one could suffer in those days (2 Sam. 10:4). But this is not an instance of the genocide of a whole people. God will act through the Assyrians merely to humble and warn Israel of their danger, always allowing them time to return to him in repentance.

7:21-22 These verses describe the poor and desolate situation of the land and of the people left upon it. A person's total possessions will then be at most one cow and two sheep. By the grace of the LORD, however, they are still kept alive. Due to the very small population they will still have abundant curds and milk, a pointer to the ancient traditional food in the wilderness. Such then will be the situation of the country, now almost void and greatly devastated.

7:23-25 There will not be enough people to cultivate the land. Even a valuable and well-kept vineyard, worth a thousand shekels of silver, will have become a wilderness full of briers and thorns, and so a mere hiding place for wild beasts. Only with bows and arrows will people dare to make their way to it. And their domestic animals will be limited to roaming the hills.

Chapter 8 is written partly in prose (vv. 1-4, 11-22) and partly in verse (vv. 5-10). The whole is interrelated and has as its historical background the outbreak of the Syro-Ephraimite War and the attack of the Assyrians against Jerusalem.

The Sign of Maher-shalal-hash-baz (8:1-4)

This sign is made with reference to the two enemies of Judah, Damascus and Samaria. It warns of the destruction of these enemies by the Assyrians (cf. 7:9, 16).

8:1 The prophetic message was to be written with "common characters," meaning clear and neatly written letters, so that everybody could read them easily. These strange-sounding Hebrew words cannot, of course, be rendered exactly in English. In the Hebrew they are onomatopoeic; that is, it is their sound rather than their meaning which is meant to hit home to the heedless passerby. We might render them, but only with less daunting English words, by "Plunder's hastening, booty's irrupting." The words "belonging to" should be kept in mind till two verses later; they tell us that this awful message is to be the name of the boy soon to be born.

8:2 This sign, possibly something like a billboard, was to be witnessed by two reliable persons, Uriah and Zechariah. As the sign was directed at Ahaz in particular, the witnesses would need to be persons known to and trusted by the king. In this connection Uriah may even be the priest mentioned in 2 Kgs. 16:10, 11, who at Ahaz's request built an altar in Jerusalem according to the pattern of a foreign altar at Damascus. The second witness is named Zechariah the son of Jeberechiah. He is most probably the one mentioned in 2 Kgs. 18:2; 2 Chr. 29:1, 13, where he is identified as the father-in-law of Ahaz.

So these two witnesses were people belonging to Ahaz's own circle. They have to attest the truth of Isaiah's prophecy, first before and then after the actual fulfilment occurs. Their attestation was all the more important because the time would come when Isaiah would for a period cease proclaiming the word of God.

8:3-4 Isaiah's wife is here called "the prophetess," possibly because in this connection she plays an active part in the proclamation of the word by bearing the child who is then called *Maher-shalal-hash-baz*. It now becomes clear that the mysterious words written on the tablet are meant to be the personal name of Isaiah's own son who will function as a sacred sign for both the people and for Ahaz.

In Isaiah's day people took a name seriously. Usually it bore a meaning obvious to others. This poor little boy was thus destined to be laughed at by the neighbors while still little, but to be regarded with awe as he grew older for being the bearer of a divine threat that had then come true in history. Yet before the son was born, there was first his mother. She had a unique place to fill in the divine plan. As a prophet, Isaiah *spoke* the word through lips cleansed by God (6:7-9). But the "prophetess," his partner, did more. She was the instrument that God now used whereby that word might become flesh. Isaiah's own name means "Yahweh is Savior (or 'Salvation')." Thus even as he collects an audience his name preaches for him. So too with Isaiah's family. As a family, even in the silence of God that was soon to come, they have become witnesses to his word to Israel.

This second sign, given a few years before the outbreak of the Syro-Ephraimite War, proclaims the fall of the two kingdoms as an act of the LORD, in accordance with his plan. Isaiah could see it all coming to pass, not only through "faith" but also through his political awareness. A baby may mumble "Mama," "Dada," perhaps by the end of his first year, so the kingdoms' demise was indeed imminent. This message once again proclaims the LORD as the LORD of history and of nations. It provides hope and comfort for the faithful in Israel although they must continue in a most miserable situation. On the other hand it proclaims God's terrible judgment upon those who plan evil against his covenant people.

The Assyrian Invasion and the Truth of Immanuel (8:5-10)

The Assyrian invasion will also affect Judah because "this people have refused the waters of Shiloah that flow gently and melt in fear before Rezin and the son of Remaliah" (v. 5).

The waters of Shiloah flow out from the spring at Gihon in the southeast wall of Jerusalem and flow gently and smoothly into the pool of Siloam. It is a small stream and at first sight looks to be insignificant in comparison with the mighty and magnificent river Euphrates.

Yet this water from the well of Gihon has an important theological significance. Solomon had been anointed there as king (1 Kgs. 1:33ff.). Refusing the gentle stream of Shiloah, theologically speaking, therefore meant refusing the promises of the LORD. To the dynasty of David the water of Shiloah as such is thus a symbol of the sure and steadfast kingdom of God and of the stability of the house of David amidst a turbulent world. Judah's attitude should be that of faithful tranquillity and trust in the LORD (cf. Isa.

30:15). Instead, Ahaz took refuge with Assyria, basing his action on his own political strategy. At John 9:7 the name Siloam has a symbolic and messianic meaning pointing to the mission of Jesus as the One who is sent. In connection with this gentle stream of Shiloah see also Lam. 3:26.

8:7-8a The Assyrian power is then described as the mighty river Euphrates, overflowing its banks and creating destructive flooding everywhere, inundating even the land of Judah, sweeping everything in its way, the water "reaching even to the neck"!

The gentle waters of Shiloah are as nothing compared with these roaring and sweeping waters of the mighty Euphrates! The kingdom of God is indeed like a tiny grain of mustard seed (Matt. 13:31-32; Mark 4:31-32; Luke 13:18-19).

8:8b-10 The problem we face here concerns the relationship between Isa. 8:8a and 8b. In v. 8b a new picture is suddenly made visible, that is, a picture of the "outspread wings" covering the whole land. Whose wings are they? Assyria, pictured as a colossal eagle? Or the LORD'S wings giving sure protection (cf. Ps. 17:8; 36:7; 57:1; 61:4; 63:7)?

R. B. Y. Scott *(IB)* and John Bright (Peake) tend to distinguish Isa. 8:8b from the preceding vv. 5-8a because it is thought to have a different background. Moreover vv. 8b-10 are closely related in thought to Ps. 46, which speaks of the sure protection of the LORD, using the refrain: "The LORD of hosts is with us; the God of Jacob is our refuge" (Ps. 46:7, 11).

Isaiah 8:8b-10 are probably part of a liturgical poem quoted here by Isaiah when Judah was suffering under the Assyrians. In this sense these verses are meant as a word of comfort and assurance about the ultimate victory of the kingdom of God (cf. 7:7). That is to say, for those who accept the sign of Immanuel (7:14) there is still hope for deliverance. The LORD will remember his people, and he will spread out his wings over them to provide them with safety and protection. Consequently, basing his message upon this Immanuel prophecy, Isaiah declares that all the efforts and counsels of the peoples (i.e., of Assyria and its subjected peoples) "will come to nought" (8:10). Human promises "will not stand." Thus here we learn of the ultimate victory, no matter how incredible and unrealistic such faith may sound to unbelieving ears! But the truth and the wonderful reality of that victory will be proven by the LORD of history, who is no less than Immanuel, the "God who is with us" (see RSV mg).

Let Him Be Your Fear and Your Dread! (8:11-15)

The attitude and message of Isaiah are in strong opposition to that of Ahaz and his wrongheaded people. Why and on what authority? The prophet bases his message upon his prophetic calling and upon the word of God he must proclaim—whether he himself likes it or not, whether the people will listen or not. "The LORD spoke thus to me with his strong hand upon me" (v. 11). The strong compelling authority of the LORD had been felt as a heavy prophetic burden on his shoulders (cf. Amos 7:14, 15; Jer. 20:9). The divine authority is all-conquering, so that he has the courage to proclaim the word without fear or favor as he opposes Ahaz and his policies and "the way of this people" (Isa. 7:12; 8:6). As such he has to persevere, to be alert and critical in his prophetic mission, that is, offer a prophetic interpretation of the ways of God both from his faith and from a measure of political wisdom.

8:12-13 The conspiracy of Pekah and Rezin, which aimed at an allied attack against Jerusalem, makes people tremble and their hearts shake as the trees in the forest (7:2). Those who are faithful, however, are called upon not to be dragged along in fear and trembling. Their conspiracy is not the real decisive danger for the fate of Jerusalem. The LORD of hosts is the real and the all-decisive factor in the situation. "Let him be your fear, and let him be your dread"! To him is due all glory and honor above all things!

8:14-15 The holiness of the LORD has a twofold power: to save and to destroy. For those who fear the LORD and honor his holiness, the LORD will be as a place of refuge or a "sanctuary." A sanctuary is a holy place *set apart* as a place of safe refuge (cf. 1 Kgs. 1:50-53; Ps. 27:5), for blessings, peace, and joy in the fellowship of the LORD (Ps. 65:4); it is the "place" yearned for by all who believe in him (Ps. 27:4; 43:4; 84:2).

But on the contrary, for those who are unfaithful the holiness of the LORD will have become a "rock of stumbling" or a "snare," causing them to stumble, fall, be caught, and brought into exile. For God is a jealous God (Heb. *el qanna'*; cf. Deut. 6:15).

Such is the basic message the prophet has to proclaim; it is intended not just to please his hearers, but to make them realize the reality they face. In many parts of the world today the full gospel message and the whole word of God are facing the danger of mutilation. In the church to which I belong in Indonesia, people like to hear pleasant and humorous sermons when they can feel happy and enjoy themselves, laughing at the many anecdotes and illustrative stories (many of them artificially out of context) proclaimed from the pulpit. I wonder whether there is still a place for a real message of the LORD'S holiness at all. The prophetic voice and proclamation in this matter is what the world really needs today.

A Land without Dawn (8:16-22)

8:16-18   The LORD hides his face from Judah. After Ahaz and his people clearly reject the word of God (cf. 7:10-12; 8:6a), the LORD declares that he will hide his face from Judah (v. 17) as an indication of his dismay and anger. For the time being he will cease to speak to Judah; yet he will continue to act to prove the truth of his Word.

Isaiah calls upon his disciples—and these would include his family—to "bind up" and "seal" the messages he has given to the king (cf. 29:11). Isaiah believed that his oracles had been given to him by God (cf. 7:3; 8:1, 11). Consequently they must be "alive" even as God himself is the living God. His words, now written on a scroll, could well be brought to light again in God's good time when they would speak validly and creatively in a wholly new situation (cf. 29:11). So it is that, 180 years later, Deutero-Isaiah seems to have believed that these oracles of Isaiah were indeed still alive and valid. He believed that through his lips they were being addressed to the Israel that was even then being purged in the "fires" of the Exile (cf. 42:18-25; 44:26; 48:3; 49:8. He uses at 50:4 the very word for "disciples" *[limmud]* that Isaiah had employed at 8:16).

However, Isaiah and his sons and daughters remain as signs and portents for Israel. They serve as living witnesses and prophecies which can never be silenced; on the contrary they function as "open letters" among the people (cf. 7:3; 8:1-4). Moreover the continuing presence of the LORD in their midst is emphasized when Isaiah declares that the LORD of hosts still dwells on Mt. Zion, where the temple of God was located.

8:19-22   The connection with the preceding verse is rather obscure. The wording and contents, particularly of 8:22, show rather a closer connection with 5:30, and it might be well to consider this section as a sequel to 5:30. In a time of anguish and panic, due to the wrath of God, people take recourse only too easily to mediums and wizards. But as the prophet observes, it is ridiculous to consult the dead on behalf of the living.

The practice of consulting mediums and wizards (cf. 3:2-3) was always a temptation for the people in Israel, notwithstanding that it was prohibited by the law (cf. Deut. 18:11; Lev. 19:31; 20:6-7). It is clear that Isaiah was very much opposed to all forms of spiritism, such as was practiced by Saul at Endor (1 Sam. 28:3-11; Isa. 8:20).

The terrible fate that could overtake the people is therefore described in vv. 21-22, if it takes place in a land where "there is no dawn" (cf. 6:11-13; 7:23-25). Instead there is hunger, thirst, and misery showing itself in physical as well as spiritual deprivation. The people's hearts are darkened and their spirit greatly disturbed. They get enraged and curse their sinful king and the God whom they have forsaken; in fact they live without hope and any consolation. Whether they turn their faces upward or cast their eyes down to the earth, they will see only distress and darkness, while they themselves will be thrust into thick darkness (cf. Exod. 10:22; Deut. 28:29). Such darkness penetrates right into the heart and soul and renders the continuation of human life impossible.

The Prince of Peace (9:1-7)

In total contrast to the preceding chapter, the prophet now proclaims a new message of hope and consolation. It is directed to "her that was in anguish." We are surprised to know who "her" is. For "her" (i.e., the Galilean area) the gloom will vanish and the light of God's grace and blessing will shine upon her.

The land of Zebulon and the land of Naphtali are located between the Sea of Galilee and the Mediterranean Sea. This area had suffered greatly from the invasion of the Assyrian armies during the Syro-Emphraimite War (734-733 B.C.) and had become an Assyrian province. The inhabitants had been taken into exile and new peoples from other areas of the Assyrian Empire had been brought in to replace them; that then was why it was known as "Galilee of the nations."

Next the LORD will "make glorious the way of the sea, the land beyond the Jordan." This "way" was the ancient highway running from Damascus to the coast of the Mediterranean Sea, which goes westwards through the land east of Jordan and Galilee of the nations.

It is interesting to note that it is Galilee in particular that is to be glorified. It is not Judah or Jerusalem, nor is it Ephraim or Benjamin that is to receive the light. The people of Jerusalem in Jesus' day rather despised the people of Galilee because it was of mixed race even then—it was still "Galilee of the Gentiles" (Matt. 4:15). This passage, placed as it is here in the book of Isaiah, can be considered a continuation of the message of the Immanuel sign (Isa. 7:14; 8:8). Consequently it is of the very greatest theological significance.

We have seen that Isaiah had immediate access to the king (7:13). He may well have been either a "court" prophet, as was Nathan in the days of David (2 Sam. 12:1), or—more likely—a "cultic prophet." The temple employed priests to handle the sacrifices, but, although we are not told so explicitly, the authorities seem to have employed "ministers" as well. These may have preached sermons and given pastoral counseling to pilgrims from the country. But they may have had still another function to perform on special occasions. While we have no explicit reference to the practice, Israel quite probably administered an institution that we do know some other nations maintained. That was to hold an annual "re-enthronement" festival in Jerusalem, conjoined with the celebration of New Year, such as is hinted at in some of the Psalms (e.g,. Pss. 47, 96–99). Thus it may well be that this oracle was actually addressed to the king by Isaiah on one such occasion, such as on the anniversary of his accession to the throne. If this is so, then Isaiah regarded Hezekiah as a prophetic symbol (another "sign") of a messianic king still to come (cf. Pss. 2, 21, 72, 110, 132). He actually then addresses him as such. On a similar occasion, at John Kennedy's installation as president of the United States, the poet Robert Frost addressed the new president in idealized language as if he portended the ultimate perfection of a president for whom the world awaits. Hezekiah was thus a "sign" of the perfection of God's plan that would some day surely come to pass.

9:2-3   "The people who walked in darkness" is evidently in parallel with "those who dwelt in a land of deep darkness." As we have seen, they were in the darkness of anguish and of spiritual death (cf. Isa. 8:22; 9:1; 60:2; Jer. 2:4-8). The great light that they will suddenly see and which will shine upon them, however, will be able to penetrate this deep darkness. It is the light of a new life, the light of glory and of a new hope (Luke 2:32; John 1:5; 8:12; Isa. 49:6). Consequently the great joy they are to experience will be both glorious and spontaneous, like the "joy at the harvest" known to the peasant when all is safely gathered in, or the joy "when they divide the spoil" that has been abandoned by a retreating army. Yet it is primarily joy before the LORD, spiritual joy, that they will experience as God's grace showered upon his faithful ones.

It is noteworthy how this image and concept of light permeates the whole biblical revelation. God's creation is described as the victory of light over darkness (Gen. 1:3). God the Creator reveals himself as "light" because he is the Light of light, the source of all life (Ps. 27:1; Mic. 7:8; Isa. 60:20; cf. Exod. 3:2). He is the light of Israel (Isa. 10:17). No wonder the messianic idea in the NT is connected with light, because Jesus Christ, hailed as the Messiah, is known as "the light of the world" (cf. John 1:4; 8:12; 12:35, 46; 2 Cor. 4:6; Rev. 21:23). As believers, members of his body, we in our turn must walk in the light of Christ and therefore become ourselves a light for the world (Matt. 5:14; Eph. 5:8; Phil. 2:15).

The concept of light was much favored in the non-Christian world of the early Church, especially in Gnosticism. Even in recent times, in the traditional life of some people in Indonesia, pearls (as a symbol of light) are inserted into the eyelids of the deceased to ensure that in the life beyond the dead one would "walk in the light," here meaning eternal joy and salvation.

9:4-6 The grace of the salvation to come is expressed in various ways. Three reasons for the people's joy in salvation are mentioned (each introduced by *ki*, "for"), leading to a great climax.

1. Galilee will be delivered from the "yoke" of the Assyrians (cf. Isa. 10:24-27). Israel is pictured as an ox under that yoke, being whipped to move along by the staff of the driver. Israel is to be liberated from the weight of this yoke in a "wonderful" way, and from the pain received through the blows of Assyria's staff. This kind of liberation has taken place before, in the days of Midian (Judg. 7).

The story of Gideon's victory culminates at Judg. 7:21-22, where we learn that his army did not strike a single blow to gain its freedom from the Midianite hordes. What happened was that the Midianites obligingly slew one another! Yet Gideon had his place, for Judg. 7:23 reports that his army pursued after Midian. Accordingly when we read "the rod of his oppressor, *thou* hast broken as on the day of Midian" (Isa. 7:4), we see that the new liberation to come will be the LORD'S doing and initiated by him. Consequently it will be "marvelous" (meaning "beyond our understanding") in our eyes (cf. Ps. 118:23).

2. We shall see not just the destruction of weapons of war, but of our human desire to use them. God will then burn them in the "fire" of his wrath.

3. Yet this mighty act of God will come about, paradoxically, through the birth of a baby (!), a "son" who will be given by God. The government of Israel or of the world will be "upon the shoulder" of this baby! Surely his task will be the government of the kingdom of God, and not that of mankind. Isaiah gives this son four titles, each of which is composed of two words:

(1) *"Wonderful"* in the Hebrew means "not of this world." A *counselor* was a wise man who applied his knowledge to the government of his people. This son then would possess that "wonderful" wisdom which the early chapters of the book of Proverbs actually seeks to personify. There we read: "the LORD by wisdom founded the earth" (Prov. 3:19), so that wisdom was itself divine. This son-counselor was to apply the wisdom of God to the human situation. Isaiah speaks of the divine wisdom again at Isa. 11:2 (cf. 25:1).

(2) The divine nature of the son is clearly expressed in the title *Mighty God.* He is pictured as a victorious hero, defeating all enemies. This aspect of his person is inseparable from the preceding one through a correlation of wisdom, courage, and power. He has a tremendous task to face and a fierce battle to fight. But the term "mighty God" needs adjustment to our picturing of him in English. Throughout the OT Israel's God is known as *elohim,* a plural term. What we have here, however, is *el,* a singular noun. We might best translate it as "the Divine Being," since *el* is the root word for divinity in all the Semitic languages. Consequently *el* is a concept that all the gentile nations could appreciate. We may best use the English phrase "divine warrior" to express the original, the victorious hero who can defeat all his enemies (cf. Exod. 15:3).

(3) He will reign as a *"Father"* over his children, for his reign will be based on fatherly love and care (cf. Isa. 1:2-3; 22:21). His is that faithfulness which is *everlasting.*

(4) As for the title *Prince of Peace,* both Isaiah and his hearers were aware that "peace" *(shalom)* meant more than what the newspaper today means by the term. This lovely word comes from a root meaning "wholeness, harmony, completion." "Peace" thus means all these things and more, and must not be limited to a mere absence of hostilities. People will be living in harmony with God, with each other, and with nature. This is the culminating aspect of the "kingdom of peace" that is yearned for by all nations (cf. 2:4; 57:19; Zech. 9:10; Luke 2:14).

9:7   The Prince of Peace will be a king "upon the throne of David" and so a legitimate king for whom Israel is longing. In his person all the promises of God that were given through the prophet Nathan to David would be fulfilled (cf. 2 Sam. 7:12, 13, 15-17; Luke 1:32-33). Unlike either Ahaz or Hezekiah, this king will establish his kingdom "with justice and with righteousness," meaning that he will uphold the rule of law and order, thus rendering Jerusalem at last as the "faithful city" of Isa. 1:26. Here then we see a close relationship between power, justice, righteousness, and love.

Such a vision is too wonderful for Israel—and for us!—to grasp. Yet the hope of it is no mere fantasy, because "the zeal of the LORD of hosts will do this" (cf. 37:32).

This last line, probably from the hand of the editor of the book, shows a full appreciation of Isaiah's message. "Zeal" (Heb. *qin'ah*) expresses urgency, passion, or jealousy in the sense of claiming exclusive rights and so even of fury. How different Isaiah's God is from that of those theologians of the third Christian century (who were regarded as heretical) who declared that God was impassable and so could not "feel" and that he was immutable in that he could never change. How powerful this word *qin'ah* is may be seen in John 2:17, where in a quotation from Ps. 69:9 it is applied to Jesus.

GOD'S ANGER AGAINST EPHRAIM (9:8–10:4)

This long passage is well ordered. It is divided into four parts, each part ending with the same awesome refrain (vv. 12, 17, 21; 10:4). In various ways the prophet describes God's anger and punishment leading to the fall and destruction of Ephraim.

First Strophe (9:8-12)

In this first oracle "Jacob" occurs as the personification of its descendants, that is, of Judah as well as of northern Israel. But from the second verse it becomes clear that Ephraim, with its capital Samaria, is here primarily the object of God's anger (v. 8).

9:8-10   God's anger "lights upon Israel." It comes as a "word" issuing from the mouth of God. Actually, the LORD has "sent" it "against Jacob" or "into" Jacob, and it will fall upon Israel. The word of God is alive, even as God himself is the living God. God's word therefore is always effective. It hits its target like the arrow shot by a bowman. In hitting, it does the will of God. In this case God's will is that "all the people will know. . . ."

The people's pride in their capital city was basically self-esteem. Like the builders of the tower of Babel (Gen. 11), they believed they could build their civilization without God. As the "Greeks," who liked to declare that "Man is the measure of all things," they rejected the guiding love of their loving God. If the enemy destroyed their city, they could build it themselves, like the small boy who rejected his mother's help with the words "I can do it myself,

Mother"; and they could rebuild it to be more glorious than ever. Yet as Isaiah says, "they will know. . . ."

9:11-12   The Syrians and the Philistines had been enemies of the two houses of Israel for generations. New attacks by these hereditary enemies against Ephraim seem to have taken place not long before the outbreak of the Syro-Ephraimite War during the reign of Menahem of Israel (742-738 B.C.), since his policy was strongly anti-Syria. Menahem was too weak to avert this allied attack, so that he was "devoured with open mouth." This was a bitter lesson for Israel. But God's anger had not yet been turned away, and new disasters were still to follow.

The vivid couplet that ends this oracle, which sounds again as a refrain at Isa. 9:17 and again at v. 21, pictures for us God's arm stretched out still. He is never-endingly concerned for his people in both judgment and in mercy at the same time (cf. Zeph. 1:4).

Second Strophe (9:13-17)

The smiting of Ephraim was intended to bring them to repentance. The call to repentance had been proclaimed continually (e.g., Amos 5:4, 6) throughout Israel's history, but Ephraim would not seek the LORD either through a prophet or through a priest (cf. Gen. 25:22; Exod. 18:15; 1 Sam. 9:9). In the wider sense of the word, Ephraim continued to refuse to worship the LORD (cf. Deut. 4:29; 1 Chr. 16:11; Ps. 10:4; 119:10).

What is so very difficult for modern Western society to accept is the OT's concept of the "solidarity" of mankind in sin. Isaiah believed that if a people such as Israel was under judgment then innocent babies and defenseless widows would necessarily suffer along with the leadership that was responsible for setting the nation's policy. Of course modern warfare shows us how truly Isaiah spoke and how unbiblical is our theology if we expect the innocent, just because they are innocent, to escape the judgment that rests upon the whole "family" of the nation. There are Christians now who suppose that the salvation God offers individuals is just to rescue them out of an evil world. God's salvation is of all creation, of all the powers of evil, such as those unjust structures that bring oppression, torture, and hunger to great numbers of people.

9:14-16 In consequence, there will be an all-inclusive punishment from the LORD: "head and tail, palm branch and reed." The leaders and the authorities, the people and the false prophets will one and all be cut off together in one day. The execution of judgment is radical and will occur all of a sudden.

9:17 The whole population has become godless evildoers, and "every mouth speaks folly," blasphemous *nebalah* ("foolishness"). There is no place at all for God and his Word in this totally degenerate society! Included are the "young men" who have also been totally spoiled, unable to be used as "cannon fodder."

Third Strophe (9:18-21)

The people's wickedness is pictured as a fire that consumes everything before it. From a localized fire in the scrubland it spreads to "the thickets of the forest." The last line of Isa. 9:18 reads like a description of a nuclear explosion! All layers of society go into the flames.

In v. 19 we meet with a contradiction between the fire of sin and godlessness, and the fire of the holiness of God that judges sinners. Humankind is responsible for its own sin, and so in all disasters that occur one has to see the hand of God outstretched (cf. 1:31; 5:24; 6:13; 9:15-16). The conflagration grows ever more serious because "the people are like fuel for the fire." Once they rebel against God, they then hate one another and fight even against their own brother! No sense of brotherly love and family relationships can survive. Such is the climax of human degeneration and social disorder. There is vexing famine and chaos everywhere; all ethical norms are relinquished. There is fighting, snatching, and stealing, just to get something to eat. "Each devours his neighbor's flesh" (v. 20) is a colloquial expression which need not be taken literally (cf. 2 Kgs. 6:28, 29; Ps. 27:2 [RSV mg]; Jer. 19:9); rather, it denotes a situation of complete anarchy.

This chaos is also evident in the relationship between the tribes of Israel. Manasseh and Ephraim are two brotherly tribes, both descendants of Joseph. After the death of Jeroboam II there was chaotic strife for the throne. Pekahiah was murdered by Pekah, a man from Gilead in the geographical area of Manasseh. But like

Ephraim the Manassites were hostile against Judah, and together the two tribes attacked Judah during the Syro-Ephraimite War. In all these continuing confrontations between the tribes, therefore, we see the hand of God outstretched still.

Fourth Strophe (10:1-4)

This fourth threat of punishment is directed against the "head" in the sense we saw at Isa. 9:14, that is, the leaders who were responsible for the social welfare. As such it may be compared to some of the oracles of the prophet Amos.

10:1-2 It was well known that the law court in Judah and Israel was very corrupt. The judges used to add "iniquitous decrees" to oppress the poor (cf. 1:17, 23; 3:14; 5:7, 23). Such is true in many countries today. A law-and-order society is often enough one that oppresses the poor and the powerless. Not only was this so in the law-giving ("writing oppression"), but also in the exercise of justice. The judges accepted bribes, used threats and intimidations, employed false witnesses, and exerted illegal pressure. So the poor were deprived of all justice and right. It is clear that their legal decisions (in the sense of case law) contradicted the Mosaic law, for the latter defends the poor and the weak.

3-4 The oppressors often forget that they are just small, weak creatures and that ultimately they will have to deal with God himself, for he remembers the fate and the misery of his oppressed people. "What will you do on the day of 'visitation?'" as the Hebrew has it—that is, the day of judgment—for he will be coming like "a storm . . . from afar." "To whom will you flee for help?" he asks. "Your wealth," accumulated by means of wickedness, will prove to be totally useless. As we say today, "You can't take it with you." All that will be left for them to do will be to "crouch among the prisoners" or "fall among the slain" (cf. 2:11, 17). The storm that is coming from afar points to the mighty armies of Assyria, which as we see in 10:5 are to be the instrument of God's fury. And so the refrain of 9:12b, 17c, and 21b is repeated once more with terrible emphasis.

PROUD ASSYRIA WILL BE HUMBLED;
COMFORT WILL BE GIVEN TO ZION (10:5-34)

Woe to Assyria Who Exalts Himself! (10:5-19)

It is theologically significant to note from this passage that Yahweh is indeed the LORD of history and of the nations. Here Isaiah uses vivid picture language. In his almighty power God can use Assyria as an instrument held in his hand to pass judgment on godless peoples—even including his own people, Judah. From the viewpoint of the Assyrians, they certainly did not realize they were being so used.

The historical background of these oracles is most likely from the period of Sargon of Assyria (722-706 B.C.), when the Assyrian Empire extended from the Euphrates to the Mediterranean Sea. At that time Hezekiah was king in Judah (725-687). The Assyrian armies succeeded in occupying part of Judah, but they were not able to conquer Jerusalem (cf. Isa. 36–39). So this passage has a different historical background from 9:8–10:4.

10:5-6 The mighty army of Assyria has now been described several times in various ways: as a cruel and mighty host, equipped with terrible weapons (cf. 5:27-28); as a young lion seizing its prey (5:29); as bees settling down and destroying the whole country (7:18); as a hired razor (7:20); and as the waters of the Euphrates overflowing the country (8:7-8a).

According to God's plan Assyria is to be used as a "rod" or stick to execute God's anger, not only against the nations but actually against his own people of Judah. "I send him . . . ," says the LORD. Assyria, that godless people, that symbol of world power, God employs temporarily to carry out his mission.

10:7 Assyria is not a mere passive instrument; "he" is not without personal responsibility for his own deeds. The godless Assyrians did not have the least notion that God was working out his plan through them. Assyria was of course no better, no more moral, than Israel or Judah. The Assyrians pursued their own sinful ambitions by oppressing the nations they had subjected with cruelty beyond measure. Here we see once again the mystery of

Assyria's "mission," which is both condemned and justified at the same time!

10:8-11 The arrogance of the Assyrian king is expressed here. All his army commanders made themselves kings over the subjugated nations reaching from the Euphrates to the Mediterranean Sea. But the Assyrian king exalted himself over them all as "king of kings and lord of lords."

In v. 9 the Assyrian king is boasting about the victories his armies have won during the reigns of Tiglath-pileser III and Sargon II. The names mentioned here are those of capital cities north of Canaan. The king's argument is that great nations have been conquered and subjugated. Are they not stronger and mightier than Jerusalem? Do they not have more idols than all the graven images of Jerusalem and Samaria put together? This is a tragic misconception on Assyria's part. Note that they supposed:

> a. The number of idols and gods a people possesses has to be decisive for that country's security.
>
> b. Yahweh, the God of Israel, is on the same level as the many idols and gods of the nations.
>
> c. The gods of Assyria are the most powerful, far more so than all other gods, including Yahweh, the Holy One of Israel.

But if they were to capture Jerusalem the Assyrians would not meet within it any idols or graven images; rather, they would meet with Yahweh, the LORD of hosts! Although King Sennacherib of Assyria besieged the city so tightly in 701, he did not succeed in conquering it; his mighty army was fatally stricken by the LORD of hosts (see chs. 37–38).

10:12-14 Isaiah 10:12 is probably an editorial intrusion. Unlike Isaiah's great address above, this verse is in prose. It sums up, however, what Isaiah has just announced and underlines the fact that God will eventually punish Assyria's haughty pride. And so there follows once again the record of the blasphemous boasts of the "king of kings," as Isaiah puts the latter's thoughts into his own words.

In vv. 13-14 Sennacherib (see ch. 36) considers himself to be both almighty and all wise, relying on "the strength of (his) hand"

and on his own wisdom and understanding. He is very proud of his arbitrary actions, that is, he had "removed the boundaries of the peoples" as if he were God himself (cf. Deut. 32:8). He had plundered and overthrown thrones of kings like a "bull" mad with rage. He had plundered freely and arbitrarily all the possessions of the frightened and helpless peoples he had overrun. He had helped himself to their wealth "as men gather eggs." No parent bird could protect its nest; it could not even "chirp" in protest at the outrage.

10:15   How foolish of the Assyrians to exalt themselves over the LORD. It is as if an axe were to "magnify itself" over the one who handles it. Assyria was just an instrument, a rod or a stick in the hand of God.

At various points in his addresses to his audience Isaiah speaks of the "plan" that God is "working out" in and through his covenant people. Deliverance is God's "work." In light of this the Reformers declared that a person's true "work" was not the manner in which he earned his bread but his obedience to God by allowing himself to be an *instrument* of God's saving work in the world. By allowing itself to be God's instrument of judgment upon his own people, Assyria was thus unwittingly sharing in this "plan" of God, as was King Cyrus of Persia in the days of Deutero-Isaiah (Isa. 45:1-4). This theme is one of the threads linking all the sixty-six chapters of "Isaiah" as one continuing piece of revelation.

10:16-19   Because of this arrogance God will send a "wasting sickness" that will sweep away the glory of Assyria. What will happen is that beneath his glorious exterior—that is, beneath the panoply of his mighty army, fully equipped for war—God will kindle a "burning," like the burning of fire. By this imagery Isaiah shows how the judgment of God works in with the nature of man. The prophet calls God "the light of Israel." As light himself God can say, "Let there be light," and light becomes (Gen. 1:3). The NT has no quarrel with this OT representation of God. For example, according to 1 John 1:5 "the message we have heard from him" is that "God is light and in him is no darkness at all"; and of course Jesus called himself "the light of the world" (John 8:12). Yet light and fire are but two aspects of the one reality. As we have noted already, Isaiah himself speaks of God as a "devouring fire," "everlasting burnings" (Isa. 29:6; 33:14). In the NT John the Baptist witnesses to this reality in the case of Jesus (Luke 3:16-17). So now at Isa. 10:17 Isaiah puts the two pictorial concepts together: "the light of Israel will become a fire, and his Holy One a flame"; and as a forest fire can devour many "glorious" (v. 16) standing trees, so will the fires of the wrath of God penetrate beneath Assyria's glorious panoply of war and "in one day" devour "his stout warriors" as if they were "thorns and briers." The light of Israel is the creative love of God, but at the same time it is the judgment that penetrates beneath a humanity's arrogant show of egoism and lets it destroy its own soul and body. And yet there is always hope, even for arrogant Assyria. The remnant *(she'ar)* of the trees, that word of hope addressed to Israel also (7:3), may indeed be few in number but there will still be a remnant.

A Remnant of Israel Will Be Saved! (10:20-27a)

This message of hope rests upon the nature of God, as we have just seen in the above but separate oracle. Yet it is also a serious admonition for Judah not to lean upon Assyria, but only upon the Holy One of Israel. For a while Hezekiah had followed the policy (which was pro-Assyria) of King Ahaz, his father. But afterwards he distanced himself from Assyria and sought affiliation with the Philistines, Phoenicians, and Babylonians in opposing Assyria. In consequence the Assyrian king Sennacherib took military action and Hezekiah had to surrender and pay heavy tribute. However, the Assyrian pressure on Jerusalem increased, and finally they besieged the city (701 B.C.). Throughout all these events Isaiah proclaimed the word of God, saying that the Assyrians would not succeed in conquering the city (2 Kgs. 18–20). It is most probable that these oracles have this as their historical background.

10:20-21 In view of the Assyrian threat of 701, Isaiah once again expresses a message of hope for a people in anguish (i.e., the message of the sign of She'ar-jashub; 7:3) but applies it now to the critical situation before Hezekiah. Isaiah is deeply concerned and convinced about "the remnant which will return" and believes that the destruction of Assyria would open the way for this return to take place. And so here he expands upon the significance of the cryptic name he gave his son in 7:3.

Who then are these remnant people? They are those of Israel who have experienced the mighty acts of God in history, and have learned from the bitterness brought about by their own foolish policy of leaning upon Assyria or upon any other foreign people. Finally they will come to their senses and lean on the Holy One of Israel "in truth." The root meaning of "truth" *(emet)* points to the reliability and faithfulness of God. In other words, reliance upon God alone offers ultimate security and the certainty that "a remnant will return."

10:22-23   Thus the remnant are the people whom the mighty God (v. 21, employing one of the titles applied to the "messianic" king to come; see commentary at 9:6) had promised to love and guide for ever (Exod. 19:6). In Moses' day God had offered his eternal covenant to the one people whom he had chosen to serve him in the world. Yet that covenant had actually been preceded by another, a covenant that enclosed a promise which God had made to Abraham many generations before. According to Gen. 22:17 the latter's descendants would be "as the sand which is on the seashore."

In cryptic language Isaiah now handles a deep theological issue. Could the "faithful" God possibly break the promise he had given to Abraham? For alongside that promise God had also set his "decree" against his own covenant people should they ever "rebel" (the word used at Isa. 1:2, where the whole of ch. 1 sets the issue of God's judgment and mercy together) and turn their back upon the calling to which they were called. Their calling was to "be a blessing . . . and by you all the families of the earth shall bless themselves," or "shall be blessed" (Gen. 12:2-3).

Now Isaiah unravels the cryptic name of his second son, *Maher-shalal-hash-baz* (which means something like "Speed spoil, hurry prey," employing onomatopoeic words that seek to sound like what a rampaging army does to the villages it passes through; Isa. 8:3). This son's name speaks of an eruption of destruction ending in desolation (cf. Luke 21:20) which was to come about by the "decree" of the LORD (cf. Acts 2:23). The LORD of hosts, the God of the whole earth and of all mankind, was bound to make "a full end," an immutable finish "in the midst of all the earth." The nations of mankind had not received the blessing God had promised them through Abraham. Isaiah implies that it was the fault of Jerusalem that it was so. The chosen people had manifestly failed God and his plan. In consequence, since all mankind is one family, each being responsible for the other, all the nations would necessarily suffer along with rebellious Israel.

Three amazing words in this passage resolve the paradox that God had made a promise to love Israel for ever, even while he had decreed that he would destroy them from off the face of the earth. Isaiah declared that the "eruption" to come would be *"overflowing with righteousness"* (Isa. 10:22). In these terms Isaiah reiterates the extraordinary revelation made throughout the whole Bible, from Genesis to the cross of Christ, that while the God of justice and love must necessarily punish evil wherever it occurs, yet being the "mighty God" (v. 21) he can bring good out of what appears to be ultimate and total disaster. And so "a remnant of them will return," having been purified and refined like silver in the terrible heat of the zeal and love of God.

"Righteousness" *(tsedaqah)* here is rendered by the feminine form of the word that Isaiah (as later both Deutero- and Trito-Isaiah) employs to describe what God has brought about in the human heart as the result of his "terrible purification" and at the cost of the unspeakable pain of the fire which he has suffered in his own "heart" (cf. Hos. 11:8-9). *Tsedaqah* describes that kingdom of love and justice among the covenant people which can be envisaged by *shalom,* the word used in the fourth and last descriptive title of the "messianic" king to come, "the Prince of Peace."

10:24-27a   Understandably then Isaiah draws the consequence of his theological discussion by following it with the strong word "Therefore!" But he continues his thesis by employing the theological title "Zion" for the city and inhabitants of Jerusalem. Though God's punishment, he says, must necessarily be executed upon Assyria (cf. Isa. 10:5-7), at Zion there will certainly be salvation and a refuge—for that is the place where "my people dwell" and as such is the "dwelling-place" of God himself (cf. 8:18). God's indignation, carried out through Assyria as a rod in his hand (10:5), will soon come to an end, when it will be Assyria's turn to be punished for overstepping their task when they exulted in cruelty and destruction (vv. 15-18).

The LORD will deliver Israel in a wonderful way (cf. 37:36 and the events of 701). His deliverance would be comparable with that which Israel experienced in the days of the Judges, when "the LORD smote Midian at the rock of Oreb" (Judg. 7:21-22) and when God brought his people out of Egypt in the days of Moses.

Isaiah does not raise here the question of why God does not always act in this manner. In many a personal "lament" (e.g., Pss. 3, 5, 6, 7, 42, 51) or in communal laments (e.g., Ps. 74) and in the book of Lamentations, the decisive term is "why?" The Nazi Holocaust in our era reminds us of countless terrible horrors in history and of the inscrutable cruelty of life such as the biblical Job experienced. Other poet-theologians, however, such as Habakkuk and Zephaniah (see volumes on these prophets in the *International Theological Commentary*) struggle with this issue in their individual ways. Today we are called upon to discover that biblical theology is like the various colored elements in the rainbow, which only when taken together reveal the pure white light of the wholeness of revelation.

At this point, however, Isaiah was insistent that God's great gift of "salvation" was many-sided. It included his total forgiveness; it meant his receiving his people back to himself once they "returned" to him in penitence and hope. It meant that God himself knew pain and suffering in his own "heart" as he experienced the rebellious behavior of his chosen people.

Isaiah Now Uses History To Interpret Theology (10:27b-34)

But before the great deliverance (Isa. 10:24-27a) came Judah would have to suffer first from an Assyrian invasion, which is described vividly by the prophet. The excited style of the poem is like that of an ancient ballad (cf. Judg. 5). The Assyrians came from the north, moving southwards towards Jerusalem. The places mentioned here lie north of Judah in the area of Samaria. Most of them cannot be pinpointed today. Nor can we date the invasion, whether it was in the past, in perhaps 734, or a decade later.

Moving swiftly from the north the Assyrians reach Michmash, where they store their baggage. As they head further southwards the road becomes more difficult; they must cross a steep and rocky ravine before reaching Geba, where they could encamp before the battle.

The panic in Judah increases as the Assyrians move towards Jerusalem. The countryside is full of refugees, crying and screaming for help. These move from one place to another, but no one can provide them with a safe refuge (Isa. 10:30-32).

But the LORD puts a halt to the invasion at "this very day." This happens at Nob, located in the vicinity of Mt. Scopus just outside the city of Jerusalem. So on "this very day" the LORD interferes and renders the Assyrians powerless; all they can do is shake their fists at Jerusalem. Here we see an example of that faith in God of which Isaiah had spoken at 7:4.

10:33-34   The Assyrians did not reckon with the power of the LORD of hosts, the Holy One of Israel. He sets limits to human capacities (cf. 7:7). Now he has only to raise his hand for the Assyrian advance to stop (cf. 10:12-13). Once again the proud king of Assyria is pictured as a thick forest, as at vv. 18-19. This is a picture, however, which could be applied to any secular kingdom in all its glory. The mighty high trees will be lopped down, and the thickets will be hewn down with an axe.

So the LORD humbles the arrogance of people and the pride of all secular kingdoms.

THE "MESSIANIC" KINGDOM WHICH IS SOLID AND PEACEFUL (11:1-16)

The Messianic King and His Kingdom (11:1-10)

In this chapter the discussion concerning the remnant of Israel is focused on the house of David and on a king of Davidic descent. The greatness and glory of this king transcends that of all secular kings and can be applied only to the king-deliverer figure who is described in Isa. 9:6.

Once again we are to envisage one of the three great festivals held annually in the temple precincts, the crowds spilling over into Jerusalem's streets which now swarm with country folk as well as the citizens who know their way around. Most probably it was at the New Year festival (end of September) that the temple authorities re-enacted the enthronement of the king. Quite possibly a priest repeated in a loud voice as he faced the throne of the king the great promise of God made to David, the words of which we read at 2 Sam. 7. At the same time also the people seem to have renewed their loyalty to the Covenant imposed on them at Sinai. Such a festival, as we saw at ch. 9, seems to be echoed in some of the psalms (cf. 2 Kgs. 11:12).

On one such particular solemn occasion our (court?) prophet Isaiah may have stepped forward and spoken the poem recorded here. In its position in the book of Isaiah the poem immediately follows the historical description of what the words "overflowing with righteousness" (Isa. 10:22) will mean for the remnant that will survive the Assyrian invasion—or, for that matter, any remnant that will survive any traumatic catastrophe in any age of mankind. Chapter 10 had ended with the felling of majestic trees before an axe. All that is left in the ground then is the mere stump of one single tree.

11:1   Isaiah begins his poem by referring to such a stump. At first glance one supposes the former majestic forest (10:34) to be nothing but a collection of dead trees. Such appeared to be the judgment of God upon Israel (cf. 6:13), in that God's people would certainly sustain divine punishment for their apostasy. But that judgment was "overflowing with righteousness" (10:22). Isaiah had already declared that "a remnant will return" *(she'ar yashub)*. Now he announces that the promised remnant would be embodied in just one person, who would be the direct descendant of the king who was facing him at the moment, just as he in his turn was the direct descendant of the great king David whose line God had chosen "for ever."

The stump of a felled tree looks to the human eye to be dead. But one day a "shoot" appears through the dry ground from one of the tree's roots perhaps a meter away from the stump. That shoot then eventually becomes a new tree—new, yet rooted in the old. Incidentally, the word "branch" cannot be a correct translation of *netser*, for branches grow only on standing trees. The shoot here must have been, to Isaiah's eye, something like a "sucker" that can develop from the root of a rosebush (cf. 53:2) in modern gardens.

This symbolism is emphasized in still another way. David had been the great king. His father, Jesse, however, had been a "nobody," just one of the seemingly dead trees in the forest. Thus it was from God that the coming Davidic king would receive his calling, with the person of Jesse only the vehicle through whom God was now purposing to act. The "shoot from the stump" from which the remnant of sinful Israel would be reborn was to be a new kingdom ruled by a Davidic king. In other words, the remnant would be the Davidic king *and* the forgiven and renewed element in Israel. If the king sitting enthroned before Isaiah was the great Hezekiah, who was remembered by later generations for his piety and his loyalty to the Covenant, then Isaiah so much as declares that Hezekiah is in fact a sign and a promise of one still greater than he who was still to come.

11:2-3a   We often read in OT history how the Spirit of the LORD was granted to special individuals like Moses, Gideon, Samson, and David, as well as to other kings and prophets. In the days to come, then, the Spirit of the LORD will be poured out upon the king and his forgiven people (Isa. 32:15; Joel 2:28). A closer look at the Spirit of the LORD shows seven characteristics:

1. The Spirit will descend from above and rest upon the king (cf. Isa. 32:15). The Spirit will remain on him permanently, and will sanctify, activate, and guide him in fulfilling all his tasks. (Compare this promise with Jesus' baptism and with the outpouring of the Holy Spirit at Pentecost).

2. The "spirit of wisdom" is the divine wisdom that is the gift of the Spirit (Prov. 8).

3. Wisdom and reason go together. Endowed with the "spirit of understanding," this king will know and see with all clarity into the heart of any matter and know how to solve the problems inherent in human life.

4. The "spirit of counsel" is that of the counselor, who interpreted the Torah, the law of Moses, the revelation that God had already given of his will for Israel.

5. The "spirit of might" is also a description of God himself, so the king will act even as God does (cf. Isa. 10:21).

6. The "spirit of knowledge" fills the king with the "knowledge of God" *(da'at elohim)*. This is not so much intellectual

knowledge but rather knowledge based on fellowship with and obedience to God, as was expected of a king (2 Sam. 23:2; 1 Kgs. 3:9).

7. The "spirit of the fear of the LORD," a synonym of *da'at elohim,* means the true and reverent worship of God. Such is the foundation of all wisdom (Prov. 1:7).

11:3b-5   The messianic king will judge in righteousness. Judges and kings who were called to uphold justice and righteousness often did the contrary. In their judgment they were often influenced by prejudice at the expense of the weak and the poor. This prejudice could be mixed with sinful desires, self-interest, arbitrariness, and all kinds of temptations to selfish gain (cf. Isa. 10:1-2), as may be seen in the case of King David with Uriah (2 Sam. 11), King Ahab with Naboth (1 Kgs. 21).

On the contrary, the messianic king, being filled with the spirit of wisdom and understanding and knowledge, can penetrate the hearts of humans and see sharply into the crux of a matter (1 Sam. 16:7). Consequently he can judge in justice and "righteousness."

This last word, *tsedeq,* is difficult to translate. As noted above, in its feminine form *(tsedaqah)* it describes how a person is to act toward his neighbor once he has been enabled to do so by God's initial act of *tsedeq* to that neighbor. Yet here this human person, this "messianic" king, will evidently do what only God can do—judge the depressed with saving, creative love! *Tsedeq* means much more than the modern word "righteousness" if it implies the idea of moral goodness. Actually the king's judgment will be a creative judgment, for (to return to the root meaning of the word) he will "put people right" with God! That then is what the succeeding expression, used in parallel with this declaration, means in similar terms. The messianic king will make an "upright" decision for the world's poor, for that is something they cannot do for themselves. Finally at Isa. 11:5 we note again that the king will do what God does—what only God can do, in fact—for he will share in the righteousness of the holy and faithful God. Thus when we read that he will "smite the earth with the rod of his mouth," we are to recognize that he himself is acting as the very Word of God that issues out of his mouth.

It is possible that "earth" *(erets)* is a misreading for "arrogant"

69

('arits); if so, then we have a better parallel between the last two lines of v. 4.

11:6-9   The reign of the messanic king will bear the fruits of peace. This will be an all-comprehensive peace *(shalom)* existing between human beings, animals, and nature, as was the case in Paradise at the creation (Gen. 2). All forms of life in nature will demonstrate harmonious peace and an atmosphere of friendliness. The old enmity between human and serpent (Gen. 3:15) will vanish; even the "suckling child" need not fear the asp and the adder (Isa. 11:8). Nature will be delivered from vanity and death, and so from its bondage to decay (Rom. 8:19-22).

Lack of respect towards nature and its resources, towards the common welfare and peace between the nations, has become today a burning and vexing global problem. It should be solved comprehensively by the nations. There is an urgent call to the present-day "rulers of the world" for repentance: the amazing technocrats, the powerful politicians, the colossal industrialists, the wealthy capitalists, the mighty super powers with their nuclear weapons. The majority of the world population is living in unrest, struggling against terrible hunger and poverty, suffering from injustice, the color bar, and maltreatment; it needs help, brotherly love, and sympathy, until "the whole earth is at rest and quiet, and they break forth into singing."

Moving towards this eschatological era, the gospel message of the coming of the kingdom of God in Jesus Christ forms a basic reality and fulfillment, from which the Christian calling for social justice, peace, and welfare should be viewed. It is to be regretted that today people are too rationalistic and secularized to live with these perspectives.

It is interesting to note that at Isa. 65:25 the author of the third part of the book of Isaiah, writing some 170 years after our Isaiah's death, can "quote" this verse, secure in his belief that he is expressing the theology of his master in this his now totally different situation. He is living in the period of the Restoration as one of the "remnant that had returned." This "new," restored people of God were not being permitted to see the firstfruits of the messianic vision given us here in ch. 11.

11:10   This can be considered as a closing verse praising the glory of this king, who again is called "the root of Jesse" (cf. v. 1). However, the RSV (also John Mauchline, *Isaiah 1–39*) connects this verse with the following passage (vv. 11-16). This is because v. 10 may be understood as a later addition since it is in prose; also, it commences with the typical expression "in that day . . ." Also, this royal figure was to be the gathering-point of the nations: "him shall the nations seek," and not only "the Holy One of Israel." His dwellings shall be *kabod,* again a word used only of the "glory" of God himself.

The Messianic Age (11:11-16)

11:11   With the help of still another theologian, "that day" is described in a short prose passage in terms of a second exodus. The first had been from slavery in Egypt in the days of Moses and was now an historical fact. Consequently God's act was thereby the guarantee that he would do so again, and again . . . and again. Thus there was to be a far greater ingathering of the remnant. They would come from the north and the south, from the east and even from across the Mediterranean. Deutero-Isaiah, in his turn, based his vision of the return from Babylon upon this verse, seeing it as a new act of God's *tsedeq*; but he does more. He sees the release of the remnant from Babylon (51:9-11; 49:8-23) as a spiritual renewal as well as a physical return—almost, we might say, as a sacramental occasion. We can only suppose that such is what Jesus had in mind when, at the Transfiguration, he "spoke of the exodus (not 'his departure,' Luke 9:31 RSV), which he was to accomplish at Jerusalem."

11:12-14   In this poem we are assured of a reconciliation between the tribes of Israel. The old struggle and enmity between Ephraim (representing the northern kingdom with the ten tribes) and Judah (along with Benjamin) will be no more. Possessing the strength of a united nation, they will be able to subjugate their old enemies as in the great days of David. Like a great swarm of birds they will "swoop down upon the shoulder of the Philistines," meaning that they will race down the Judean hills sloping westward to the land of the Philistines. Then they will proceed to the

71

area east of the river Jordan to subjugate Edom, Moab, and the land of the Ammonites as they did in the time of the great King David (cf. 2 Sam. 8:13-14). This does not mean that Isa. 11:14 is to be taken literally. Isaiah, who has given us the vision of the coming reign of peace, is not thinking in these terms. Rather, he is saying in a manner such as the simple peasantry of Judah could grasp that "in that day"—once the Davidic king has begun to reign—there will be a return to the authority and rule known to Israel in David's day.

11:15-16   Again Isaiah uses history to interpret the purposes of God. "The tongue of the sea of Egypt" was the "Reed Sea" through which the Israelites had crossed under Moses' leadership. "*The* River" is the river Euphrates which runs through the land of Babylonia. Never again, declares Isaiah, shall there have to be an exodus *from Egypt*. As once God brought his people out of Egypt, so he will accompany them now as if in a joyous caravan on a well-built highway. This exodus would then be seen to be an acted promise by God that a second exile would indeed take place. Later ch. 35 makes use of this vision of the "highway" leading home (35:8).

Moreover it is clear that the real fulfillment of this vision will not be limited to any Jewish national expectation alone. Believers from among the Gentiles will also "come home" to Zion (2:2-4) and become one Israel with the remnant of whom Isaiah speaks (Gal. 6:16). The ancient city of Jerusalem will then be understood eschatologically (Rom. 11:17-24) as the firstfruits of a spiritual and a heavenly city that God has in mind as the "home" of all who desire to dwell with him for all eternity (Heb. 11:10).

Maimonides († 1204) has provided us with a digest of rabbinic law in words which are now considered to be the official Jewish doctrine: "The pious of the Gentiles will have a share in the world to come" (see A. Cohen, *Everyman's Talmud* [1949; repr. New York: Schocken, 1975], 369). And Islam has a special place, alongside its own true believers, for the future of those whom they designate "the people of the Book," namely, Jews and Christians.

A Song of Thanksgiving to the Lord (12:1-6)

The first collection of Isaianic prophecies (chs. 1–12) is beautifully closed with a doxology and an exultant response for all the blessings received from the LORD, including that of well-deserved judgment. It starts with a song of praise and thanksgiving (12:1-2) and is followed by a psalm of exhortation to witness to the glory and the majesty of the LORD (vv. 4-6).

The song follows directly after the closing verse of the preceding ch. 11, which makes reference to the Exodus event. Perhaps it is placed here to show that it is in line with the Song of Moses and Song of Miriam (Exod. 15) sung after the Exodus had been completed. The song in Isa. 12:1-2 will be sung once the Return from Assyria is complete—*she'ar yashub* ("a remnant will return").

12:1-2   Unified Israel is here addressed as a single person ("you," singular). Israel knows that God's holy anger is just and right. The anger of God towards his people is never meant as an end in itself; it is rather a discipline in love. Therefore, God's anger does not last forever (Ps. 30:5; 103:9). God's anger has now been turned away; he even comes with comforts and new blessings (Isa. 40:10-11). Consequently Israel can yield and put their trust in him and abandon all fear (Ps. 118:6; Rom. 8:31). Note the quotation from Exod. 15:2; it occurs again at Ps. 118:14.

"God is my salvation" ("God" is singular in the Hebrew) is an exclamation of astonishment and joy intended to be heard by the nations. We should read instead "The divine Being *(el)*".—whom all peoples acknowledge—"is actually my Savior!" Then Isaiah adds, again for pagan ears to hear, "I declare (understood from the particle *ki*; RSV 'for') that *the* LORD GOD (our very own God [plural] of Israel) is my strength and my song." Moreover, "he has *become* my salvation." Our God of the Covenant is the same God yesterday, today, and for ever. Yet he keeps moving along with his pilgrim people on the "highway" back home to Zion. He never lets his people go (cf. the refrain in Ps. 136). He "becomes" their Savior (Exod. 3:12 uses the same verb as here) even as they submit to him and, like the Prodigal in Luke 15, return home to him as *Shear-jashub*.

73

12:3   The plural form of "you" means "each and all of you"—no matter how many you may be. You will draw water "with joy." Since there is an overabundance of water you will be able to draw it up from the well with ease and without any trouble and at no cost to yourself. At times water bears the symbolic meaning of the abundance of God's gracious blessings. Here this water comes "from the wells of salvation," that is, from the LORD himself, for he is the God of salvation (cf. John 7:37, 38; 4:13-14).

Note that the significance of Isaiah's name is brought out twice in Isa. 12:2-3. "Salvation" is wholly of God. Mankind can in no way save themselves. So now Israel is to proclaim *God's* name among the nations; that is, they will tell the world that in the *Lord God* there is salvation for all peoples. Israel will then be singing a new "song of the well," as their ancestors had done after their rescue from Egypt (Num. 21:17-18).

In later times these verses were sung by pilgrims as they went up to Jerusalem to celebrate the Feast of Tabernacles; during the ceremony the pilgrims drew water from the well of Shiloah (Isa. 8:6). This verse thus forms a good introduction to the following psalm.

12:4-6   We find expressions in this psalm which are also found in some other psalms (e.g., Pss. 148, 150, 66, 67). Note the excited calling for thanksgiving and proclamation and praise. God's name and deeds should be proclaimed "among (all) the nations," and he should be exalted as the Holy One of Israel! This psalm thus calls upon all nations on earth to recognize what God has "done gloriously" in the sight of all mankind.

The holiness of God has made such a deep impression on the prophet that he closes this, his first series of prophecies, by proclaiming again that Yahweh is "the Holy One of Israel" and his people are the holy, redeemed people. They are such—sanctified—because the Holy One is always present "in your midst"! Such then is the essence also of the Christian presence in the world today, for it requires obedience and courage in the fear of the LORD to bear Christian witness in the most effective and relevant way! Moreover, the Church today can do so because of the reality Isaiah expresses here, that God is at the same time both transcendent in his holiness and immanent in his holiness.

PART II
THE NATIONS UNDER GOD'S JUDGMENT

Isaiah 13:1–23:18

These chapters, which contain judgments against the nations, have a significant place in the Isaianic prophetic tradition. Yahweh is concerned with the history of the nations because he is the LORD of history. Yahweh is not merely a national god. On the contrary, his sovereignty extends far beyond mankind's national boundaries. The wide range of Israel's ancient neighboring peoples here under the judgment of Yahweh represents the whole world of nations. It is significant to discern the universal aspect of Yahweh as the almighty sovereign God who is totally different from the local or national gods of Isaiah's day.

The following is a collection of divine oracles. The editor of the book of Isaiah has not thought it necessary to present them in chronological order. Indeed, they seem to originate from various periods of Isaiah's prophetic activities. Moreover, their Isaianic authorship is even questionable in some cases. So far as they can be ascribed to Isaiah, they seem to originate from the period 715-705 B.C., after the death of Ahaz, who had rejected the prophetic message of Isaiah; thereupon Isaiah was called to proclaim God's judgments against Philistia (Isa. 14:28-32). The situation in Judah had improved once Hezekiah became king. For the time being there seemed to be no reason for Isaiah to pass judgment against his own people. Then again, some oracles here have been added later and have been attached to the authentic Isaiah oracles. It is worthwhile noting that similar oracles of judgment are also included in the book of Jeremiah (Jer. 46–51) and in the book of Ezekiel (Ezek. 25–32). In both cases the relevant collection of oracles against foreign peoples comes in the middle of the book in question. They are enclosed symbolically in what God has to say in the first place to his own people Israel.

ORACLES CONCERNING BABYLON, ASSYRIA, AND PHILISTIA

13:1–14:32

AGAINST BABYLON (13:1-22)

The historical references here point to the middle of the 6th cent. B.C., most likely after the death of Nebuchadnezzar of Babylon (562), and so these oracles were uttered by a later disciple of the master. Babylonian power began to crumble preceding the enthronement of Cyrus of the Medes (550) as king over the former Babylonian Empire.

Isaiah 13:1-22 is a literary unit, though it reveals some unifying redactional activity. Verses 2-16 proclaim in general the wrath of the LORD "in that day," in a manner similar to the prophecies of the "later" prophets (cf. Joel 2:1-11; Zeph. 1:14-18; Zech. 14:2, 6). It is only in Isa. 13:17-22 that the prophetic message of a terrible judgment in general becomes connected particularly with the circumstances of Babylonia after having been defeated by the Medes (cf. Jer. 50:1–51:58).

Title (13:1)

The Hebrew verb for "oracle" is *massa'*, derived from a verb which means "to lift up." Most modern interpreters understand it as "to lift up the voice" when solemnly proclaiming the Word. As such it is also understood as "divine utterance." This prophetic utterance is usually short and concrete, containing a message of judgment.

This is an oracle "concerning Babylon." Not before Isa. 13:19, however, is the name of Babylon mentioned. The reason for this may be the influence of the similar prophecy of Jeremiah (Jer. 51:24-32), where Yahweh is said to avenge Babylon because of its iniquities against Judah. This relationship points therefore to the later origin of this oracle in the Isaianic tradition. The epithet "Isaiah the son of Amoz" has been given to it because Isa. 13:2, 5, 6, 11 all echo Isaiah's previous language.

The place of Babylon in the theological view of Judah was connected with the fall of Jerusalem, the Exile, and the termination of the kingdom of Judah. As such Babylon was considered as a symbol of all worldly powers that rebelled against God by thwarting his plan to use Israel as his chosen instrument. Babylon as a symbol of evil is taken up in the books of Daniel and Revelation and in much Jewish literature.

The Lord Summons the Armies of the Nations (13:2-5)

By raising a signal, using a loud cry, and by "waving the hand" (i.e., by pointing and gesticulating), the LORD as the "commander in chief" makes an urgent call to the armies of the nations to assemble "on a bare hill" (vv. 2-3). The armies are to come from afar (cf. 5:26). They are called to invade "the gates of the nobles," for it was at the gates of the city of Babylon that the power and wealth of the nobles were concentrated.

It is most surprising that these are called "my consecrated ones." Aren't these foreign nations worshipping their own idols? This expression recalls the ancient "holy war of Yahweh" as known at the time of Joshua and the Judges. Those who were recruited for the holy war were subject to the ritual laws of consecration (cf. Deut. 23:9-14). They were consecrated because Yahweh purposed to use them to serve his plans, namely, to execute his anger against God's enemies. As such they are described as "proudly exulting ones." In this context those "consecrated ones" were the Medes (Isa. 13:17), insofar as they served God's purpose.

This creates a great problem in missiology. On the one hand, how do we consider people of other faiths who show themselves to be earnest and faithful to their particular religions? On the other hand, how do we consider so-called Christians who may exercise abominable practices? The challenge and danger for Christians is that they behave as the "proudly exulting ones" (v. 3), which in no sense serves God's purpose. The Church must remember that it is first of all *God* who "gathers the outcasts," but

that he does so by working through his people's loving service of
the nations (56:6-8).

13:4-5   A great multitude, composed of the armies of the nations of the East, now gather together on the mountains with great
"tumult." These mountains were presumably located in the land of
the Medes, northeast of Babylon. The great multitude of armies
consisted not only of the Medes, but also of various nations which
were subjected to Babylon and who now joined the Medes under
Cyrus. They came from afar, "from the end of the heavens" (13:5),
which means the uttermost distant point human eyes can see. Considered from the point of view of Palestine, where the prophet
lived, the farthest Eastern country known was Persia. Actually, at
that time the Persians joined the Medes and together they founded
the kingdom of the Medes and Persians.

Behind all these political upheavals and human ambitions cherished by the Medes and the Persians the LORD of hosts was working out his own plans. Their secular war becomes the war of
Yahweh, who "is mustering a host for battle" (v. 4). They become
"the weapons of his indignation" serving God's purposes. Such is
the way Yahweh chooses at times to work and intervene in world
history.

". . . To destroy the whole earth" (v. 5) cannot be taken in a literal geographical sense. In line with the total contents of this chapter, it is obvious that the whole Babylonian kingdom is meant here.
As such this kingdom represents all worldly power, the kingdoms
that covered "the whole earth," the known world of the ancient
Near East. It is the prophet's intention to show that even this
mighty Babylonian kingdom and the new emerging world power
of the Medes and Persians are all under God's sovereign control and
subjected to God's purposes, yet without eliminating their own responsibility.

The Day of the Lord Is a Day of Destruction (13:6-16)

This was already one of the most important messages of the 8th
cent. prophets (cf. Amos 5:18-20). "On that day" the holy God of
Israel will execute a universal judgment; he will vindicate his holiness and glory by showing his anger against all rebellious peoples,

including those who have been unfaithful in Judah and Israel. For them the day of the LORD will become a day of wailing and destruction, anguish and agony. All the strength, courage, and pride of mankind will melt away, and instead they will "look aghast at one another" (Isa. 13:8) in total frustration and confusion.

The last line of v. 8, "their faces will be aflame," produces difficulties in interpretation. The Indonesian version of the Bible (LAI) reads "their faces like feverish," which means feverish red. In such circumstances of panic we rather expect to see pale faces! But on the other hand, the reddish color of their faces could also be understood as relating to the ultimate efforts and anguish of a woman in travail. So we may read: "With agony on their faces."

13:9-13   The fierce anger of the LORD will be poured out against the earth and all that is on it. It will even affect the whole universe, which is considered as one entity, everything in it being interrelated. Therefore the earth will be destroyed and made desolate. All life on earth will cease, and there will only be deadly silence. What is the ultimate reason for this destruction, and to whom is God's fierce anger directed? It is because of the sin of the humanity that occupies the earth. Who are they? They are the arrogant, the ruthlessly haughty of mankind (13:11; cf. 2:9, 11, 17). And so the simple, the poor, being "bound up in the bundle of life" of the universe, must suffer along with the ruthless.

The glory of the heavenly bodies will vanish; instead there will be only deep darkness (cf. Amos 5:8). Without light life is impossible and everything will revert back into chaos, as it was in the beginning (Gen. 1:2). Astral worship proves to be vain. According to the psalmist this terrible darkness as a sign of God's anger is likened to the effect of an earthquake (Ps. 18:7). Nature, sea, and the mountains will all tremble, and the foundations of the earth be laid bare (Ps. 18:15). This OT image finds its echo also in the NT (Matt. 24:29; 2 Pet. 3:10; Rev. 6:12-17).

13:14-16   The panic on earth will have various aspects. Here it is described in terms of war and of disaster and of the cruel destruction caused by human enemies. The local situation is given therefore as a sample. No particular enemy or city is mentioned here. The generality of the picture might thus be related to Isa. 13:1-2.

The inhabitants of the invaded city will have to flee like a "hunted gazelle" or as "sheep" without a shepherd. ". . . Every man will flee to his own land" indicates that these are strangers who have made their fortune in the city that is under siege. Referring back to v. 2, these might well be the nobles of the city of Babylon; indeed, there were many such nobles there, who were appointed as local kings over subjected peoples. The destruction is cruel and total; no one can escape. Men and babes are slain and women ravished before being cruelly killed (vv. 15-16). Their luxurious homes will then be plundered.

This whole passage (vv. 2-16) proclaiming universal judgment (cf. 18:3; Amos 8:9), originally derived from the prophecies of Isaiah, has now been applied to the destruction of Babylon. The editor has recognized that the word of Isaiah is the Word of God and that therefore it is alive in every new situation.

The Fall of Babylon (13:17-22)

The second part of this chapter is important and helpful for a better understanding of the first part. Here the destruction of Babylon by the Medes is clearly stated. This distinctly points to the 6th cent. After the death of King Nebuchadnezzar of Babylon (561) the unified kingdom of the Medes and Persians became a mighty and undefeatable nation under Cyrus (from 560). This united kingdom defeated Babylon in 539.

13:17-18   The LORD has now "stirred up" the Medes, a cruel but courageous people well trained in war, against Babylon, which had been weakened by internal strife. The Medes were driven by revenge, hate, and lust against Babylon. This was not merely lust for the plentiful gold and silver available there. In a merciless way the Medes slaughtered all men, women, and children—even "the fruit of the womb" (Isa. 13:18; cf. Amos 1:13; 2 Kgs. 8:12; 15:16). This they did on their own responsibility, not God's, and in accordance with their natural lusts.

13:19-20   The Babylonian Empire was indeed glorious in its time. It was seemingly undefeatable, and its domain stretched from the Euphrates to the Mediterranean Sea; its splendor and pride were due to its spiritual and cultural wealth and treasures. Marduk, its chief god, was considered to be the sustainer and vindicator of all world order, and therefore was of universal importance. The city of Babylon was full of magnificent buildings, temples, palaces, and fortresses. But this proud kingdom was to be overthrown and turned into ruins and desolation. The fate of Babylon would thus be that of Sodom and Gomorrah. Its ruins would remain, but the city would never be built up again. No Bedouin would stop over there, nor would a shepherd seek shelter for his flock among the ruins.

13:21-22 "Wild beasts" *(tsiyyim)* will have taken over the ruins. The city will also be inhabited by "satyrs" *(se'ir,* meaning "male goat" or "the hairy one"), evil spirits in the form of a hairy male goat that was believed to hide in desolate places and attack human beings (cf. Luke 11:24); in those days it could be difficult to distinguish between animals and evil spirits. In other words, the powers of evil, destruction, and darkness would dominate the ruins of Babylon.

". . . Its time is close at hand" (Isa. 13:22). In reality the fall and destruction of Babylon in 539 was only the initial event in the whole process of fulfillment of this oracle. During the reign of Darius a generation later Babylonia tried to rebel, but it was soon overwhelmed and the city was destroyed once again. Alexander the Great tried but failed to rebuild Babylon in 330, and ever since then it has been left out of the history books. However, the fall of Babylon as a symbol of anti-God world power has an eschatological significance beyond the historical event. That is why it is referred to again in Rev. 18:2ff.

God's involvement in world history cannot be thought of apart from Israel. Babylon, which put an end to the kingdom of Judah, is mentioned first in the whole series of judgments. But at the end (ch. 23) the universal renewal is also connected with the Return and renewal of Israel "in that day."

There still remains, however, the problem of the execution of God's judgment through a wicked and sinful medium such as were the Medes. Although employed as God's agent, this evil instrument will also be judged eventually because of its wickedness. The Medes are called the "consecrated ones" (13:3) but not the "holy ones."

83

Holy are those who really serve God in full fellowship and faithfulness to him. As such they are more than merely "consecrated" tools or agents; they are the chosen "people of God."

Chapter 14 contains a satire on Babylon (Isa. 14:4b-21), preceded by an introduction (vv. 1-4a) that briefly expresses reassurance for Israel and offers insight into the reason for Babylon's fall and its meaning for Israel.

Words of Assurance (14:1-4a)

Yahweh will remain the faithful God of Israel. He had given his Covenant to Israel and made promises to the patriarchs in the past. He had showed his faithfulness when his people suffered in the house of bondage in Egypt. This steadfast love of his is thus the ultimate reason and motivation for his redeeming acts. What does this mean then for Judah in the present situation? Four points should be noted in this theological introduction to the satire against Babylon.

1. The LORD will once again "have compassion on Judah" and will still *('od)* "choose Israel." It is remarkable how Judah and Israel are mentioned together to denote the unity of the chosen covenant people. They are to be reunited as one new people, experiencing a new exodus and new blessings (cf. Isa. 41:18-19; 40:2).

2. The promise of "their own land," which has been overrun by the Assyrian and Babylonian armies, will also receive new fulfillment (cf. 10:20-22; Ezek. 37:14).

3. The people of the new covenant will transcend its traditional and national limitations, because "aliens will join them and will cleave to the house of Jacob" (Isa. 14:1). Thus Israel will be a blessing to the nations as God had promised Abraham they would be (cf. Gen. 12:2; Isa. 11:10-12).

4. The house of Israel will be glorified above all other nations. In the new age to come all roles will be reversed. The house of Israel as one reunited new people of God will "possess" their former oppressors in "the LORD'S land" (understood in a more general sense as his "kingdom") and make them servants of God in serving Israel: ". . . they will take captive those who were their captors (making them 'proselytes' of the faith, 2:3; Zech. 8:20-22), and rule over those who oppressed them" (Isa. 14:2).

It seems more likely that we should interpret these verses in a general eschatological sense rather than in a literal one. They seek to show the glory of the new people of God, the new Israel, consisting of all believers who will inherit the kingdom. This process of renewal and the coming of the new age will serve as concrete signs and pledges of the ultimate fulfillment of the promises. Thus along this glorious perspective v. 2 serves as an appropriate prelude for the taunt song in the following passage.

The pain, travail, and hard service pressed upon the house of Israel, mentioned in v. 3 (and see 40:2) seem to refer to those with past sufferings which culminate in the Babylonian Exile. The fall of the Babylonian Empire therefore means a new era for the liberated people returning to their homeland. Thus we are dealing with a vision in the Isaianic tradition years after the death of our prophet.

A new era of rest and peace then will follow upon the terrible judgment that will have been accomplished in that day (cf. 13:6, 9; 25:8). This picture should be understood once again in an eschatological sense. After the destruction of all worldly power and pride (represented here by the king of Babylon), the people will magnify the LORD as the almighty victor and redeemer. But at the same time a taunt song against the kings of all the Babylons of history will be raised (14:4a).

Satire on Babylon (14:4b-21)

Differing from the previous verses which were written in prose, this pericope has been written as poetry and then appended to the prose passage.

The poetic satire, deriding in a most lively way the fall and the death of a world-king, does not mention the name of God, except in v. 5, nor the name of any king or kingdom. As such it could be considered as originally independent poetry, which has been aptly applied to the fall of Babylon.

14:4b-8 First we hear the earth rejoicing because of the death of an "insolent" king. The object of the taunt here is obviously the king of Babylon and all the rulers in the Babylonian Empire. "Staff" (or rod) and "scepter" are symbols of authority and oppressing power (cf. 10:5ff., 24; 14:29). Therefore this Babylonian oppression reminds Judah of the ancient slavery they had undergone in Egypt (Exod. 2:11; 5:14, 16). But now, those "unceasing blows . . . with unrelenting persecution" (Isa. 14:6) have ceased. How is this possible? It is because "the LORD has broken the staff of the wicked, the scepter of rulers" (v. 5). Consequently the whole earth is now quiet and rejoices at the death of the tyrant. Due to the "unceasing blows" and "the insolent fury" of "the oppressor" (v. 4), the world has suffered, mourned, languished, and withered, been polluted and laid waste (cf. 24:3-5). For ages the cypresses and the cedars of Lebanon have suffered from the greedy hewers coming up from Assyria and Egypt (14:8), plundering the forests for building material for royal palaces. But now the glory of Lebanon will be restored (cf. 35:2b; 60:13).

A century ago the German scholar Bernard Duhm declared that this oracle revealed a "revoltingly arrogant expectation." But much study of biblical theology has been done since then. In Duhm's day most scholars in the West were accustomed to take for granted the "Greek" philosophical division between matter and spirit. The "Greeks" thus separated between the real and the actual, body and soul, heaven and earth, politics and religion and read these suppositions into the text of the OT. But unlike the civilizations of virtually all the peoples of the ancient world, the Hebrews (followed by the NT) never thought in this manner. The modern evangelist who declares that God loves "you" but hates your sins is out of tune with the biblical revelation. For Isaiah it is the sinner, not his sins, who is under the judgment of the God of love. Thus, since all humanity is composed of sinners, all must come under the judgment of God. (This is the substance of Paul's argument at Rom. 8:1-4 and 11:32.)

Violence against nature and pollution due to misuse of power by greedy and unscrupulous people is an old problem. The LORD is not careless about this human sin. Respect for nature and its resources, concern for the common welfare and for peace between the nations—these have become burning and vexing global problems. They should be solved comprehensively by the nations. An urgent call to the present-day "rulers of the world" must be heard: to the amazing technocrats, the powerful politicians, the colossal industrialists, the mighty superpowers with their nuclear weapons. The majority of the world's population—living in unrest, struggling against terrible hunger and poverty, suffering from injustice, the color bar, and maltreatment—cries out for help by means of brotherly love and sympathy until "the whole earth is at rest and quiet" and "they break forth into singing" (Isa. 14:7; cf. Zech. 1:11).

14:9-10   How does Sheol welcome the deceased king? It is most ironical that not only the whole earth reacts to the death of the king, but also in Sheol, the netherworld of the dead and of the shades, derision is heard (v. 9). According to the ancient Israelite imagination Sheol was located in the depths of the earth; it is the "underworld," where there is only silence and inactivity. But in this pericope, according to the imagery of the poetic satire the situation on earth is still continued in Sheol, since God's creation is one unity. The deceased kings occupy a special place there, sitting on their thrones and surrounded by the shades of their servants (cf. Ezek. 32:22-23). Those shades sitting on their thrones are supposed to be the leaders of nations and kings who know the deceased tyrant, and have suffered from him on earth. Now in a most ironical way those shades on their thrones revive and even get excited; they rise up "from their thrones" (Isa. 14:9) to welcome the royal entry of the mighty king! The rest and tranquillity of Sheol has been disturbed! However, it is not a warm hearty welcome of homage and honor that the shades give; on the contrary, it is an ironical welcome full of revenge and accusations. They all rejoice in the death of the tyrant and allocate to him the deepest corner of the Pit (v. 15; cf. Ezek. 32:23).

14:11   Now the poet begins his conclusion, expressing the vanity of human pomp and power. The picture has now shifted to the situation in Sheol. During his life on earth the king had been surrounded by all manner of royal splendor and glory in his palace and served by countless servants. He had been to sleep on soft mattresses and covered by luxurious blankets. But all this has now changed in the grave. Now maggots and worms become his bed and covering.

14:12-15   He who exalts himself shall be abased. This is wholly true for the Babylonian king, who is pictured here as the "Day Star, son of Dawn" (Heb. *helel ben-shahar*). This is the eastern star or the star of the dawn. Dawn's son Helel has been too ambitious and haughty, having aimed to ascend to heaven above all other stars in order to set up his throne on "the mount of assembly (of the gods)" in the far north. His ultimate goal is to overthrow the Most High *(el elyon)* and achieve absolute power and sovereignty over the universe (cf. 2 Thess. 2:3-4). Helel, the star of dawn, acts just before dawn, shining proudly and brightly in the eastern sky. But at daybreak when the rays of the rising sun are peeping through the reddish sky on the eastern horizon, the star of dawn grows paler and paler until it finally vanishes from sight. According to this Canaanite mythology, which our poet has adapted for his purposes, when Helel was in the act of rising the sun-god Shamash arose to chase him and cast him down to earth. In such a manner, then, the haughty king of Babylon will be thrown down into the deepest deep, that is, into Sheol. There the deepest corner of the Pit will be his abode.

In Isa. 47 Deutero-Isaiah applies the theme of ch. 14 to the Babylon of his day. He names the queen "the virgin daughter of Babylon." She (or Babylon) had boasted: "I shall be mistress for ever" (47:7). "I shall be" is Heb. *ehyeh,* God's own name for himself at Exod. 3:14, for it can be rendered by either "I shall be" or "I am." But in Isa. 47 the queen follows the declaration with the words: "I am, and there is no one besides me" (47:8, 10). We are therefore not surprised to hear the prophet pronounce judgment upon her in the words: "Disaster . . . and ruin shall come on you" (v. 11).

The profoundest sin that mankind can entertain is expressed in the boasted desire: "I will make myself like the Most High" (14:14). This reminds us of the first sin of mankind in the garden of Eden, of the temptation of the Serpent, and of mankind's sinful nature as it is expressed also in the story of the tower of Babel. This mythological picture then came, in later centuries, to represent these evil worldly powers that rebel against God, or the anti-God world power of the anti-Christ (cf. Dan. 11:36; 2 Thess. 2:4).

14:16-20a   On earth people look with disgust and contempt upon the miserable corpse of the king. From earth down to Sheol and from Sheol back up to the earth the sounds of taunt and wonder are still heard. On earth the scene is pictured like a terrible battlefield where the unburied corpse of the king is found among the slain and "pierced by the sword" (v. 19). If we take the NEB translation of v. 12 which says that the star of Dawn was "felled to the earth, sprawling helpless across the nations," then we might consider vv. 16-20a closely connected with v. 12.

The death of the king creates great wonder and excitement because of the sharp contrast between his former and his present state. Now his corpse lies unburied, miserable, and unrecognizable like "mere loathsome carrion" (v. 19 NEB), trodden under the foot of mankind. On the contrary, the kings whom he had previously held in subjection are now lying "in glory, each in his own tomb" (v. 18).

Even today traditional and honorable Chinese tombs are built on a hill overlooking a valley with its rice fields and running waters. They sit, quiet, serene, full of majesty, as if unaffected by time and history. The tomb is considered as the eternal abode of the soul, but is also the pride of the family. Here is the place where the family at large assembles at regular intervals, in the presence of their forefathers, to hold and to enjoy a family reunion.

In ancient times a tomb was considered of crucial importance, as it was closely connected with personal and ancestral honor and provided a guarantee for the well-being of the deceased spirit in the life after death. This is especially true for the royal tomb. To be left unburied is too bad a fate, because according to the ancient belief their spirits would never come to rest, always wandering and looking for refuge and for food in desolate and dark places. Again the king is equated with an untimely birth, that is, an aborted fetus, one who had never been born!

14:20b-21   The prophet now comes to the climax of the message. "The descendants of evildoers" will never be mentioned or remembered because of their disgusting reputation. "A good name is better than precious ointment" (Eccl. 7:1). Applied then to the descendants of the Babylonian king, their fate will be harrowing indeed. All the king's descendants will be slain (v. 21) and his dynasty terminated for evermore. According to the ancient view, it will be not only the guilty king who would be killed; the same fate is reserved for the whole family. Such a fate befell the dynasty of Omri (2 Kgs. 9:1–10:11) and the descendants of Zedekiah (2 Kgs. 25:6-7). This execution was meant to prevent the comeback of the dynasty, as is said in Isa. 14:21: ". . . lest they rise and possess the earth. . ." This warning reveals the close relationship and responsibility that exists between the generations (cf. Exod. 20:5; Lam. 5:7).

In this connection we note once again the ethical problem facing us today. Will future generations also lament because of our present irresponsible way of living through our exploitation of nature? Concerning this personal responsibility we also read in Jer. 31:30 that ". . . every one shall die for his own sin; each man who eats sour grapes, his teeth shall be set on edge." The prophetic message reminds people not to rely on the faith of the fathers or on the traditional false hope of salvation. In this sense the prophet Ezekiel also stresses the seriousness of personal responsibility (cf. Ezek. 18:26). But nevertheless, it is still true that the sins of the fathers can cause much suffering to their descendants. Personal responsibility requires personal conversion and fellowship with God, without disregarding the collective sense of common responsibility to future generations.

Babylonia Will Be Destroyed Totally (14:22-23)

These prose verses are the closing and concluding words of the long oracle (Isa. 13:1–14:23). They pick up the idea expressed in verse in vv. 20b-21. It is the LORD of hosts who will rise up against Babylonia and cause it to vanish from history. The picture of "Babel's" destruction mentioned at the end of ch. 13 is taken up again in 14:23 (cf. 13:19-20). All remnants of Babylonia will be swept away and their abode will be a place for "the hedgehog" (Heb. *qippod* describes some creature that lived in desolate places) or a swamp where nobody can live. As this might sound unbelievable, the strong expression "says the LORD of hosts" occurs twice. In a wider sense too, of course, the Babylonian kingdom here may speak of the universal "demonic powers" which dominate the world (cf. Rom. 8:3; 1 Cor. 15:24; 2 Thess. 2:9; Rev. 13:2; 17:13-14).

AGAINST ASSYRIA (14:24-27)

This pericope seems to be an originally independent oracle, showing some parallel resemblance to those in chs. 9 and 10 (e.g., com-

pare 14:25 with 9:4 and 10:27). The typical expression "the outstretched hand" (14:26-27) is also used in 9:12, 17, 21 and 10:4.
This pericope also shows discontinuity with the previous one, because the object of the LORD'S anger is not Babylonia but Assyria.
It might be considered as originating from the last two decades of
the 8th cent. B.C., after the fall of Samaria in 722 or during the
reign of Sargon of Assyria (722-705).

The judgment of Assyria is introduced by a solemn announcement
by the LORD of hosts saying that everything he has planned and purposed will stand (14:24). He himself will break the Assyrian power
and "trample him under foot" (v. 25). This will happen "upon my
mountains," that is, upon the Judean hills and upon Mt. Zion itself.
And it did happen in 701 (cf. 2 Kgs. 19:35, 37).

God's purpose is to liberate Jerusalem from the Assyrian siege,
but in a wider sense to liberate all the nations of that day from the
Assyrian yoke of oppression. This was not realized until 612 with
the downfall of Nineveh, the capital of Assyria.

There is a striking similarity between Assyria and Babylonia as
described here. Both are called "the rod of my anger," but both are
stricken by God's anger. Both are considered as world powers
under God's judgment. The LORD is the sovereign God over all nations. This has been evident in the past and will be so also in the
future. Behind all this drama therefore lies God's plan and purpose
that must be reckoned with. The Assyrian proof will be followed
by the Babylonian proof. For this reason the oracle against Assyria
is mentioned once again and is added as a closing pericope to the
long oracle concerning Babylonia. What Isaiah wants to make clear
is that Yahweh is the LORD of history in all ages.

AGAINST PHILISTIA (14:28-32)

The composition of this section creates some problems. Isaiah
14:30a appears to be out of context and could better be related to
v. 32b, with v. 32a standing on its own. Other problems concern
the chronological relation of the death of King Ahaz to this oracle.
Who is meant by "the rod which smote you (Philistia)" (v. 29)? It
is unlikely to refer to Ahaz; on the other hand, v. 31 declares that
the terrible oppressors come from the north. It is therefore more
likely to refer to the Assyrians. Which Assyrian king could be

meant here? The problem now is how this smiting actually happened "in the year that King Ahaz died" (v. 28).

Apparently no satisfactory solution can be found in this way. Otto Kaiser (*Isaiah 13–39*, 51-53) shares the opinion that the Isaianic origin of the title in v. 28 cannot be confirmed. According to Kaiser this oracle must originate from a much later date than the other Isaianic oracles. As a result no great value can be attached to this introductory verse to define the authorship and the historical situation and date involved.

Philistia and Judah are summoned not to rejoice too early, assuming that the rod which has smitten them has been broken. Those cruel oppressors are described in mythological symbols originating from Egypt and Babylonia, namely, "adder" and "flying serpent." These symbols denote the terrible demonic power that dominates the whole earth, applicable at the moment to Assyria (cf. 10:7-8). In the apocalyptic passages the flying serpent is called Leviathan, while the sea dragon reigns over chaos (cf. 27:1).

Who is identified by the serpent, the adder, and the flying serpent? Evidently Tiglath-pileser III (745-727 B.C.) can be considered as the founder of the great Assyrian kingdom, which dominated the whole ancient Near East (except Egypt) by the end of the 8th cent. After 739 the northern kingdom had been subjected and had to pay tribute to Assyria (2 Kgs. 15:19). At the Syro-Ephraimite War (734-733) Israel was subjected once again and devastated by the Assyrian "serpent."

Sargon (722-705), a descendant of Tiglath-pileser III, launched a fatal blow on the northern kingdom (722) as well as on Syria, which also endeavoured to stand up against Assyria. He might be identified with the adder "from the serpent's root" (Isa. 14:29). After Sargon had died a new revolt broke out in Philistia, and Judah participated in this. Sennacherib, who succeeded Sargon, once again undertook military action in 701 and Jerusalem was besieged. Sennacherib might be identified with "the flying serpent," who eventually fled from Jerusalem through God's intervention.

It has been recommended that we take vv. 30a and 32b together. In Jerusalem "the first-born of the poor," that is, the poorest and most needy people, will have enough food and will live peacefully and safely. For Zion is the symbol of safety and strength, since it has been built by God himself. He has laid in it a strong foundation of "tested stones" (cf. 28:16; Ps. 87:1), so that it becomes a sure refuge for his afflicted people.

How different it will be in Philistia (Isa. 14:30b-31)! For the Philistines there will be famine, slaughter, and death. No remnant will be left. Therefore Philistia is called to wail. The fortified cities of Philistia were well-known for their strong gates providing sure protection against their enemies. But against the Assyrians their mighty gates will fail. See the dark smoke of destruction accompanying the approaching armies from the north!

The sharp contrast between the fate of Philistia and the safe stronghold of Zion offers an important message for Judah under King Hezekiah, namely, that a bond with Philistia against Assyria will be in vain. The Assyrian domination cannot be averted, because Assyria is called a rod of God's anger! The only wise response of Judah is to repent, that is, to change their lifestyle and submit wholeheartedly to Yahweh, because eventually Yahweh will deliver Zion and establish his righteousness therein. He is the faithful God who has already promised, "I will break the Assyrian in my land" (v. 25).

The questioning sentence in v. 32a seems to stand on its own and be a later addition to the chapter. Who is meant by "the messengers of the nation"? The LXX reads merely "nations." They are most likely the messengers sent by the Assyrian king to Hezekiah demanding Judah's surrender (cf. 2 Kgs. 18–19; Isa. 36–37). The prophet disregards this demand by referring to the fact that Zion has been founded by the LORD as the city of God and is therefore a sure refuge.

Others would like to interpret those messengers as coming from Philistia to Judah with a summons to join a common revolt. Still others suggest they come from the surrounding nations, wondering about Jerusalem's liberation from the Assyrian siege; in this case the following sentence (14:32b) would be the answer given them.

In any case, the question in v. 32 requires a definite answer of faith. Political and national crises have always been a serious challenge for Israel's faith. It is the finality of faith that matters ultimately throughout the history of nations in all ages. Isaiah has more to say on this later.

THE DESTRUCTION OF MOAB
15:1–16:14

This oracle comes to us in a poetic form and can be classified as a lamentation. It describes vividly the enemy's attack and the consequent sufferings. But the enemy's identity is obscure. In Isa. 16:8 we are given only the slight indication about the enemy, who are called "the lords of the nations." From the fact that the Moabites evacuated southward, it could be concluded that the enemy in all likelihood arrived from the north; the enemy could thus be the Assyrians at the time of Isaiah. It is, however, uncertain whether the judgment passed here concerns the past or future events.

MOAB IS UNDONE IN ONE NIGHT (15:1-4)

The first two cities mentioned in 15:1 are Ar and Kir. According to Num. 21:15 Ar (Heb. *'ar moab*) is a city at the northern border of Moab at the river Arnon. Presumably it means "the city of Moab," denoting the ancient capital of Moab. Kir *(qir-moab)* was a fortified city located about 40 km. (25 mi.) south of Ar. It could be identified with Kir-hareseth or Kir-heres (Isa. 16:7, 11).

These important cities in Moab were destroyed suddenly in one night. They could be considered as representing the whole country. Evidently there was no opportunity for escape, or for invoking their god Chemosh to avert the calamity. The terrible devastation of Moab is emphasized by the Hebrew exclamation *ki* (15:1), which means "verily."

The destruction of Ar-moab created widespread panic and lamentation all over the country. Dibon, located about 6.4 km. (4 mi.) north of the river Arnon, was likely a center of idol worship. In the heart of the town was a temple to Chemosh, and outside it was another one for open-air cult ceremonies. This place on the hill was considered to be the most important holy place. In these circumstances of panic the inhabitants of Dibon fled to this holy place to seek protection and the help of Chemosh, but in vain! All they could do was to weep helplessly.

At Nebo and Medeba, north of Dibon, the situation was just as bad, full of wailing and mourning. Bald head and shorn beard were signs for mourning and disgrace (cf. Amos 8:10; Mic. 1:16; Isa. 22:12). All the people participated in this national mourning—in their homes as well as in public places.

Heshbon, the former capital city of the Amorite king Sihon, was located about 9.6 km. (6 mi.) north of Medeba, while Elealeh was located about 3.2 km. (2 mi.) northeast of Heshbon. The town of Jahaz lay about 32 km. (20 mi.) south of Heshbon. If the Moabites' cry was heard as far as Jahaz, this could not be meant literally because of the long distance. It might be possible though that those who fled crying from Heshbon and Elealeh moved southward as far as Jahaz. It is remarkable that in this short pericope nine places are mentioned and six verbs are used to denote their weeping. This means that the whole country of Moab was woefully stricken. The destruction was so terrible that "the armed men of Moab cry aloud and tremble."

FLEEING SOUTHWARD (15:5-9)

With deep emotion the prophet describes the wretchedness and sufferings of the Moabite refugees as they flee southward (cf. 22:12, 14; Jer. 9:1).

Although Moab had always maintained evil intentions towards Israel and Judah, the prophet nevertheless had deep sympathy with Moab (15:5; cf. 16:9, 11; 21:3, 4). Its people had now fled towards Zoar at the southern end of the Dead Sea, abandoning Kir-moab which had been destroyed and laid waste.

The name Eglath-shelishiyah creates some difficulty in interpretation. As the name of a particular town it is unknown. Literally it means "three-year-old calves." It may be a later addition to describe the panic of the refugees, as if they were young calves fleeing from danger, frightened and helpless. With loud and heartbreaking cries, the fugitives went up the hill of Luhith and then down to the road leading to Horonaim.

To make the situation even worse, the waters of Nimrim dried up (15:6), and consequently the grass withered and all greenery vanished. Apparently the enemy cut off all watercourses in the north. The waters of Nimrim might be identified with Beth-nimra at the Jordan Valley close to the Moabite hills, where there was much verdure and a stream running down into the Jordan River. At this sight the people's fear, anguish, and despair increased.

Under this miserable situation the Moabite refugees proceeded southward carrying all their belongings, "the abundance they have gained" (v. 7). They crossed the Brook of the Willows (Wadi Zerek) at the southern border of Moab; and so they plod heavily on.

The whole country was full of crying (v. 8). The exact location of Eglaim and Beer-elim is unknown. Perhaps Eglaim was on the southern coast of the Dead Sea (cf. Ezek. 47:10), while Beer-elim may be identified with Beer (Num. 21:16-17), located north of the river Arnon. Thus these two names denote the extreme borders of Moab.

Isaiah 15:9 presents trouble because of its lack of clarity. The MT uses the name Dimon instead of Dibon, which is used in the Vulgate. Several translations retain the MT version (e.g., NEB, NIV, KJV), thus distinguishing it from Dibon (v. 2). According to Otto Kaiser (*Isaiah 13–39*, 69) Dimon could be considered as identical with Kirbet Dimneh south of the river Arnon. Edward J. Young (*The Book of Isaiah*, I, 460) considers it identical with Madmen (Jer. 48:2).

The situation at Dimon was terrible because the waters there were "full of blood." Nevertheless, "I will bring upon Dimon even more" (Isa. 15:9). What this would be is not further clarified.

Verse 9b seems to stand on its own and does not show a clear connection with v. 9a. The enemy is pictured here as a lion, ready to pounce on the Moabite refugees. "The remnant of the land" would then also be a victim of that "lion." Thus even more disasters would follow.

SEEKING REFUGE AT ZION (16:1-5)

This pericope does not reveal itself as a clear literary unit. The second verse rather disturbs the sequence as it goes back to describe the sorrowful situation of the daughters of Moab at the fords of the river Arnon. Verses 4b-5 do not supply an answer to the supplication of the refugees. That answer is given only in v. 6. It has been suggested that this is due to an insertion by a later redactor.

The sending of lambs by the refugees from Moab to the "ruler of the land" (v. 1) indicates their humble request for refuge sent to the king of Judah at Jerusalem. Those lambs were sent from Sela ("stone" or "rock"), presumably the capital of Edom. Even in this, their capital rock city, the refugees felt unsafe and looked for a better refuge at Mt. Zion. It is hard to believe that the Moabites, who were worshippers of Chemosh, had such a strong trust and faith that Jerusalem would provide them with a safe refuge. How did they come to entertain such a hope?

Verse 2 looks back to the situation of panic among the fleeing refugees at the fords of the river Arnon. As such it could be considered as complementary to the circumstances at 15:5-9. The "daughters" who fled from the north are now described as "scattered nestlings," fluttering around and not knowing exactly where to go. They were still weak and unable to take swift and long flights.

Isaiah 16:3-4a, on the other hand, continues the picture given in v. 1. They contain a request addressed to Zion. Who made this request? Presumably they were the messengers sent to bring the lambs to the ruler of Zion (v. 1). They acknowledged that only at Mt. Zion were counsel and justice for the nations to be found (cf. 2:3-4). Yahweh's help and protection are thus described as a "shade like night at the height of noon" (cf. 25:4), as a perfect sure refuge for "the outcasts" (cf. 26:6).

There is, however, a possibility that this appeal to Zion came from the prophet himself, who had every sympathy with the refugees. He considered it most appropriate that those poor Moabites should come to Zion, because Zion was the center of the world and of the nations and was a safe stronghold for the helpless. If so, we meet with eschatological overtones, thus raising the suggestion that 16:3-4a may be a later insertion in the text.

The contents of vv. 4b-5 are of general significance. These verses aim at showing the eschatological glory of Zion and of the "tent of David." They picture the situation where the powers of evil and of destruction have vanished, thus offering new hope and comfort

97

for all oppressed peoples. The LORD'S faithfulness would once
again establish the throne of David forever (cf. 2 Sam. 7:13; Isa.
9:7)—a kingdom based on the love and faithfulness of Yahweh,
and his justice and righteousness. "Steadfast love" here is the *hesed*
God will continue to show to David's descendants in days to come
(Isa. 55:3). However, these verses do not give an answer to the request submitted before. Therefore, in line with 16:3-4a, it is likely
we have here a later addition exhorting the Judean people to remain faithful and to treat all refugees with humanity and merciful
kindness. So then this oracle provides an important message and
appeal to Judah and revives in exilic days the eschatological hope
and comfort that belong in Yahweh's covenant commitment to his
people.

A WAILING FOR THE DESTRUCTION OF MOAB'S VINEYARD (16:6-12)

This pericope closes the long oracle concerning Moab. Apparently
this wailing was caused by the refusal of Moab's request for asylum
(v. 3). Moab had to pay the price of their pride and insolence.

In vv. 6-7 we hear the answer and judgment uttered by the inhabitants of Zion. If Moab wished to be saved they had first to
humble thenselves earnestly before the LORD. But evidently Moab
still remained as ever before: proud, arrogant, and insolent. The
Hebrew MT text reads: "Let Moab wail for Moab," which means:
"Let the Moabites wail together for the terrible fate of Moab."
They were fully responsible for the situation they were in. Being
utterly stricken, they mourned for "the raisin-cakes of Kir-
hareseth." The famous vineyards there would never produce sweet
grapes again, because they were utterly destroyed.

The terrible fate of Moab is now described in an exaggerated
fashion (vv. 8-11). The devastation of the vineyard extends to the
whole land of Moab. Heshbon and Sibnah were located near each
other at the northern border of Moab. Jazer was even farther north.
Moab's branches also spread eastward and strayed as far as the
desert. Its shoots even spread abroad, spread westward over the
Dead Sea! This means that the whole fertile land of Moab languished and the glory of the land was taken away by "the lords of
the nations," that is, the Assyrians (v. 8).

The prophet could not withhold his emotions, and in sympathy he shared in the weepings of Jazer and Sibnah. In a dramatic way he describes how all the joy and gladness of harvesttime has disappeared. At Heshbon and Elealeh (cf. 15:4) the shouts of joy suddenly turned into mourning and wailing because they were robbed of their harvest, leaving the winepresses desolate.

The emotional outburst of the prophet is expressed in many exaggerated ways (16:9, 11). He seems to have a deep sympathy for Moab even though the punishment that befell Moab was well deserved. But human feelings and solidarity have now evoked a strong compassion in the face of human wretchedness (cf. Abraham's prayer of intercession for Sodom, Gen. 18:16-33; and Jesus weeping over Jerusalem, Luke 13:33-34). This is in sharp contrast with the attitude of the prophet Jonah towards Nineveh!

Isaiah 16:12, which may be a later addition, presents a conclusion and teaching concerning the vain efforts of Moab to save itself. Moab's worship of the god Chemosh (cf. 15:2) on the high places was of no avail, even when the Moabites wearied themselves in their sanctuary with praying to their idols. Yahweh the God of Israel is the only true God, and only at Zion is there refuge and salvation for mankind (cf. 17:7-8; 46:1-2).

THE END OF MOAB WILL SOON BE REALIZED!
(16:13-14)

These closing verses, which could be a later addition, must be distinguished from the previous pericope. Isaiah 16:13 contains an explanation of events, declaring that the previous oracle concerns Moab *in the past*. "But now . . ." (v. 14) denotes a definite short time within which the end of Moab is to be accomplished, namely, within three years. Then Moab will disappear from history and be absorbed into the tribes of Arabia.

These closing verses show a close similarity to the closing verses of ch. 21. It is not impossible that they originate from the same redactor.

ORACLES CONCERNING DAMASCUS, EPHRAIM, AND ASSYRIA

17:1-14

The significant relationship existing between Israel and Damascus came especially to light in the context of the Syro-Emphraimite War, when a coalition of kings Rezin of Syria and Pekah of Israel revolted against the Assyrian domination.

A JUDGMENT ON DAMASCUS AND EPHRAIM (17:1-6)

The fact that Damascus and Ephraim are mentioned together points to the Isaianic origin of this pericope at the outbreak of the Syro-Ephraimite War. However, it is worth noting that in v. 1 only Damascus is mentioned, although the fate of Ephraim is addressed. A number of explanations are possible: (1) As political and military allies Damascus and Ephraim were considered one entity. (2) The fate of Ephraim was entirely dependent on Damascus (cf. 10:9). (3) This pericope is separate and is but one part of a series of oracles dealing with foreign nations.

17:1-3 Throughout history Damascus was known as a large and prosperous city, watered by the rivers of Abana and Pharpar, which were "better than all the waters of Israel" (2 Kgs. 5:12a). In Isa. 17:2 the MT reads "the cities of Aroer" (MT *'arey 'aro'er*; so NIV). Indeed, there were two cities bearing the name of Aroer, one in the land of Moab and the other in Ammon, both located on the eastern side of the river Jordan. So this expression could be understood to refer to the area east of Jordan in general. As such it would express the total destruction of the area around Damascus from north to south. Others prefer to follow the LXX, as does the RSV which translates Heb. *'adey 'ad*, meaning "for ever." There is, however, in principle no objection against either version or translation.

100

The first mention of Ephraim occurs in v. 3. By "the fortress" of Ephraim is meant the capital city of Samaria, which was indeed a very strong fortress built on a hill. This fortified city would disappear from Ephraim and would become a heap of ruins at the fall of Damascus. "The remnant of Syria" (i.e., Damascus) would disappear together with "the glory of the children of Israel." In fact, about ten years later Samaria did fall and the northern kingdom of Israel vanished from history.

17:4-6 These verses should be distinguished from those which precede because originally they seem to have stood on their own. The opening phrase "And in that day . . ." usually denotes a later time. Three features stand out in the picture presented here: (1) "the glory of Jacob will be brought low" (v. 4), (2) as with the remaining "ears of grain" at the time of gleaning (v. 5), (3) and with the few remaining "berries" after the olive tree has been beaten and gleaned (v. 6).

In the first picture northern Israel is personified by Jacob, their most honored ancestor (v. 4). "The glory of Jacob" as such was manifested in Yahweh's faithful relationship with his people as LORD of the Covenant. Politically this glory was related to the extensive kingdom of Israel during the reign of Jeroboam II (786-746 B.C.). Under Pekah (737-732) this glory showed a low profile, partly due to the coalition with Damascus and the common efforts of these small nations to revolt against Assyria. But now, this "glory of Jacob" is pictured as a fat man who later becomes thin and feeble due to some incurable disease. In actual fact Assyria was to come and launch the fatal blow.

The second picture (v. 5) is that of grain brought in at harvesttime. The reapers gather the standing grain and harvest the ears. After the harvest the glory of the field disappears and only a few ears are left for the gleaners. The valley of Rephaim is located outside the southeastern part of Jerusalem, just outside the city gates. This valley is mentioned because it is fertile ground and good for fields of grain.

The third picture (v. 6) concerns the time of harvest and the gleaning of the olive trees. Olive trees were shaken or beaten to let their fruit fall down. Finally only a few berries were left at the top of the highest boughs. This remnant would also be gathered by the gleaners. This means that even the few survivors of Israel would be deprived of the glory they had once known.

This oracle must have sounded quite shocking, in that Israel was to be treated equally with Damascus—as a heathen people. The insertion of this pericope in this context seems to be a serious warning for Judah not to rely on other nations for salvation (as did northern Israel) but on Yahweh alone, the God of Israel.

THE LURE OF FOREIGN GODS (17:7-11)

17:7-9 These verses do not show any clear relationship with those preceding them. Instead they contain only a rather general message. "In that day . . ." is obviously related to the terrible judgment of Yahweh. In that day people will only realize their own weakness and wretchedness and humbly turn to "their Maker," "the Holy One of Israel." This typical Isaianic expression declares on the one hand the distance separating the holy God from sinful mankind, and on the other hand God's gracious close relationship on which mankind can always rely.

"In that day" their idol worship and altars made by their own hands and fingers would be of no avail, and people would be totally helpless in face of God's judgment (cf. 40:18-20; 41:29). The reference to the Asherim and the altars of incense points to Baal and the goddess Ashtoreth, who were worshipped in the Canaanite fertility cult (cf. Deut. 16:21).

Isaiah 17:9 gives some textual problems. Instead of ". . . the Hivites and the Amorites . . ." (RSV, following LXX), the MT reads ". . . in the wood and the highest bough . . ." (cf. NIV ". . . thickets and underbrush"). Apart from this variant reading, the relationship of v. 9 to the previous and to the following verse is not smooth; it could be better related to vv. 4-6.

The mention of the Amorites and the Hivites points to the ancient history of Canaan. In OT usage these peoples constituted the pre-Israelite population of Canaan; indeed, when the Israelites came to Canaan the population was called Amorite and, occasionally, Hivite. The Hivites were a people from northern Mesopotamia at the time of Abraham. Their influence on Amorite culture was very strong in the 18th cent. B.C., when the Amorites dominated the whole Fertile Crescent (of which Canaan was a part). At the time of the Israelite invasion the Amorite cities were destroyed and left totally desolate, remaining so for ages, and became places truly abandoned to thickets and underbrush (NIV).

Such a total destruction, then, will also befall Israel because of its unfaithfulness, so that "the glory of Jacob will be brought low" (v. 4).

17:10-11   The root evil of Israel is mentioned here. "Forgetting God" has a deeper and stronger meaning than the English conveys; it means betraying God by committing adultery with alien gods. In what follows the prophet describes the apostasy of Israel. The "pleasant plants" in the orchard denote the worship of alien gods, because they are in fact alien slips imported from abroad. They point to the pleasant gardens dedicated to the god Tammuz (or Adonis), worshipped in Babylonia and Assyria. These slips were placed in pots to force quick growth. When ready they were flung by groups of women into a pool of water as a kind of rain charm. The pots were meant to symbolize the female sex organs, and so this ritual was performed in order to stimulate both the soil and the woman herself. The beauty of spring does not last long in these countries, because the heat of summer comes quickly. The Adonis flowers in Greece were a symbol of vanity—they "blossom in the morning that you sow" (v. 11)—but the flowers quickly wither and no harvest can be collected. This might be caused by a sudden heat "in a day of grief and incurable pain." This sudden calamity will thus happen "in that day" when God executes his judgment, and the people will be carried away into exile. In this respect the Adonis garden symbolizes the fate of Israel, which is frequently pictured as an adulterous woman (cf. Hos. 1–3; Isa. 57:3ff.; Jer. 3:2; Ezek. 23).

AGAINST ASSYRIA (17:12-14)

Again these verses do not show any direct continuity with those which precede. There is no mention of one particular nation but of "many peoples." However, it seems clear that Assyria is meant here. The mighty Assyrian army indeed consisted of many subjugated peoples and nations. If so, these prophecies seem to point to a later period than that of the Syro-Ephraimite War, because the enemy here is, described as those "who despoil us" and "who plunder us" (Isa. 17:14). To be more precise, they probably originate from the time just before the Assyrian siege of Jerusalem in 701 B.C. At the same time these verses can be considered as an introduction to chs. 18–20 to follow, where it is announced that eventually Ethiopia and Egypt will also be punished by God's judgment. Isaiah is saying it is futile for King Hezekiah to rely on those nations for help. Yahweh is the only God of redemption and salvation! Hezekiah must thus take this message seriously.

The passage begins with the Hebrew word *hoi,* which is used in Jerusalem to announce a death. The Assyrian armies, consisting of many peoples, march forward threatening and frightening "like the thundering of the sea" and the "roaring of mighty waters." There is no explicit explanation as to who this enemy is, but the contemporary reader would surely recognize who is meant.

According to Otto Kaiser (*Isaiah 13–39,* 88), this picture seems to have a mythological background and so symbolizes the revolt of the oceanic forces against the divine cosmological waters. But "he will rebuke them" (v. 13), that is, the LORD of hosts, the mighty God of the universe will rebuke the roaring waters that represent the forces of evil (cf. Gen. 1:6-7; Mark 4:39-40).

Accordingly, the lot of those mighty armies is described in terrible language. They will be like chaff and dust, whirling before the storm of God's rebuke (Isa. 17:13b-14). God will chase them away in just one night (cf. Ps. 46:5-6; 2 Kgs. 19:35). Truly, Yahweh is the triumphant God of salvation, the Rock of refuge and of redemption.

ORACLES CONCERNING
ETHIOPIA AND EGYPT
18:1–20:6

Chapters 18–20 form a unity. During the reign of Hezekiah Ethiopia and Egypt were closely related to each other; they presented a united front to face the ever-growing Assyrian power. Yet Ethiopia succeeded in dominating the Egyptian kingdom. Hezekiah, who at times demonstrated his anti-Assyrian attitude in a revolt (713-711 and 703-701 B.C.), sought political ties with those two affiliated countries. It is at this point then that the prophet Isaiah raised his warning voice declaring that Assyria, Ethiopia, and Egypt would fall by means of God's judgment. The traditional interpretation suggests the second half of the 8th cent. as the historical background of these chapters. However, it should be admitted that some eschatological features in this passage cannot be ignored; for example, no particular people is mentioned, a universal perspective is presented (18:3), and the subjection of earthly kingdoms to the LORD of hosts at Mt. Zion "at that time" is declared (v. 7).

AN ORACLE AGAINST ETHIOPIA (18:1-7)

18:1-2 What country is meant here by the "land of whirring wings"? The usual interpretation relates these whirring wings to the tsetse flies which proliferated in Egypt and Ethiopia. Furthermore, the land is described as located "beyond the rivers of Ethiopia," which would mean the upper Nile region. Therefore, it would not be wrong to identify this land here with Ethiopia.

Ethiopia had sent messengers by the Nile. They had come sailing swiftly in papyrus vessels, probably aiming to persuade Hezekiah to join a common revolt against Assyria. The Judean king most likely consulted the prophet on this matter (cf. 37:2, 3, 21). In 18:2b we hear the answer and message of the prophet to his king. It is as if the prophet had said, "Let the Ethiopians leave Judah alone, because Judah possesses the Rock of refuge and the God of salvation!"

18:3-4   The universal summons in v. 3 reminds us of the similar call to the nations made at 11:10; 13:2, which is characteristic of the holy war of Yahweh. The LORD of hosts called upon all nations to participate in his holy war to aid Judah. But for the moment Judah should remain quiet and put all their trust in the LORD (cf. 30:15) because he will not leave the wicked unpunished but will have dominion forever. The LORD will look quietly from his heavenly dwelling at all the iniquities and confusion going on in the world, knowing precisely when to act. This divine attitude is further described in a figurative way:

- The "clear (NIV 'shimmering') heat in sunshine." This clear heat at noontime suggests quiet conditions, in that neither wind nor rain is mentioned.
- The "cloud of dew in the heat of harvest." At harvesttime a cloud of dew often hangs over the fields for a long while, refusing to move away.

Chapters 18 and 19 emphasize the unpleasant human feeling in such situations from which people look forward to be relieved. For a while it seems nothing will change, but this does not mean a permanent situation because the LORD is not inactive. He is acting in history, even though often it is not visible to human eyes. This quietness of God requires also mankind's quietness in faith (cf. 28:16). But for the enemies it means the quietness before the storm of God's judgment.

18:5-6   God's act of judgment will come all of a sudden. Just before harvesttime, when the grapes are becoming ripe, the LORD will cut off the shoots and the spreading branches (cf. John 15:2, 6). The vineyard is left desolate and there will be nothing but heaps of wood and unripe grapes (cf. Amos 7:1-3).

The vineyard which was once a pleasant and well-kept garden now becomes wild and desolate. Wild beasts and birds of prey find habitation there all summer and winter. Likewise Assyria will be destroyed.

18:7   The oracle concludes with a prophecy concerning a bright future for Ethiopia, when it will come to Mt. Zion to worship the LORD of hosts.

This verse is most likely a later addition inspired by a messianic expectation saying. At "the end," it appears to be saying, the glorious and almighty LORD will subjugate all great nations (such as Ethiopia and Egypt), however great and mighty they may seem to be (cf. Ps. 68:30; 76:12). No wonder God is twice called "LORD of hosts" *(YHWH tsebaot)*, at the beginning and at the end of this verse.

It is worth noting that Zion is called here "the place of the name of the LORD of hosts." This expression, according to Otto Kaiser, has been influenced by the Deuteronomic theology concerning significance of the "name" (Heb. *shem*) of the LORD. This "name" makes a distinction between the LORD in heaven and his abode on earth. It is particularly related to the temple worship at Jerusalem, where the "name" of Yahweh is called upon (Otto Kaiser, *Isaiah 13-39*, 97). At a later stage of development the theological reflection on "the name" tended to use the term as a substitute for the LORD himself, and eventually it even became hypostatized (cf. Isa. 30:27; Deut. 12:5; 2 Sam. 7:13; 2 Chr. 20:8).

AN ORACLE CONCERNING EGYPT (19:1-25)

The prophecies in this chapter seem to be related to the anti-Assyrian tendency of King Hezekiah, who at that time tried to enter into association with Egypt. The prophet warned Hezekiah about his policy, because Egypt itself was about to be seriously punished and brought into confusion.

It is not easy to determine whether this prophecy points to past events or to the future. If we consider this chapter to be closely related to both the preceding and the following chapters and that it functions as a serious warning to Hezekiah, then it is more likely that it points to future events in Egypt. The opening verse announces that the LORD is coming to Egypt "on a swift cloud." The economic collapse due to the waters of the Nile drying up (vv. 5-10) also points to a future event. But in describing the prophecies the prophet employs pictures from the past, from the 23rd and 24th Dynasties when Egypt experienced severe decline.

However, the sins of Egypt are not mentioned; it is the glory of Egypt that will be finally destroyed. Nevertheless, the prophecy ends with a bright eschatological perspective for Egypt.

This chapter can be divided into two parts, the poetic part (vv. 1-4, 5-10, 11-15) and the prose section (vv. 16-25). The poetic part announces the terrible confusion that will result from God's judgment. The prose section prophesies a bright future for Egypt as well as for Assyria, which together with Israel will then worship Yahweh. The LORD does indeed punish, but he also graciously blesses with peace and prosperity.

19:1-4 Yahweh is described as the almighty Creator, lifted up high and sitting on a swift cloud coming to Egypt (cf. Ps. 68:4, 33; 104:3). The use of this mythological picture is to show the glory and almightiness of Yahweh as the living God, active and swift in his actions. There is, however, no indication when and from where Yahweh comes.

The coming of Yahweh produces a double effect: "the idols of Egypt will tremble . . . and the heart of the Egyptians well melt within them"; both become powerless before the holiness and glory of Yahweh. The melting of hearts indicates total confusion, in that the heart is considered as the center of human life in all of one's emotional and intellectual reactions (cf. Isa. 7:2, 4; Deut. 20:8; Ps. 22:14; Josh. 7:5; Isa. 13:7).

Along with this spiritual frustration and mental confusion, which culminates in a state of anarchy and civil war, there is no longer brotherliness or even friendliness. People oppose, suspect, and kill each other. Such anarchy spreads over the whole country, each city considering itself an independent city-kingdom. Centralized authority will cease. Such a chaotic situation had indeed developed during the previous 24th Dynasty. But the history of Egypt to follow was not exempt either from social and political troubles (Isa. 19:2).

There is a close relationship between the function of the heart (Heb. *leb*) and that of the spirit *(ruah)*. If the heart of the Egyptians melts away (v. 1), then their spirit declines and becomes "emptied out" (v. 3; Josh. 2:11; 5:1). The empty spirit becomes vain and meaningless and leads even to despair. In such circumstances of panic people become totally confused in their minds, and they consult idols, sorcerers, and wizards for help (cf. Isa. 8:19).

Finally, God's punishment would be fatal for Egypt, because they will be delivered into the hands of "a hard master," meaning an alien king who is cruel and merciless (19:4). There have been various attempts to identify this ruler, for example, the Assyrian king Esarhaddon who defeated Egypt in 670 B.C. or the Persian king Darius I who defeated Egypt in the 6th century.

19:5-10   God's judgment on Egypt also touched and paralyzed the whole economic life of the country. The river Nile was the source and radial artery of life in Egypt, because it provided both fertility and food for the country. Normally the Nile never dries up; it receives water from the melting snow of the African mountains, and in summer from the heavy rainfalls in Ethiopia. This causes regular floods, when the water level can rise up 7 to 10 m. (23 to 33 ft.) high, inundating the surrounding areas. In such a situation the river looks like a "sea" (cf. 18:2). Therefore, it would be quite amazing were the Nile to dry up. This would be the greatest disaster that could be imagined by the Egyptians, and a proof of the vain results of idol worship (19:3b).

Ever since ancient times Egypt has been famous for its canals; these conducted the waters of the Nile to all parts of lower Egypt. The irrigation works were ingeniously built and became the national pride of ancient Egypt. But, declares the oracle, all these canals and branches of the Nile shall dry up and become foul and stinking because of rotting fish and dead animals. This will result in epidemic diseases (vv. 5-6).

The land around the banks of the Nile is broad and fertile, especially at the Nile Delta where the land of Goshen was located. At the time of the prophet many sown fields were there. This part of the country was considered the national grain barn of Egypt. But what would happen? All this would dry up and the seeds that had been sown would be blown away and be no more (v. 7).

Fishery would also suffer badly (v. 8). Fish were much favored and were a cheap food. Fishing was thus an important source of income for the people. When all had dried up, the fishermen could only "lament" and "languish."

But the general populace also would suffer. The employers and the employees at weaving industries would become unemployed because no basic material would be available. Clothing material would become scarce (vv. 9-10).

Verse 10 presents some problems. Following the MT, the RSV reads "pillars of the land," meaning the leaders of the country. But with respect to the context of the preceding verses this reading seems unlikely. It would be better to presume that this phrase was a parallel to "all who work for hire" (v. 10b). So it might be better to follow the reading of the LXX, which uses a slightly different word meaning "workers" or "laborers" (cf. NIV). Together with all wage earners, they would be "crushed" and "grieved." But it would be a great mistake to think that the wealthy and powerful classes would then be exempt from suffering; indeed, they would experience it even more!

19:11-15 Under God's judgment, the spiritual leaders of Egypt would be put to shame. Egypt had long been proud of its traditional wisdom which had been inherited from the people's "ancient kings," the pharaohs. That wisdom was legendary throughout the ancient Near East; Moses is said to have been educated in "all the wisdom of the Egyptians" (Acts 7:22).

Isaiah 19:11-13 ridicules the foolishness and stupidity of the "princes of Zoan" (Tanis in the Nile Delta, since ancient times the capital of lower Egypt) and the "wise counselors of Pharaoh" (including those of Memphis, the capital of upper Egypt).

The priests were the counsellors to the pharaohs, owing to their special relationships with supranatural powers; therefore they were imbued with spiritual authority and wisdom. But evidently all these counsels proved to be false and foolish. Therefore, they too would be put to shame (v. 3). Yahweh the LORD of hosts overruled all this wisdom. Indeed, they were completely ignorant about the purposes of Yahweh against Egypt. The only thing they could do was to lead people astray (v. 13). The LORD had poured into them a spirit of confusion, rendering Egypt like "a drunken man" who skids and falls in his own vomit (v. 14). The expressions "head or tail, palm branch or reed" in v. 15 refer to all people of all ranks and files.

19:16-25 Written in prose, this pericope may be divided into five parts, each introduced by the specific phrase: "In that day . . ."

110

(vv. 16-17, 18, 19-22, 23, 24-25). Such a phrase is often used for apocalyptic and eschatological prophecies, when they announce the implementation of the LORD'S judgment against the enemies of Israel and the manifestation of God's glory and redeeming power. According to many scholars this kind of prophecy in most cases is of a later date, added onto the older existing prophecies. The contents lead us to regard this pericope as a continuation and climax in the prophetic line of thought, leading as it does in vv. 24-25 to the emergence of a new multinational people of God.

19:16-17   Verses 16-17 seem to fit well into the preceding context. The Egyptians are described as terrified women trembling with fear because of "the hand which the LORD shakes over them." This uplifted hand is ready to punish them repeatedly, just as Egypt had already experienced it in those ancient times around the Exodus event. The preceding pericopes also show clearly how terrible the LORD'S judgment is against Egypt. It is little wonder that the land of Judah becomes a terror to the Egyptians, because the "hand of Yahweh" is actually identical with Judah, the people of God! Every person in Egypt to whom the name of Judah is mentioned is filled with fear, because this reminds him of the purpose of Yahweh against the Egyptian people.

The implementation of this judgment relates to one particular period in history. Following from the preceding pericope (vv. 11-15), these verses give the impression of being motivated by fanatic nationalistic views. Yet what is hinted at is that the whole history of Egypt is being viewed as one unfolding scene. If Egypt is described as a terrified and trembling woman, then this only describes what Egypt eventually became, that is, a nation overrun by the Assyrians, the Persians, the Greeks, followed by the Romans in 30 B.C., and, finally, by the Arabs who in A.D. 641 came to dominate that country and remained to do so throughout the succeeding centuries.

This derisive passage against Egypt has emphasized once more what Isaiah has had to say about each of the nations in turn. Unfortunately, modern mankind can dip into these prophetic denunciations and without seeing them in context come to the conclusion that the God of the OT was merely a cruel, wrathful, and vindictive monster.

Yet we must remember that the context of the prophet's denunciations is his name, "Isaiah" *(yesha' yahu),* "the LORD is Savior." The descriptions of the LORD'S terrible judgments that we have heard in chs. 13–19 were made upon evil plans and selfish, violent purposes such as emanate from the hearts of all people in all nations of the earth—even including the covenant people of God. Isaiah's descriptions form an exposition of what every one of the prophets believed about our human nature—and in fact what the whole Bible believes, as we see from the words of Jesus: "For out of the heart come evil thoughts, murder, adultery, fornication, theft, false witness, slander" (Matt. 15:19).

The primal story that lies behind the whole history of the covenant people records God's detestation of sin and his determination to "blot out man whom I have created from the face of the ground" (Gen. 6:5-7). For of course "sin" is not a "thing" in itself. It is always an action performed by a sinner. The "holy" God (Isaiah's great word) must therefore necessarily be at war with human wickedness in all its aspects. God's holiness and mankind's evil cannot dwell together. This is especially true since, as Isaiah had declared, God is Immanuel, "God *with* us," God in total proximity to this creature who has rebelled against him.

Yet God is the God of love, and the meaning of Isaiah's name ("the LORD is Savior") speaks of his desire that all people should know and love him in return. In consequence, we who read the book of Isaiah cannot begin to appreciate the height, length, depth, and breadth of that love until we have first grasped the terrible extent of humanity's sinful activities. And on these God must first pass judgment. Only then can he begin to redeem the sinner and bring him home to himself.

As his instrument to this end God elected the people of Israel to work *with* him, or rather he elected them that he might work *through* them but *with* their cooperation. In order to do this God made himself present *in* Israel (Isa. 43:1-5; 45:14-15; see G. A. F. Knight, *Servant Theology*) by binding himself to her even as a husband binds himself to his wife (54:5; Hos. 2:16; Jer. 31:32). In consequence, God experienced Israel's rebellion against the bonds of the Covenant as being upon his own "Person." Thus Israel's sin was worse than the evil displayed by the nations, for in her rebellion (Isa. 1:2) Israel was actually thwarting God's plan to be the Savior of the world. So we hear the terrible utterance of God through the lips of Amos (Amos 3:1-2): "You only have I *known* (in the deep sense of union in marriage) of all the families of the earth; therefore I will punish you. . . ."

19:18   With this verse we reach forward to hear how, once God has forgiven his people their indescribable evil in thwarting the plan of God, God has totally forgiven and renewed them (Isa. 40:1) and will now go forward to redeem the nations in and through his elect people. What terrible judgments he had proclaimed upon the two great world powers Assyria and Egypt, one on each side of little Israel. How then is all of this to take place?

There are to be five cities in the land of Egypt which "speak the language of Canaan." The prophet Jeremiah mentions just four cities as Jewish settlements in Egypt, namely, Migdol, Tahpanhes, Memphis, and Pathros (Jer. 44:1). The name of the fifth city given here is rather uncertain. According to the MT it is *ʿir haheres* (so JB), which means "the City of Destruction"; as such it could be identified with Leontopolis. But considering the religious status of these five cities (as Jewish settlements), this name is rather strange. Some other manuscripts of the MT along with the DSS have a different reading which means "the City of the Sun" and may be understood as Heliopolis (Jer. 43:13 RSV). But in that famous Egyptian city people worshipped the sun-god, not Yahweh. The Greek text (LXX) has another reading meaning "the City of Truth." This noble name would thus virtually compete with the lofty status of Jerusalem and Zion (cf. Isa. 1:21b). Which city in Egypt is meant by this name then is uncertain.

If we follow the MT reading "the City of Destruction," the name of this city could be interpreted as pointing to future oppression and suffering (19:2). But this would result in the repentance of the Egyptians there and their turning to the worship of Yahweh.

19:19-22   So Yahweh will be worshipped in Egypt. If vv. 16-17 have been influenced by the Exodus tradition, the present pericope might in some way be influenced by the patriarchal tradition. In ancient times the patriarchs used to build altars in Canaan for the worship of Yahweh who had manifested himself at a particular place. So in the midst of the land of Egypt Israelites would build

113

an altar to Yahweh. At this altar they would bring sacrifices to the LORD.

Further, the Israelites would build a pillar (monument) at the border of the land. The building of a pillar *(matseba)* recalls again the patriarchal tradition (cf. Gen. 28:16-22), as well as the Mosaic tradition (cf. Exod. 24:3-4). This pillar signified that only Yahweh was to be worshipped beyond this point. It functioned as "a sign and a witness" at the border of the land, most likely at the northern border of Egypt east of the Nile Delta and close to Palestine. It seems to have had a symbolic meaning for people crossing the border, for it declared that Yahweh was the only God who is to be worshipped in Egypt as well as in Palestine. The penetration of this Yahweh worship into Egypt is also symbolized by the building of an altar "in the midst of the land of Egypt." Thus Yahweh will have displaced all the many gods of Egypt.

So "at that day" the Egyptians would "know" Yahweh, even as Israel "knows" him, and worship him with sacrifices and burnt offerings. They would no longer be considered as enemies but as a people of God. In days of tribulation Yahweh would hear their cry and send them a savior. The altar and the pillar may have been erected by the Israelites, who by this period were now living permanently in Egypt. Had Israel now perceived the meaning and purpose of their election? God had made covenant with them in order that they might be "a light to the nations, that my salvation may reach to the end of the earth" (cf. Isa. 49:6; Gen. 12:1-3). In other words, God had called Israel with the intent that they should be a missionary blessing in the Diaspora which they would soon have to undergo. And since the Church is the Israel of the new covenant people of God in Christ, this passage in Isaiah reveals that within the New Covenant God is not just calling us to be "saved" but to implement the command of Christ to "go and make disciples of all nations" (Matt. 28:19). Thus in Indonesia, for example, the author's Church seeks to meet the missionary challenge in the various transmigration areas where church people have been spread throughout the whole archipelago.

Yet there is something more to add. The "language of Canaan" (Isa. 19:18) may not refer to the Hebrew language as such. The phrase may be a way of speaking about the language of love, care, and compassion that only Israel knew through its covenant relationship with a loving, caring, and compassionate God. Or the phrase may mean both ideas at once. The LORD will treat Egypt as a father treats his dear son. Punishment is at times necessary and helpful for the sake of well-being. This educational pattern was true for Israel as well as for Egypt (cf. Hos. 6:1; Isa. 40:2). "In that day" Egypt would understand the blessed meaning of suffering and they would "know" Yahweh, not only as the punishing God but also as the hearing and healing God (Exod. 15:26). How great and wonderful is God's mercy, even to Egypt!

19:23 Throughout history Egypt and Assyria were continually hostile to each other. For example, Egypt had to suffer badly from Assyrian domination under the reign of the Assyrian king Esarhaddon (670 B.C.). Consequently Egypt always sought for allies to avenge itself against Assyria. On the other hand, both countries were hostile to Judah! However, "in that day" something "miraculous" would happen: all those countries would become reconciled with each other and have peaceful and friendly relationships with each other (Isa. 19:23).

There was indeed an ancient highway from Egypt through Palestine to Assyria. But the "highway" foretold here should be understood symbolically. The two large countries mentioned, Egypt and Assyria, should be understood in a wider sense as representing the countries and nations of the world living in a hostile situation, just as today we could speak of the First World and the Second World. The direction of this highway from south to north is significant. Egypt (in the south), which has now turned to the LORD, would be no longer revengeful but would have the spiritual and mental strength to take the initiative to meet and to extend a hand of friendship (north) to Assyria. Where God's grace is accepted all hostility disappears, even in a pluralistic society; it is replaced by mutual love and appreciation. This is the way that nations and superpowers in the world can always meet each other, respecting and accepting each other in a friendly and brotherly manner.

In this new age the Assyrians would come to Egypt, no longer as an invader but now as a respected friend. In reverse the Egyptians would come to Assyria not as a vengeful enemy, but as a brother in the LORD. Finally, they would both worship Yahweh together along with Israel. Such is the key to the wonderful peace among nations that is God's plan for his world.

What is prophesied here could be considered as a counterbalance to the "Babylonian confusion" (Gen. 11). It finds its essential fulfillment in the day of Pentecost when the Holy Spirit was poured forth, reuniting peoples of other nations and tongues. There is in consequence a close relationship between world mission and world peace.

19:24-25   These verses contain one of the finest prophecies to be found in the OT. Israel is reminded of their initial calling as it was revealed to Abraham, namely to be a blessing for all the families on earth (Gen. 12:2-3). According to Otto Kaiser (*Isaiah 13–39,* 110), these prophecies can be considered on the same level with Isa. 2:2-3; Zeph. 2:11; 3:9b-10; Isa. 45:20-21. According to this prophecy, Israel will be on a par with Egypt and Assyria, and they will worship Yahweh together. To Israel is not given the privilege to be the *primus inter pares*; rather, "Israel will be the *third* with Egypt and Assyria . . ." Israel would be the "Third World"! However, the eminence of Israel in past history cannot be denied, because through Israel the LORD had revealed his purpose for all mankind.

Therefore, the blessing and the promises initially granted to Israel can now be applied to Egypt and Assyria too. Israel is still regarded as "my people" (cf. Hos. 2:23; Jer. 7:23; 11:4; Ezek. 36:28), but Assyria is called "the work of my hands" (cf. Isa. 60:21; 64:8; Deut. 32:6). Israel itself, based on its long history through father to son, is called "my heritage" (Ps. 94:5; 28:9; Mic. 7:14; Deut. 4:20). These all will have become one new people of God. This will happen at the consummation of the ages, when the glory and vindication of the kingdom of God will be fully realized. This good news of universal blessings is echoed in the gospel of Jesus Christ.

AN ORACLE AGAINST EGYPT AND ETHIOPIA (20:1-6)

In ca. 713 B.C., when there was a general revolt against Assyria, Ashdod presumably sent messengers to Hezekiah with an invitation to join in the revolt. The situation became the more critical when Hezekiah considered accepting the invitation. Similar to what Isaiah had advised Ahaz, he now warned Hezekiah that he should neither join the revolt nor expect any help from Egypt. It seems that this advice was not acceptable to Hezekiah. In such a situation the LORD spoke to Isaiah, instructing him to perform a symbolic act (cf. Ezek. 24:15, 17; 33:21-22). This act was to be performed with attention to detail, in order to expose clearly its symbolic meaning. Isaiah was to loosen his sackcloth from his loins and take off his shoes from his feet (Isa. 20:2).

In verses 3-4 it is not clear when Isaiah carried out this instruction—whether at the outset of hostilities or at their end. Presumably it was done at the outset after Ashdod had been punished by Assyria in 713.

The LORD now calls Isaiah "my servant"; this is an expression of honor for his faithfulness and obedience in his prophetic task, even though at the beginning the meaning of this symbolic act might not have been clear to him.

The prophet, being naked and barefoot, attracted everyone's attention. He was now wearing only the loincloth permitted to a prisoner or a slave. The people simply wondered what had happened to him, but Isaiah seized the opportunity to proclaim the meaning of this symbolic act. His whole demeanor and physical condition thus became "a sign and a portent" for the people. Through it he proclaimed the lot of the Egyptians and Ethiopians, who in a few years time would be led as captives into exile. They would be driven out shamefully, "naked and barefoot," as a sign of total capitulation. The message of the symbolic act was clear: it was absolutely vain to rely on Egypt for salvation.

In verses 5-6 we hear the tragic response of Judah, now "dismayed and confounded." Who is meant by "the inhabitants of this coastland"? That area comprises not only the Philistines but also the Judeans who had joined the revolt at Ashdod with the help of Egypt (cf. 30:1-3, 7; 31:1-3; 36:9). In this way the Judeans had identified themselves with the heathen by renouncing their trust in Yahweh and by relying on human saviors with their horses and chariots.

"And we, how shall we escape?" (20:6). This cry of despair might be applicable to the Judeans (and Philistines) as well as to the Egyptians and Ethiopians themselves. Both will realize their own helplessness, their vain hope in idols, in human power, and in mighty weapons. Sharing the faith of Isaiah the psalmist can say: "It is better to take refuge in the LORD than to put confidence in princes" (Ps. 118:9; cf. 146:3).

ORACLES CONCERNING BABYLON, DUMAH, AND ARABIA

21:1-17

AN ORACLE CONCERNING BABYLON (21:1-10)

21:1-5 This oracle concerning Babylon differs from the previous ones (cf. chs. 13–14, 15–19) with respect to the dubious title it bears.

The prophet trembled at the terrible vision with the accompanying sounds of a sandstorm coming from the Negeb, the "terrible land" in the south. Such a sandstorm is often accompanied by terrible heat and can be quite disastrous (cf. Job 1:19; Hos. 13:15). This sinister calamity illustrates the coming invasion of Elam and Media to defeat Babylon.

This vision also illustrates the great confusion among the subjected nations that preceded the fall of Babylon. There were revolts, betrayals, plunderings, and sufferings throughout the Near East. Babylon, which was much occupied and weakened by internal strife, allowed all these catastrophes to occur.

In the meantime the threat from Elam and Media in the east became more serious as they made ready to invade Babylon. "All the sighing . . . I bring to an end," says the LORD (Isa. 21:2). It was Yahweh who would bring liberation. Yahweh was acting behind the uproar of the nations, the downfall and the rise of kingdoms, making an end to the suffering of oppressed peoples.

In a most emotional way this prophet, who lived a century after Isaiah of Jerusalem, describes his feelings of distress even though the fall of Babylon resulted in the liberation of Judah (vv. 3-4). He compares himself with "a woman in travail" suffering from birth pangs; he suddenly feels as if his stomach is attacked by painful spasms, so that he is "bowed down" in dismay. Even the twilight, which was usually appreciated as a time of leisure and for the en-

119

joyment of family life, now causes his mind to reel and his body to
tremble because of the horrible prospect of the darkness the night
would bring.

On the other hand, the court life at Babylon continued in lavish
fashion, full of splendor and gaiety, its courtiers completely disregarding the critical situation of their country (cf. Dan. 5: Jer.
51:39, 57). But all of a sudden the nobles were summoned to arise
and leave for battle. Due to their negligence they even had to oil
their shields first!

21:6-10 With this announcement from the watchtower the
prophecy concerning Babylon reaches its climax. The prophet
regards himself as observing events like a watchman in a tower
waiting for the word of God (cf. Hab. 2:1). He had to announce
objectively what he would see; all subjective emotional thoughts
on the fall of Babylon were to be avoided. Instead the prophet had
to listen "very diligently" to receive the word of God. However, it
is not clear whether all these events struck home to him through
ecstatic vision or from physical observation from the tower. The
latter interpretation would be more feasible, considering the precise instructions he received and the prediction of the scenes he
would see (Isa. 21:7). For in his mind's eye the prophet saw a multitude of armies coming, consisting of chariots, horsemen, and
riders on asses and camels. Some think that these asses and camels,
animals commonly used for transport of provisions and weapons
as well as for spoils, were employed by the Medes to create confusion among the enemy under attack.

The watchman showed his discipline and perseverance by
watching nights and days continuously. But what he saw eventually (v. 9) was something rather different from what he had seen as
described in v. 7. Now the riders on asses and camels are not even
mentioned! In his excitement he seems to neglect the details and
instead concentrates his attention on the message to which he had
to listen diligently. The sentence "And he answered . . ." (v. 9a), or
better "one" answered, presupposes a preceding question raised by
the watchman. If so, the prophetic message came through the answer of one of those horsemen. Presumably he was one of the returning army that had defeated Babylon. They were returning tri-
umphantly with asses and camels fully laden with booty. Thus the

fall of Babylon meant the fall of all its idols and images as well, for these were now lying shattered on the ground (v. 9b; Jer. 51:8; cf. Isa. 46:1-2); Babylon's power had been totally paralyzed and would never rise again. "Fallen, fallen is Babylon . . ." (21:9).

In the Bible Babylon sometimes symbolizes any world power opposing God and his people (cf. Gen. 11; Rev. 18:2). Therefore, the fall of Babylon conveys an eschatological message concerning the victory of the kingdom of God which involves liberation and salvation for the oppressed peoples of the earth.

Judah has suffered from Babylon and is now called "the threshed and winnowed one" (Isa. 21:10); that is, Judah is put through a sieve! For Judah the fall of Babylon would bring some relief but not yet total liberation. The process of threshing and winnowing has not yet come to an end. Only a remnant of Israel is to be saved. Therefore the prophet, as he looked farther ahead in history, could not yet rejoice fully concerning the liberation of Judah. The only thing of which he could now testify was what he had heard and announced as coming from the LORD of hosts himself.

It is worth noting that in v. 9 the word came through the horseman's answer, to which the prophet had to listen diligently. Now we can understand why emphasis is put on the word "diligently," because it is not easy to recognize the Word through human words. Diligent listening through the ear of faith is only possible in communion with God and in the fellowship of all believers.

An Oracle Concerning Dumah (21:11-12)

Dumah means literally "silence." But according to many interpreters it should be understood as a wordplay on Edom (cf. NIV; LXX: Idumea). This is quite possible because the question in v. 11 is put to the prophet from Seir, the hill country southeast of the Dead Sea in the land of Edom.

In the silence of midnight someone calls from Edom "to me," the watchman, that is, the prophet: "What is left of the night?" (NEB, NIV). Then the watchman answers: "Morning comes, and also the night," meaning that as yet it is still dark. "If you will (meaning 'would like to') inquire (about dawn), come back again (after some hours)" (v. 12). The questioner from Edom is longing for daybreak, because in the OT the darkness of the night illustrates suffering and disaster (cf. 8:22; 9:2; Amos 5:18, 20; Nah. 1:8); therefore the darkness is frightening (cf. 1 Sam. 2:9). Conversely, light illustrates life, salvation, and liberation (cf. Isa. 9:2; Ps. 27:1; 90:14; 97:11).

When did Edom undergo such distress, and who was the oppressor? If we relate this oracle to that concerning Moab (Isa. 15–16), then it may belong to the period of Assyrian oppression. Others, however, think of the Neo-Babylonian oppression, before the downfall of that state.

During the Exile the Edomites more than once plundered Judah, but later on they seemingly came to the prophet of that day asking for help and relief (cf. 15:2-4). The prophet answered that release would indeed come, but as yet they had to realize fully their present darkness of misery.

AN ORACLE CONCERNING ARABIA (21:13-15)

Because of the Assyrian invasion (second half of the 8th cent.), the main caravan highway had become insecure. The Dedanites, an Arab tribe who were largely merchants, lived in the northern part of Arabia that adjoins Edom and were believed to be descendants of Abraham and Keturah (Gen. 25:3; 1 Chr. 1:32). The caravans of the Dedanites had now to hide "in the thickets of Arabia" and lodge there presumably near the land of Tema (Isa. 21:14) to escape not from Arabian robbers but rather the plundering Assyrian soldiers.

The oracle shows the merciful attitude of the prophet towards those refugees fleeing from the hardship of war. The inhabitants of Tema, another commercial center on the caravan road and friendly to Dedan (Jer. 25:23), are here encouraged to help the Dedanites in their hiding place, although to do so would endanger the life of Tema itself. Indeed, to extend help to those in misery sometimes requires risk and even sacrifice. This then is a picture of self-giving love for the sake of others.

21:16-17 The relation of these closing verses in prose to the preceding oracle preserved as a poem concerning Arabia is not clear. But considering their form and style, they show affinity with Isa. 16:13-14. They may in fact, however, be a later addition.

According to Gen. 25:13 Kedar was the second son of Ishmael.

The tribe of Kedar had become a strong and influential Arab tribe in the northern part of Arabia, occupying the Syrian-Arabian desert east of the Jordan. They were known for their wealth and for their ability as archers. The Arab revolts against Assyria in northern Arabia were led by warriors of Kedar. In the 6th cent. the various Arab tribes were largely allied and headed by Kedar. Dedan and Tema were also located in this area, and they too were related to Kedar. It might be for this reason that the oracle concerning Kedar is added, like closing verses, to what precedes. It declared that in short time (there is no figure specified in the MT) the pomp of Kedar would come to an end.

It is difficult, however, to determine the date of this event, or even whether it occurred during the Assyrian or the Babylonian domination. The expression "The LORD, the God of Israel, has spoken" guarantees that this oracle is indeed trustworthy and will come to fulfillment eventually.

AN ORACLE CONCERNING JERUSALEM

22:1-25

This chapter can be divided into two parts, vv. 1-14 containing an oracle concerning the "valley of vision" and vv. 15-25 containing a prophecy on Shebna and Eliakim.

THE VALLEY OF VISION (22:1-14)

The first part of the chapter is rather heterogeneous and creates some problems relating to the historical scene and time. Some verses can be assigned to the Assyrian siege against Jerusalem and its miraculous deliverance in 701 B.C. (vv. 2, 9-11, 13). Some verses, however, could be related better to the Babylonian attacks against Jerusalem in 597 and 586, resulting in exile and despair (vv. 3, 4, 12, 14) and so be the words of a later prophet. In addition, the typical expression "in that day . . ." (vv. 8b, 12) usually has an eschatological reference. It seems that a later redactor compiled these various materials into one unity under the title of "the valley of vision," cited from v. 5. Nevertheless, as a whole it can be considered a prophecy in the Isaianic tradition exhibiting a clear theme and message to Jerusalem.

22:1-4 There is uncertainty about the location of the "valley of vision." According to John Mauchline *(Isaiah 1–39)* it must be one of the several valleys around Jerusalem. Edward Young *(The Book of Isaiah)* saw its mention as an identification of the city of Jerusalem where the prophet lived, received visions, and heard the word of God. Standing on the surrounding hilltop or at the top of the Mount of Olives, one can look down on the city as if it lay in a valley.

The release of Jerusalem from the Assyrian siege created exultant joy in Jerusalem (vv. 1b-2a). All of the city's former suffering seems to be forgotten. But vv. 2b-3 show a sharp contrast, remembering all that had happened. Many young people had been slain not as heroes in a battle, but without honor through sickness or famine. Jerusalem's rulers had "fled far away" as cowards but had been captured and treated shamefully. Such a miserable situation is in line with that described in vv. 12-13.

The prophet has fully realized that this exultant city was moving towards total collapse. There was no sign of penitence, and they "did not look at him [the LORD]." Consequently the prophet felt extremely sad and complained: "Let me weep bitter tears . . . and do not labor to comfort me" (v. 4). "The daughter of my people" (v. 4) simply means "God's people."

22:5-8a The prophet continues to give the reason why he felt so sad. Ultimately "the defenses of Judah are stripped away" (v. 8a NIV, "laid open" NEB). Thus one day Yahweh will deliver Jerusalem into the hands of the enemy. Then there would be a great tumult of war and the battering down of the city wall, the trampling of advancing soldiers' feet and hurrying people fleeing for refuge, total confusion leading to anarchy. The people's noisy shoutings would be heard from the tops of the surrounding hills (v. 5).

The Elamites (Elam lies to the east of Babylon with its capital Susa; cf. 21:2) were well known for their excellent archers. They now come in full array "with chariots and horsemen." The location of Kir is rather obscure (cf. Amos 1:5; 9:7). It has been suggested that Kir may have lain east of the river Tigris and close to Elam. As such it is still difficult to determine whether these enemies were Assyrians or Babylonians, because in both cases Elam and Kir were employed as soldiers.

The valleys around Jerusalem were "full of chariots," and the enemy horsemen took up their position in front of its gates. They were ready for combat. Jerusalem was powerless like a bird in a cage. The city was stripped of all its "covering" (Isa. 22:8a)—of all means of defense. What a shameful situation for "the daughter of my people" (v. 4) to be in (cf. also Nah. 3:5; Lam. 1:8).

22:8b-11 This pericope describes in an "intermezzo" the efforts of Jerusalem to withstand the enemy. (The line of thought of Isa.

22:1-8a is continued in vv. 12-14). In this critical situation Jerusalem has relied on its own resources and its own defense system. First, the city looked to the weapons stored in "the House of the Forest" (cf. 1 Kgs. 7:2-5). Since the time of King Solomon this "house" was used as an arsenal to keep hundreds of gold-plated shields (1 Kgs. 10:17), and served as Judah's main arsenal. Second, Jerusalem looked to the many breaches made in the walls of the city of David. Those breaches had been caused by either Assyrian or Babylonian attacks and had remained unrepaired, presumably due to the enemy's prohibition of any restoration. The "city of David" (cf. 2 Sam. 5:9) was the southeastern part of Jerusalem (known as "Zion") on which, in ancient times, the fortified city of the Jebusites had been built (i.e., the Mount of Ophel). After David had captured it he reinforced the ridge with a strong wall, and this site became his royal abode. The inhabitants could not get materials from outside to rebuild these walls; so they set out to count the houses in Jerusalem that could be pulled down in order to get materials for the restoration (Isa. 22:10). This was indeed a drastic but yet urgent step to reinforce the defenses of the city. Third, they looked to the water supply system. Jerusalem contained two important pools. The "lower pool" lay just outside the wall on the east side. The "old pool," near the well of Gihon at the Kidron Valley, lay just outside the city wall on the west side. So the inhabitants channelled the waters from the two pools into a big reservoir inside the wall. This reservoir (perhaps the work of King Hezekiah mentioned at 2 Kgs. 20:20) became known as the pool of Shiloah. In this way the people of Jerusalem sought to secure the water supply even in time of siege.

The limitations of human skills and modern technology induce human beings to remain humble before God. The dramatic failure of the launching of the space shuttle Challenger is one such example. Erosion of religious truths and values are evident in many parts of the world, partly due to the fascinating rapid social changes and developments of our time, and to revolutionary changes created by modern technology in all fields of life throughout these last few decades.

All those preventive steps were most necessary and praiseworthy. But Jerusalem's leaders neglected the one most important and all-decisive factor, namely, Yahweh himself. For it was Yahweh "who did it" and "who planned it long ago" (Isa. 22:11). They did not reckon with the LORD, did not look to him, or have any regard for him. So here we see once again the sin of Ahaz described earlier in ch. 7. It seems to be a deep-rooted sin in human nature to ignore God in human deliberations and skillful calculations. Ingeniously planned programs for national development and welfare are nowadays expressed in neat designs and well-calculated ciphers. But important as these may be, human beings only too often tend to disregard God and ignore decisive spiritual factors in life. Faith primarily reckons with God. Mankind proposes but God disposes! (cf. Prov. 11:4; 14:34; 16:5; Jas. 4:13-16).

22:12-14 In these verses the prophet gives the real reason for his mourning and weeping (Isa. 22:4). The people of Judah had been called to weeping and mourning, not primarily because of the tragic misery of their situation but because they had forsaken the LORD. They ought therefore to express true repentance. For this purpose they must shave and gird themselves with sackcloth.

But what was the people's response? They ignored the call of the prophet and instead found relief and pleasure in banquets, in eating and drinking without restraint just to forget the crisis and the terrible future that loomed before them (v. 13). The prophet rightly quotes their frivolous slogan: "Let us eat and drink, for tomorrow we die." Such a slogan is still heard today: "Let us be merry and enjoy life today; forget about the day after tomorrow. Why should we bother with God and his commandments!" The apostle Paul repeats this warning against such a frivolous lifestyle (cf. 1 Cor. 15:32). In the secular world, both in the affluent society of the West and in some corrupt circles in developing countries, this kind of popular "hymn" is still to be heard.

A PROPHECY ON SHEBNA AND ELIAKIM (22:15-25)

Differing from the previous pericope, the prophet now deals with particular persons, namely, Shebna and Eliakim. These names are also mentioned in 2 Kgs. 18:18 and Isa. 36:3. In these latter verses Eliakim ben Hilkiah is called the "palace administrator" (NIV) and Shebna is called the "secretary." But in 22:15 it is Shebna who is the

127

palace administrator. It has been suggested that the present pericope precedes 2 Kgs. 18:18, because in the latter Shebnah seems to have been degraded.

22:15-19   The prophet here reveals the life situation at the royal court; it appears that the high officials there were also corrupt. The prophet is sent to Shebna, the highest official ("steward") responsible for the household at the royal court, in order to accuse him. Concerning the identity of Shebna there are different opinions. One sees him as an Israelite and his name an abbreviated form of Shebaniah (Neh. 9:4; 10:4). Others think he was of Egyptian descent because his name is rarely found and the name of his father is never mentioned, which is not according to Jewish custom. But if he was an alien, how was it possible that he managed to occupy such a high and responsible office at the royal court? At any rate, this problem has not yet been solved.

The first part of Isa. 22:16 can be translated according to the NIV: "What are you doing here and who gave you permission . . . ?" The prophet, it seems, had met Shebna outside the royal court, probably on Mt. Ophel. There Shebna was supervising the carving of a tomb for himself hewn out of the rock. It was customary for Israelite nobles and for the royal family to have such tombs as a sign of dignity and honor. But it was reprehensible for Shebna, amidst this national crisis, to think first of an honorable tomb for himself. The prophet did not consider him appropriate for such an honor. This is the more obvious if it was true that he was virtually of alien descent.

What the prophet had to announce was terrible and shocking for Shebna, because it was contrary to the steward's own plans and desires. The LORD would hurl him away violently, round and round as one whirls oneself round before "putting the shot": "O you strong man"—that is, strong in your own estimation—"there you shall die, and there shall be your splendid chariots, you (who are the) shame of your master's house" (v. 18). The "wide land" where Shebna would die disgracefully might even be interpreted as the great Assyrian and Babylonian plain. Apparently Shebna often misused his high position and employed the royal chariot and other royal facilities for his own personal benefit. So he was to be deposed and ousted from his position and office (v. 19). God hates corrupt officials. It has been suggested that this dismissal from office was because of Shebna's political attitude, which was pro-Egypt, and because he had tried to persuade Hezekiah to look to Egypt as an ally.

The message of the OT here is loud and clear once again. It is one that must be proclaimed fearlessly in all lands. Corruption in all its forms, such as the falsifying of weights and measures and so today of falsifying the accounts, is a temptation that attacks officialdom in many lands at all levels of administration. Severe economic pressures, paired with social insecurity, can lead to this corruption. Structural problems such as we meet in developing societies and uncontrolled greedy ambition need to be confronted by this prophetic message and so by a more holistic and comprehensive approach to such issues in society. The situation keeps reminding the Church of its social calling in the various contexts in which it finds itself.

22:20-23   Shebna will be replaced by Eliakim (meaning "God will affirm"), the son of Hilkiah. This Eliakim is to be distinguished from other men bearing the same name (cf. Neh. 12:41; 2 Kgs. 23:34; Matt. 1:13). He is here called "my servant," strong in his own estimation as noted above.

The LORD will clothe Eliakim with the "robe" and "girdle" of Shebna as a symbol of honor and authority (Isa. 22:21). But unlike Shebna, Eliakim would be a "father to the inhabitants of Jerusalem and to the house of Judah." This means that his authority would be fully accepted and respected inside as well as outside the royal court. This "father" idea also implies a close relationship, one of love and of influence. So we are reminded of the position of Joseph at the royal palace of Pharaoh (Gen. 45:8). In a word, Eliakim would be a servant to the LORD and a father to the people.

"The key of the house of David" signified the office of stewardship at the palace. As such Eliakim would be authorized to open and to shut the royal court and so to have full authority in all aspects of the business of the royal household (cf. Rev. 3:7). In the Bible the phrase "the house of David" has a particular meaning and a special place in relation to God's kingdom; in this respect, Eliakim showed some messianic features. It is interesting to note with Edward Young (*The Book of Isaiah*, II, 114) that the key of the house of David was not put "in his hand" but was placed "on his shoulder" (cf. Isa. 9:6).

Eliakim was to be guaranteed a firm and lofty position in the government of God's people and be a "throne of honor to his father's house" (22:23). He would be like "a peg in a sure place," "sure" here being the Hebrew word *ne'eman* that was given a central place in God's promise to David and to his line. 2 Samuel 7:16 reads: "And your house and your kingdom shall be made *sure* for ever before me." So was it to be with Eliakim. As a peg in a secure place he would be expected to bear every weight that the people of Jerusalem would hang upon him.

22:24-25 These closing verses are worth serious attention. In the preceding verses (22:20-23) Eliakim has just been described in his glorious position as a messianic type. But there are still limitations. The name of Eliakim is not mentioned again; we are given merely the image of the "peg."

A peg has its limitations; it cannot be used arbitrarily. Yet this is what did indeed happen. The whole weight of Eliakim's father's house and of his offspring and issue are to hang on him alone. We are shown how all kinds of interests and business, from the weighty to the trivial, would hang on this peg.

This undue weighty burden would then finally result in Eliakim's downfall (v. 25). This would be brought about by the sin of those people who manipulated and misused his lofty position. Verses 20-25 show a certain longing for a truly messianic leader, one who would be an "everlasting father" (cf. 9:6) to his people. But on the other hand these verses show disillusionment with human capabilities, no matter how strong and lofty these might look. For all people, without exception, have feet of clay.

ORACLES CONCERNING TYRE AND SIDON

23:1-18

This is the last chapter of the long series of oracles concerning the nations (Isa. 13–23). It can be divided into two main parts, 23:1-14 dealing with the destruction of Tyre and Sidon and vv. 15-18 concerning the future restoration of those two city-states. There is, however, still uncertainty concerning the dating of the oracles. Opinions vary from the 8th to the 4th cent. B.C. In addition, the text is not always clear, therefore making interpretation difficult.

THE DESTRUCTION OF TYRE AND SIDON (23:1-14)

23:1   In the ancient Near East Tyre was a center of world commerce and the important harbor of the Fertile Crescent. It connected the lands of the Near East with the countries around the Mediterranean Sea. As such Tyre held a key position in international commercial life. Because of the city's strategic importance this whole oracle bears the name of Tyre (v. 1a), although some verses embedded in it are related to Sidon (vv. 2-4, 12).

It is rather strange that v. 1 addresses the "ships of Tarshish" and not the inhabitants of Tyre. These ships were big vessels built for commerce and able to traverse the Mediterranean Sea as far as Tarshish at its western end. They were owned by rich merchants of Tyre and were most important for the city's welfare. Sailing back from Tarshish carrying rich cargos, they might have put in at Cyprus to discharge and then reload. However, in the very moment that they left Cyprus, heading for the harbor of Tyre with great joy, they were meant to hear this oracle of doom.

131

23:2-4   These verses address the "inhabitants of the coast" and the "merchants of Sidon." Those who lived along the coast of Phoenicia (including Tyre and Sidon) were mostly merchants. Now they are called upon to be silent, because the message of doom would mean a halt to their whole business.

Sidon was the second center of international commerce. It dealt in many products from Egypt (v. 3). "The stronghold of the sea" in v. 4 seems rather obscure; the phrase might be a later addition. Most probably however it refers to Tyre. If so, then not only is Sidon called upon to be ashamed but so is Tyre. The destruction of these two most important harbors on the Phoenician coast caused even the sea to lament. It is depicted as a barren woman, humiliated because she has produced no offspring. Such barrenness and humiliation are now to be the fate of Sidon and Tyre. None of their commercial ships would sail and pay honor to the sea, which thus has also become desolate and "barren."

23:5   The fall of Tyre and Sidon, which here represent the whole of Phoenicia, causes Egypt also to tremble because it means that the mighty enemy (Assyria) is drawing ever closer. Besides, Egypt will lose important markets for its merchandise.

23:6-9   Here the prophet calls to the Phoenicians to flee to Tarshish. Why to Tarshish? Perhaps this was the farthest away place in the West known to him, and probably at that time there was a Phoenician colony there. This call might also be related to v. 1, where it is suggested that the ships of Tarshish could not enter the harbors of Tyre or Sidon and were forced to sail back to Tarshish.

How glorious was Tyre before its destruction! It used to be a crowded trading center. Tyre was "honored" as being the oldest city on the coast of Phoenicia (v. 8). Its glory was well known in the region surrounding the Mediterranean Sea. Its people were active and diligent traders and sea-going sailors. They had settled in colonies along the Mediterranean coast as well as in Cyprus (v. 7). More than that, Tyre is called "bestower of crowns" (v. 8). This means that various high officials had been appointed by mighty and wealthy Tyre to occupy positions of authority in the colonies or elsewhere in Phoenicia. The wealthy merchants who had their businesses in Tyre were called "princes," that is, most honored persons or, as we might say, "kings of commerce."

Obviously everyone would wonder how all this glory of Phoenicia could be defiled, brought low, and put to shame. Who would be in the position to do such a thing?—the LORD of hosts (v. 9)! It was God who purposed to bring low all the haughtiness and pomp of mankind. Concerning the haughtiness of Tyre and a lamentation on Tyre, see also Ezek. 26:1–28:19.

23:10-14   Now the text is once again rather obscure. With the help of the ancient renderings of the DSS and LXX as well as of some other manuscripts Isa. 23:10 might best be translated: "Till your land along the Nile, O daughter of Tarshish, for you no longer have a harbor." If we follow this reading, the inhabitants of Tarshish are being summoned to flee away and till a foreign land because nothing could be expected anymore from sea trade. Their ships could no longer operate, as there were no harbors anymore for them to use.

Tyre and Sidon were not to regain their former position, because the LORD had "stretched out his hand over the sea" (v. 11), that element which was of vital importance for both cities and for the whole coastland of Phoenicia. According to the mythology of the day the sea was dominated by the sea-god, who had command over tremendous and terrible powers that could threaten human life. Therefore the sea was frightening in itself, so that people were always tempted to worship the sea-god. Moreover, the Israelites believed that Sheol (the shadowy netherworld of the deceased) was located deep down under the sea. The mythological sea-god (Yam, according to Phoenician beliefs) was often conceived of in animal-like form; he was known as Leviathan (Job 3:8; Ps. 74:14; 104:26; Isa. 27:1) or Rahab (Ps. 89:10).

Now in this oracle the sea with all its frightening powers would in its turn be punished, made powerless, and so would languish (cf. Isa. 23:4). Thereupon all the nations around the Mediterranean Sea would tremble. Here "Canaan" is taken in a broad sense to denote the whole Phoenician coast and to include particularly Tyre and Sidon. So the "daughter of Sidon" (meaning its inhabitants) would now have no place to rest (v. 12). The people could only flee to the colony at Cyprus, though even there they would find the same tragic situation.

133

This oracle (vv. 1-14) is now closed by repeating the words of its beginning (v. 1a), thereby emphasizing that the stronghold of Tyre is indeed "laid waste" together with "the stronghold of the sea" (v. 4). In other words, the judgment of God is absolute.

A REFLECTION ON THE FUTURE FATE OF TYRE
(23:15-18)

For some time, then, Tyre would be forgotten, but afterwards it would be rehabilitated and dedicated to the LORD. "Seventy years" indicates a fullness of time and should not be interpreted literally; rather, it is a symbolic prophetic number (cf. Jer. 25:11; 29:10; Dan. 9:24; Zech. 1:12; 7:5; Luke 10:1, 17). The interval is also called "the days of one king," that is, the span of a king's lifetime. During that period Tyre would be forgotten by the nations.

Finally, the once important and glorious city is pictured as a harlot who has lost her youthful attractiveness and is now trying hard to maintain her profession. As a lonely and unlovely prostitute she will walk the streets playing her harp and singing the old songs of long ago, in this way presenting herself to the public and so attracting men's attention to her out of pity.

The greedy and selfish motivations and goals usually attached to commerce, when people use shady means and neglect ethical as well as religious norms, could in many cases be compared with the practice of harlotry. But commerce in itself is not sinful and can serve a good purpose. This is evident from Isa. 23:17-18. After the fullness of time Tyre will regain her position as mistress of the Mediterranean but with a total change in her for good, for her activities will now be "dedicated to the LORD" (v. 18). She will show her spirit of dedication by her concern for honest dealing. She will no longer hoard the grain and "fine clothing" she has discharged into her store sheds, "cornering" them in a miserly fashion; she will release them at once into the market in honest trade.

The casual reader of the NT, however, may not notice an identical denunciation of the cities of Galilee issuing from the lips of Jesus. In fact, Matt. 11:23 clearly echoes the very words of Isa. 14:13, 15. So we are to remember that just as the name "Jesus" meant "Yahweh (or 'the LORD') is Savior" (Matt. 1:21), so too the name "Isaiah" also means "Yahweh is Salvation." Consequently in both the Old and New Testament we discover that it is only through judgment that God's saving love rescues and rehabilitates (as here in the case of Tyre). It is actually out of mankind's egotistical resistance to his love that God builds his kingdom of righteousness and peace. Moreover, he accomplishes his purpose by the "unheard-of" (Isa. 53:1) means of actually immersing himself in the sinful situation that his creature mankind has brought about in God's world.

PART III
THE GLORY OF ZION

Isaiah 24:1–27:13

THE "ISAIAH APOCALYPSE"

These four chapters, Isa. 24–27, should be taken together as one unit occupying a particular place in the book of Isaiah. Having dealt with oracles on various nations (chs. 13–23), the editor now brings together in one the announcement of the universal judgment of the LORD. No human being will be able to escape from it (24:1). Yet it is the LORD'S purpose that, in and through the judgment, Zion will be blessed and glorified when the LORD will reign there for ever (24:23). In that day all dispersed Israelites will be gathered together to worship the LORD at Zion (27:12-13); Israel will have become like a pleasant vineyard (27:2-4; cf. 5:1-7), for it will have taken root downwards and so will blossom again upwards (27:6; 37:31-32). Therefore at long last Israel will produce fruit for the nations. All praise and worship is thus due to the LORD, who will have punished his enemies and delivered Israel to be his true servant at last.

Considering the language and style of this section and its many apocalyptic and eschatological features, many scholars advocate a postexilic dating for these chapters. Others prefer to see it as the product of a period that produced the suffering of the Exile. The poetry in it can be compared with the best in Deutero-Isaiah (chs. 40–55) and in Isa. 60–62, in that it makes use of alliteration, assonance, climactic parallelism, and the like.

The section is not "apocalyptic" in the sense that some intertestamental books can be described by that term. It is a collection of what were probably independent pericopes which are eschatological in nature. These look like sermon notes which employ the kind of picture language that Jesus used in his parabolic teaching. We shall note as we proceed how the editor of these chapters expresses distinct judgments upon individual nations; but in each case the editor does so in order to illustrate how the *eternal* judgment and equally *eternal* saving love of God are *eternally* present to all mankind, here and now. (See William R. Millar, *Isaiah 24–27 and the Origin of Apocalyptic*. Harvard Semitic Monograph 11 [Missoula, Mont.: Scholars Press, 1976].)

THE EARTH AND THE NATIONS UNDER GOD'S JUDGMENT

24:1-23

THE EARTH LAID WASTE (24:1-3)

The whole earth lies under the judgment of God. The situation is pictured as utter desolation affecting young and old alike, buyer and seller, lender and borrower. The latter are specified because all of mankind's economic activities are infused with selfishness and greed; men and women can do nothing completely right, for their hearts are impure. In a lively way the prophet invites the reader to watch diligently what will happen when God punishes the earth (Isa. 24:1). "The earth" here should not be taken in a modern geographical sense, but rather in the sense of the inhabited world known to the ancient reader. In the first place the earth will be laid waste and made desolate through natural disasters, war, or epidemic diseases. The punishment then reaches its climax when the earth's surface becomes twisted and is turned upside down so that its inhabitants fall tumbling down in chaotic confusion and are scattered around like rubbish. In this poetic and pictorial manner the prophet thus seeks to show how great and terrible God's power and judgment always are, both now and at "the end"; for the eternal God is eternally present in his world.

Here we have an example of the manner in which the biblical poet tends to express the universal in the one event he is addressing. In this way he makes the contemporary event an example of the broader spectrum of activity that is always happening. Thus in ch. 24 we have "apocalyptic" writing in the true sense of that word, for it means in colloquial English "lifting the lid off" a particular moment in contemporary life to reveal the *eternal* significance of that moment. Apocalyptic can do so because of its awareness that the eternity of God overarches and infuses our world of space and

140

time; thus it is equally and simultaneously present to Moses, to Paul, and to us today. That is why here the poet can speak of "the end" as being both "now" and "to come."

Verses 2 and 3 describe the resulting total confusion. Human life in society is completely disrupted: all share the same fate (v. 2). All distinctions of class and social groups, distinctions between strong and weak, rich and poor, will no longer be recognized. The whole life of society, the cult, and the economy will suffer.

Note the contrasting comparison between people and priest. In postexilic times the position of the priests was growing stronger; they had become the spiritual leaders of the people and preservers of the tradition. As such they were much honored by the people. On the other hand, through the centuries the priests often became objects of prophetic criticism (cf. Hos. 4:4; 5:1; Mal. 2:1ff.) because of certain shameful practices and unfaithfulness to their covenant relationship with Yahweh. Therefore in this list of people to be judged (Isa. 24:2) the priest is not excluded. So this verse offers a serious warning to all cult officials and clergy at all times.

THE EARTH MOURNS AND WITHERS (24:4-13)

24:4-6   The earth is now personified and unified with its inhabitants, and so together they suffer from the judgment of the LORD. Until now the Hebrew word *ha-arets* has been used, the noun normally employed to describe the Holy Land. But here *ha-arets* is paralleled with *tebel*, which designates the whole earth. By this usage the prophet is stressing that the judgment of God upon Israel for breaking the Covenant (v. 5) has effect upon all mankind, even upon those with whom God has made no covenant. Thus Israel is doubly under judgment, as Amos 3:2 had declared only a generation before Isaiah's day. Thus it is too that Deutero-Isaiah could see, as he looked back, how the covenant people of God had to suffer double for all their sins if the rest of mankind was to be redeemed by God's grace in and through his sinful covenant people (Isa. 40:2; 49:6).

Most Western countries provide for their youth an education which features a scientific orientation. In consequence their young people naturally learn to "call a spade a spade" and so read a book such as Isaiah literally. But the genius of the Third World, by and large, is to employ poetic language to express truth, and so it may exaggerate vividly for the sake of emphasis. The Third World reads the book of Isaiah as it is meant to be read, that is, in terms of poetic phraseology. By speaking here of God wiping out both mankind and nature, the author is not declaring a verifiable fact. He is emphasizing strikingly the utter holiness of the holy God before whom no sinner can stand. The prophet feels compelled to employ hyperbole such as this to make vividly clear the "otherness" of God, in that God's thoughts and ways are absolutely other than those of sinful mankind (cf. 55:8-9). To this end, therefore, the biblical poet did not hesitate if necessary to speak in stark opposites in order to emphasize the mystery of God's unspeakable love (cf. Mal. 1:2-3; Luke 14:26).

So we are reminded of the initial sin of Adam resulting in the curse upon the earth recorded in Gen. 3:17. The earth withers, becomes barren, and is no longer productive (Isa. 24:4)—and all because of Israel's rebellion! The people of God only too often take for granted that they have been "chosen to be saved" and so rejoice in the wonder of their salvation. But as the whole book of Isaiah declares, they had been chosen—not to be saved but to serve. As Jesus put it in later years: "For whoever would save his life (his 'soul,' Gk. *psyche*) will lose it" (Luke 9:24).

The earth's resources come to an end. In the Bible heaven and earth are taken as one entity. So the heavens languish and become barren and are unable to pour down rain. This prophetic picture is nowadays receiving the serious consideration of mankind. The present universal crisis of earth's resources (e.g., from pollution and from erosion) have become a growing and ever-pressing problem that must be dealt with universally if it is to be effectively overcome. According to scientific reports and observations, the earth is *now* mourning and withering. Christian theology must face this world problem and try to detect its fundamental causes and find basic answers to it.

Isaiah 24:5 gives the basic reason for God's judgment: it is based on (1) his justice, (2) his Word, and (3) his Covenant. The LORD of hosts, Creator of heaven and earth, observes that the whole earth has been "polluted" by its inhabitants. At the very beginning the earth was created for the glory of God and was given to mankind to cultivate and till (Gen. 2:15). But behold, the earth is now exhausted, withered, and polluted in the air and the water as well. What is the basic reason for this defilement? The prophetic faith detects that it is human sin in all its forms and expressions (Isa. 24:6). According to the OT revelation, this "pollution" is related to bloodshed of the innocent (see Num. 35:33; cf. Ps. 106:38; Gen. 9:6), to harlotry and vice (Jer. 3:2), to idolatry and adultery committed with stone and tree (Jer. 3:9). Further, we are reminded of the "everlasting covenant" made with Noah (Gen. 9:1-17), totally forbidding the shedding of blood and revealing mankind's obligation to be faithful to God's regard for his natural world.

The salvation which God has offered his world is not, as some modern sects suppose, merely the renewal of individual persons by being born again into a right relationship with God. It is the redemption of the whole cosmos (John 3:16), of the whole of creation—the renewal of nature as well as of mankind (Isa. 11:6-9), in that, of course, mankind itself is part of nature (Gen. 2:7).

People in the Western world are conditioned by their schooling to accept the idea that their ideology, their philosophy of life has come from the great teachers of ancient Greece. While these teachers differed among themselves, there was one aspect of reality they held in common—that the ideal was separate from the actual, that the body was separate from the soul. Consequently, when presented with the OT view of the unity of all creation, Westerners either reject it outright or seek to read the "Greek" concepts of time and eternity into the poetic interpretation of the relation between the present and the future given us by the prophets of the OT. What we today must necessarily grasp is that the worldview of the prophets regarded the "eternity" of God as being always present in the "now" of human experience. The word *ayolam*, "everlasting," does not refer to endless time. Rather, it speaks of the element of ultimate reality which is ever present both in the here and now and in the expressions we must use to speak of God's eternity.

This then is why God's "everlasting" judgment is described in terms of fire and scorching flames, which leap upon each of the nations in turn in the here and now. For this is the pictorial understanding of God's very nature (Isa. 33:14), which is eternal.

24:7-13   These verses give a clear and detailed picture of the sufferings of mankind—not as they will be at "the end" but as they are now in their actuality. Earth and humanity mourn and wither *together* (24:7-9). The vineyards no longer produce sweet grapes. Therefore there is no wine, no sound of music and songs; naturally merry-hearted men and women no longer make merry, and even strong drink has become "bitter" and destroys people's powers of judgment. The gods and goddesses of fertility, once thought to be the source of joy and pleasure, now prove to be vain and powerless.

Verses 10-13 present a lugubrious picture of the broken city. It is called "the city of chaos" (*tohu,* the very word used at Gen. 1:2 to describe the opposite of light and of God's creative purpose). The city has been devastated and lies in desolation; all its doors are closed, its inhabitants have either died or fled, and its gates are battered down and lie in ruins. Only a few persons are to be seen staggering about the streets, crying loudly and vainly "for lack of wine," that is, for their lost sense of joy and pleasure in life. The word "city" here is that used of any town in any land in the whole world. So the picture here represents the "chaotic" situation of human civilization if here and how it does not possess the *shalom* of God (Isa. 2); the city lies under the judgment of God. It may well be that the destruction of Jerusalem in 586 B.C. is, in the view of the prophet, the "type" of the judgment of God upon all human cities in all ages of mankind.

TUMULT AMONG THE DISPERSED FAITHFUL (24:14-16a)

Consequently Isa. 24–27 form a link in the chain with those chapters of Trito-Isaiah (chs. 56–66) that speak of the creation of the New Israel of God. For at 24:14-16a we hear suddenly a surprising cry of joy and praise. Who is it doing this crying? And what is the reason for it? If we relate this to the preceding pericope, then we are inclined to think of the few who are left (v. 8). They are now heard praising the LORD for their salvation. "From the west" means the coastlands around the Mediterranean Sea, where Jewish colonies had long since established themselves (cf. 23:4). Among them, then, a few faithful men and women were still to be found. This cry from the west thus induces the prophet to summon those living in the east to respond in the same way and to give glory to the LORD (24:15). There would then be a kind of responsive cry as east and west answered each other in giving "glory to the Righteous One" (v. 16a). And so God's righteousness has been revealed through his judgment and just punishment, for these have also revealed the forgiveness of God.

INESCAPABLE JUDGMENT (24:16b-20)

This pericope may be divided into two parts. Verses 16b-18a may be seen to be a continuation of vv. 1-3 and refer to all the inhabitants of the earth. Verses 18b-20 become then a continuation from v. 4, which deals with the shaken earth.

24:16b-18a The prophet recognizes that the punishment is eternally with us. He realizes how terrible it is and how stubborn the human race is in not seeing it. The prophet identifies himself in compassionate concern with those people who are still under judgment and cries out: "I pine away." He is aware that the treacherous still act treacherously, and says so in a strongly alliterative phrase in the Hebrew. Their punishment is described in terms of panic, "terror," and "the snare," or as if they were hunted animals. They fall into a pit; and if they manage to creep out of it, then they are caught in a snare (cf. Amos 5:19). No escape is ever possible.

24:18b-20 The earth is described in a poetic and figurative manner as trembling and crumbling. According to the story of Noah (Gen. 7:11) we read that "the windows of the heavens were opened" and there came down those catastrophic rains that caused the Flood to cover the whole earth. Here at Isa. 24:18 the same expression is used to express pictorially the total realm of the sin of mankind.

"Like a drunken man" the earth staggers. Presumably the picture includes cyclones and thunderstorms so great as to shake the foundations of the earth. The earth in staggering sways like "a hut" in an earthquake (v. 20). Finally the picture is of one languishing and staggering under the heavy burden of sin and of the curse, a person who will ultimately fall, never to rise again. This then is that heavy load of transgression which finally causes the world to collapse. Genesis 6:6-7 had already expressed this issue in pictorial terms.

145

THE ULTIMATE VICTORY OF THE KINGDOM OF GOD
(24:21-23)

After the destruction, however, the world will not return to the chaos which was there in the beginning (Gen. 1:2); instead the LORD "will reign on Mount Zion and in Jerusalem" forever. But in the meantime the closing verses of this chapter announce God's judgment upon the powers in heaven and on earth which have polluted both mankind and creation (cf. Amos 8:9; Joel 3:16).

The "host of heaven" (Isa. 24:21) means all the stars, the sun, and the moon which regularly appear, disappear, and then return again in the firmament (cf. 40:26; 45:12; Jer. 33:22; Neh. 9:6). They regularly become objects of worship and are related to various gods and idol worship. The OT strongly opposes this astral worship (cf. Deut. 4:19; 17:3; 2 Kgs. 17:16; 21:3, 5; 2 Chr. 33:5). There is, however, another meaning to this expression, namely, the angelic beings who inhabit the heavens above (1 Kgs. 22:19; 2 Chr. 18:18; Luke 2:13). The OT cannot conceive of the heavenly bodies as being merely dead matter. The heavens, it is believed, were infused with life. So the heavenly bodies were merely visible, tangible signs of what Paul in later days called "principalities and powers"; and since "heaven" and "earth" together form God's creation, these powers hold sway in both at once (Eph. 1:21; 3:10; 6:12; Col. 1:16; 2:15).

This host of heaven, then, together with the earth will be punished. Again, this concept of the oneness of creation is carried on in the apocalyptic passages of the NT. According to Rev. 12:7-9 a great war arose in heaven between Michael and his angels against the dragon and his angels. The great dragon, which is also called the serpent or the Devil, the deceiver of the whole earth, was thrown down to earth together with his angels. These become the stars in heaven, deceiving the whole world and all the rulers on earth (cf. 2 Cor. 4:4). As such the lightbearers become the objects of worship of many ancient nations. They also become "the spiritual hosts of wickedness in the heavenly places" (Eph. 6:12). The rulers of the earth, being influenced by them, will be gathered together as prisoners "in a pit," from which they can never escape. After many days they will be punished.

These apocalyptical pictures contain many mysteries that are still unsolved. Why must these powers wait for "many days" before punishment comes? And when will the "end" be made manifest? Though no direct answer can be found, the theological significance of the imagery of this chapter is of great assistance. First, we must be patient in faith, knowing that all those powers have already been broken and put to shame. Second, God is even now acting towards the total renewal of all things and the full manifestation of his kingdom. Third, opportunity is still being offered to the inhabitants of the earth to repent and participate in God's work.

The closing verse (Isa. 24:23) announces the final outcome and the climax of this eschatological picture. The LORD will establish his kingdom and reign "on Mount Zion and in Jerusalem." These geographical names are employed as symbols of the center of the kingdom, the holy city of God, the heart of the renewed world (cf. Rev. 21:2-3).

The glory of the LORD will fill the whole earth (cf. Isa. 6:3), penetrating and chasing away all darkness and evil. The light of his glory shining forth from Zion will never grow dim. Therefore, light from the sun and the moon will not be needed any more because the LORD himself will be the "sun of righteousness" (Mal. 4:2).

The LORD'S glory will be manifested "before his elders" at Mt. Zion. This reminds us of Exod. 24:9-10 when God manifested his glory before Moses, Aaron, and the seventy elders of Israel; cf. also the passage in Rev. 4:4 where the glory of God is manifested before the elders who are seated on their thrones. These elders represent the congregations of the people of God on earth. What a glorious hope and comfort this all is for the faithful people of God!

SONGS OF THANKSGIVING AND PRAISE AT ZION

25:1–26:21

Just like Isa. 12, ch. 25 follows the proclamation of God's eternal judgment upon both the nations and the earth with a song of praise and thanksgiving. This song can be taken as a continuation of 24:14-16a, particularly as a response made by the elders in the face of the glory of God at Zion. This assumption finds support in the fact that the elders are familiar with God's "wonderful" deeds and "plans formed of old" (25:1b) and that they distinguish themselves from the "aliens" (v. 5).

PSALM OF THANKSGIVING AND HOPE (25:1-5)

This psalm contains not only thanksgiving because the enemy has been crushed, but also a confession of faith, acknowledgment of consolation, and hope for the suffering people.

The psalm opens with the firm confession that Yahweh alone is God. This praise and conviction is based on Israel's many experiences in the past (cf. Ps. 31:15; 40:5; 118:28, 29). Thus those who put their trust in Yahweh will not be ashamed (cf. 2 Sam. 22:31; Ps. 5:12; 16:1). God's plan is wonderful and never fails (cf. Isa. 9:6; 55:8). This reality has been experienced in history: the Exodus from Egypt, the Babylonian Exile and deliverance, and fortified cities of aliens destroyed and turned into ruins forever (cf. Ezek. 26:9; Isa. 13:19; 14:22-23). In other words, the ultimate judgment that belongs in God's eternity has already been "revealed."

Now that the significance of God's actions has at last been grasped, a new miracle will emerge, namely, the repentance of the nations. The "peoples" will desire to glorify the LORD (25:3). The triumph of God's kingdom will be universally acknowledged. The strength of these nations and cities will be based no more on

148

fortresses, weapons, soldiers, or idols, but on the fear of God alone.

For these peoples Yahweh will indeed be a safe stronghold (v. 4). The "poor" and "the needy in his distress" are those who are oppressed by ruthless rulers or are the victims of calamities. They are hopeless and helpless and can rely only on the righteousness and mercy of Yahweh. Therefore, they will gladly humble themselves before God, who is their safe refuge. Without God they can never withstand "the blast of the ruthless" because it is "like a storm against a wall, like heat in a dry place (desert)." These are indeed irresistible disasters beyond human capacities to avert. The picture of "shelter" (or "hut") and "shade" are no less important and inviting for those facing "storm" and "heat."

"The noise of the aliens," causing chaos, is subdued, and "the song of the ruthless" is stilled. In the OT the presence of God is often manifested by a cloud, for example, during the wandering in the desert. In like manner this cloud here gives a wholesome and pleasant shade for his faithful people. Who can appreciate it more fully than a pilgrim wandering in the scorching heat of a desert?

JOY IN ZION (25:6-12)

This pericope gives a further description, in poetic imagery, of the situation at Zion when the LORD will reign and reveal his glory (cf. 24:23). The psalm of praise in 25:1-5 can be considered as a kind of intermezzo as well as an introduction to the great joy and witness of the nations who will come to Zion.

The Royal Banquet for the Nations (25:6-8)

Mount Zion is the center of God's reign over the nations. People go up to this mountain to receive teaching (Isa. 2:3), and to worship and bring offerings (cf. 60:1-7; Ps. 96:8-9; 68:31; 72:9-11). Here we see another new aspect, namely, a new and perfect worship by the world's peoples, described as a royal banquet set out as a gift *from* the LORD. This extravagant royal banquet can be likened to the celebration at the installation of a new king (Isa. 24:23).

This picture of Zion indicates symbolically the abundant blessings that will flow from Zion to "all peoples" on earth (Ps. 22:27).

It will be the fulfillment of God's promise to Abraham (Gen. 12:3). There will be a lasting fellowship in peace among all nations. In line with the OT revelation, the NT also proclaims the kingdom of God by way of a banquet (Luke 14:15-24; Matt. 22:1-14; Rev. 19:6-10). The OT emphasizes the coming of the nations to Zion, while the NT puts more emphasis on the active missionary aspect, that is, on the Church's mission to the world. Nevertheless, it is the same message that is proclaimed—that all nations will be accepted by God and so will be welcomed home.

At Zion the peoples will find a consolation, life, and joy, such as they have never experienced before. There will be no more mourning, tears, or even death (Isa. 25:7-8).

The "covering" and "veil" that is cast and spread over the nations may be interpreted as the spiritual blindness which prevents them from seeing God's glory; what the nations do now is only a groping around in darkness (2 Cor. 3:15-16). With their own efforts they try to find release from this miserable situation, but they will never succeed in doing so. So there is no way left other than to flee to Zion, because it is there that the LORD will destroy the covering and the veil.

But the greatest reason for all these coverings is death. So to release mankind from all such sorrows, death is swallowed up forever (Isa. 25:8). In this verse nothing is said about the way this is to be realized. On the other hand, the NT message is clear in this respect (cf. 1 Cor. 15:54; Rev. 21:4). But both the Old and New Testaments declare that God will wipe away all tears from all faces. "The reproach of his people" is frequently related to Israel's stubbornness (Deut. 9:6) evident throughout history. A new Israel will come into being consisting of all peoples who will gather together at Zion and who will partake together of the Great Feast.

Joy in the Lord (25:9-10a)

This is the positive response of the elders and of the peoples to what the LORD proclaims at Zion. With joy and happiness they confess Yahweh as the only and true LORD and Savior for which they have longed. For the Israelites Yahweh is the faithful God of the Covenant from generation to generation (Isa. 25:1), and this new conviction is like the shout of joy of the prodigal son who finds his father waiting for him to come home. For the peoples Yahweh is the fulfillment of all their hopes and ideals. Indeed, Yahweh meets the hopes for salvation of all mankind. Therefore all people should join in this song of praise and thanksgiving from east to west and north to south (cf. 24:14-16a). They will never be disappointed because the protecting and mighty hand of the LORD will permanently rest upon this sure place of refuge, the Mount of Zion.

Moab Trodden Down in a Dung-pit (25:10b-12)

In striking contrast, the prophet describes other peoples who insist on remaining haughty and who rely on their own abilities. He selects Moab as an example of such because, according to Deut. 23:3, the Moabites and the Ammonites are rejected from the assembly of the LORD. Judgment against Moab as a wicked, haughty, and adulterous people is also mentioned in Isa. 15–16. Here the prophet points out the result of Moab's stubbornness. Even when "trodden down in a dung-pit," Moab continues to make hopeless efforts to survive like a skilled "swimmer" spreading out his hands in the mud. But the LORD will "lay low" these efforts of Moab's to live as if God had never uttered his Word.

As apocalyptic, this chapter "reveals" (or "takes the lid off") mankind's ever-ongoing response—or lack of response—to God's ever-loving approach to his world through his steadfast love *(hesed)* (cf. Ps. 136). The prophet is telling us here that those who respond to God's creative love now are *already* tasting the delights of the divine banquet. But his words "reveal" to us the *eternal* reality that those who reject the offer of fellowship with God, as did Moab, are now living hopeless and useless lives. They are like "straw . . . trodden down in a dung-pit." Consequently, thoughtful writers today can describe as "straw men" those who continue to imagine that they live useful and creative lives through "the high fortifications" they have built by using their own "skills." Unlike the people who have accepted forgiveness and from whose faces God has "wiped away all tears," they remain unaware that what they have built is a useless waste of human energy.

Apocalyptic reveals that it is not God who lays low the straw man's fortifications. Rather, such is the fate that the latter has called down upon himself and his egocentric activities. Our passage, then, is not a description of what a cruel God will do "some day," "in the end," to those who are his enemies. It is a "lifting of the lid" from off the world of humanity as it is now. It is a revelation of the reality that is humanity's present way of life in community. It points to the reality that our life can be lived either *with* God or *without* him. This means that those who here and now reject the God of revelation and who worship what their own hands, hearts, and skills can produce are merely filling in the time between birth and death, without really knowing what it means to be alive.

Chapter 26 is related to ch. 25 as a song of praise to God for Zion, Israel's safe stronghold. Yet it also shows some relationships with Ps. 24:7-10, a liturgical psalm sung at a triumphal entry into the Jebusite stronghold, indicating the glory of Yahweh entering Jerusalem and taking up its abode at Zion. As such Zion is in sharp contrast to "the lofty city" (Isa. 26:5) which has been cast down to the dust (cf. 25:12). Therefore, the lofty city could well be taken in a general symbolic sense.

SONG OF PRAISE AND JOY (26:1-6)

26:1 "In that day . . ." points to the day of judgment, particularly judgment upon haughty enemies, and at the same time offers redemption to the poor and the needy (v. 6). This is the theme of the song to be "sung in the land of Judah." It is not clear who the singer is; it seems unlikely to be the inhabitants of Jerusalem, for the city is the chief subject of this song of praise. From Jerusalem this song is to be passed on to the whole land of Judah. The "strong city" could be the stronghold mentioned in 25:4, built by the LORD himself. As such it clearly denotes Zion, the city of God, located in Jerusalem on the site of the ancient Jebusite stronghold.

26:2 This verse recalls Ps. 24:7-10. The strong city has gates in the high walls, watched over by a guard day and night. The guard opens the gates for the pilgrims who seek to enter the city. The pilgrims moving up in procession towards Zion are called "the righteous nation," one that consists of many peoples (cf. Isa. 25:6). Also, they are a nation "which keeps faith." Righteousness and faithfulness are inseparably related to each other. The righteous people in the LORD are those who are faithful to God and keep the Covenant of Grace (cf. Rom. 1:17); for if we "enter in" to God we find peace and salvation (cf. 1:26; Ps. 24:3-6).

26:3 This verse contains a confession by the pilgrims who enter Zion. Those whose minds are "steadfast" (NIV) have a strong conviction, a firm attitude, and are never "driven and tossed by the wind" (Jas. 1:6). Such persons put all their trust in God. They will be kept "in perfect peace," just as Zion itself.

26:4-6 Because of their firm conviction and trust in the LORD, those who are "in" the strong city now call upon all mankind to enter in, that is, also "to trust in the LORD for ever." The speakers fully recognize the frailty of sinful mankind, human stubbornness and insurrection against the commandments of God, and that mankind is therefore worthy of being punished by death. But on the other hand, they fully acknowledge God's love and mercy, his faithfulness through which mankind can be saved.

God's power and faithfulness are described as "an everlasting rock" (Isa. 26:4). In 17:10 God is called the Rock of refuge and God of salvation. This image is found frequently in the book of Psalms (e.g., Ps. 18:2; 31:2; 62:7; 71:3; 144:2). Yahweh is the sure and unmovable foundation on which people can stand firmly amidst the roaring waves of the ocean.

The image of the rock, however, gives a somewhat static picture. So besides it Yahweh is also praised as the jealous and dynamic God in all his saving acts throughout history. This is evident from his judgment against "the lofty city" (cf. 25:12). The pride and haughtiness of mankind are struck down at their very heart!

In an ironical way the prophet announces the fate of the "lofty" city as being "laid low." The haughty ones had trampled the faithful in such a way that they became poor and helpless. But now, after the city's downfall, the picture will be reversed. The lofty city in its turn will be cast down to the earth and its former oppressors trampled under foot, even the feet of those who had been made poor and needy. All this will happen "in that day" when the LORD will turn the sinful world upside down!

153

LONGING FOR GOD (26:7-10)

The prophet now turns his attention back to the present reality and to the challenge still to be faced by God's faithful people. He bases his declaration on the eschatological perspective that includes the total destruction of God's enemies and the redemption of the faithful, so that they will experience eternal peace and fullness of life.

What does "the way of the righteous" (26:7) look like? It looks to be both "level" and "smooth." But this does not mean always an easygoing and pleasant walk, free from all kinds of distress (cf. v. 16). It means, rather, a way leading straight to the destination that pleases God. It is a great privilege for the believer to walk on this "royal highway of God," the "Holy Way" of 35:8.

How does God level and smooth the way? We see at 40:4 how the valleys will be filled in and mountains and hills made low. This will be done through God's twofold judgment, for it will make low the lofty and haughty and at the same time lift up the oppressed and poor.

Therefore the prophet yearns for the implementation of God's righteousness. "Thy memorial name" (26:8) means that God's name shall always be remembered, not in a formal manner but confessed with true and firm conviction and gratitude to God. People will remember wholeheartedly all the saving, loving, merciful, and powerful acts of God in history, night and day (v. 9). It will be a spiritual pleasure to be in the continuing fellowship of God.

By the acts of God's judgment in world history the inhabitants of the earth will "learn" and "know" the righteousness of God in its double meaning. This judgment is the more necessary because of the stubbornness of those who believe they do not need repentance, even though they have seen God's hand lifted up. These will never see God's glory, for they will continue to act perversely even in "the land of uprightness." Nevertheless they cannot escape God's righteousness and judgment.

THE WICKED WILL BE PUT TO SHAME AND DESTROYED (26:11-14)

God has "lifted up his hand," which means that God is ready to execute his judgment (cf. 14:26, 27). The wicked sees as if he does not see, hears as if he does not hear. But eventually the wicked will be forced to see the hard reality of the LORD'S zeal for his people. He is jealous towards his adversaries, who will eventually be put to shame and be consumed by the "fire" of God's judgment (cf. Deut. 4:24; 9:3; Heb. 12:29).

For the faithful there will be peace after the accomplishment of God's judgment (Isa. 26:12). They will be delivered from their adversaries and will be reconciled with God. This "peace" is essentially the work of God himself, granted to mankind and through mankind. This is a mystery which can be understood only by faith. It is through earnest yearning for God that such a peace can be achieved (v. 9).

In Israel's history many other "lords" have been known, whether human kings or alien cults. But they were found to be false, misleading, and even oppressive, so that their subjects became poor and needy. Now those subjects' eyes are opened, and they have come to the firm conviction that Yahweh is the only LORD. Only his name will be remembered and worshipped (v. 13).

Now those other "lords" have been totally destroyed and their power terminated forever. They have become mere shades and "will not arise." This expression does not mean a denial of the resurrection from the dead (cf. v. 19a), as taught in later centuries by the Sadducees (cf. Mark 12:18). It only means that those "shades" will not become human beings again to oppress the faithful. The complete fulfillment of this prophecy, namely, the total destruction of the enemies and liberation from all their influence, may not be fully experienced as yet by God's people in the present dispensation. But in principle, as the NT declares, the final victory over "the enemies" has been accomplished through Jesus Christ (John 16:33).

THE LORD IS SAVIOR OF HIS PEOPLE (26:15-19)

Not only does the LORD liberate, but he also keeps his people in peace (Isa. 26:3, 12). As a result, the borders of the land will be enlarged. This old ideal of territorial expansion, achieved at the time of King David, together with the promises given to the patriarchs (cf. Deut. 19:8; Isa. 54:2; Ezek. 47:13–48:35) was still alive even in late postexilic times. But the fulfillment of this ideal can be seen only in a universal eschatological perspective pointing to the glory of the LORD. It will be God's kingdom at Zion, a multinational kingdom whose borders are unlimited in scope.

However, this people will in no way be a spoiled people (Isa. 26:16). They will be a people who are no strangers to suffering and distress, yet neither perish nor rebel. Rather, this people will increase in the knowledge of God. They will all the more wait for and depend on the LORD. Such has been the wandering pilgrim people of God throughout the ages.

Looking back at past history, the people remember all the sufferings and pain they had to endure "in your presence, O LORD" (v. 17 NIV). The people were like a woman in travail, writhing and crying in her pangs when the time drew near to give birth. So though the people struggled with all their might, they did not give birth to a child, but "as it were brought forth (only) wind" (v. 18). As the NIV reads the final line of v. 18, "We have not given birth to people of the world." In fact Israel has failed completely in its mission to the world. This was realized once they had glimpsed the righteousness and the glory of God the Redeemer.

Verse 19 deals with a new point concerning the resurrection from death. Some interpreters suggest that this verse is a later addition to the pericope. The traditional view, however, sees it as a continuation of the preceding verses, thereby closing the pericope.

This reference to "resurrection" may seem obscure to us. But what the prophet is affirming is his awareness that it is sin and not our physical existence that separates mankind from the love of God. Thus physical death in itself cannot mark the "end" of God's people. Throughout the succeeding chapters God's people are repeatedly called "the righteous." This word does not mean "self-righteous" or "morally good," as it is popularly thought to mean today. Rather, it translates the noun *tsaddiq,* meaning "right," "in the right." The hiphil or transitive form of the verb *tsedeq,* from which the noun comes, then means "to put right"; it is used only for an action of God. God puts us right with himself, by grace alone. He does so by forgiving us and thus renewing our personality. Since it is sin that separates mankind from life in God, now that "thou hast cast all my sins behind thy back" (Isa. 38:17), God has "put our personality right with himself." Consequently God's people are known as "the righteous" *(tsaddiqim),* those now living

156

the forgiven life. Since such is the gift of the "living" God, the righteous now live a life that death cannot touch. So we read here: "*Thy dead shall live, their bodies (nebhelah, 'corpses') shall rise*" (and the Hebrew may have read "my corpse," as the prophet excitedly allies himself with God's loved ones)—surely a reason to "sing for joy"!

The imperative calling for resurrection comes from the LORD himself. The deceased here are considered as if they are just sleeping (cf. Ps. 13:3; Job 3:13; Jer. 51:39, 57; Dan. 12:2).

"Dew of light" (Isa. 26:19) illustrates the power of God over death. "Dew" is the symbol of freshness and new life. In the OT the image of dew is also associated with youth (Ps. 110:3 RSV mg), with God himself as the giver of new life (Hos. 14:5), and with the saved remnant of Israel (Mic. 5:7). In the OT "light" illustrates life and salvation (e.g., Job 3:16; Ps. 27:1; 36:9; 56:13; Isa. 9:2).

Such dew from God provides fertility for the earth; so the fertile earth will give new life to the seeds sown in it. Isaiah 26:19 together with Dan. 12:2 and others such as Hos. 6:2; Ezek. 37:4 are important witnesses to the OT's teaching on the resurrection of the shades and the renewal of Israel as a new nation.

26:20-21 The location of these verses is debatable; should they be regarded as the closing verses of Isa. 26 or the opening verses of ch. 27? Actually they can be both at once, since 26:19 forms a good closing verse giving new hope and a perspective upon the resurrection. Verses 20-21, however, deal also with something different, namely, what should be done when God executes his judgment on earth.

Israel is called upon to hide in their chambers and close the door tightly, because the LORD will surely execute his judgment. This picture reminds us of the ark of Noah (Gen. 7:1, 16) and of the plagues in Egypt preceding the Exodus event (Exod. 12:12, 13). God's wrath will be very terrible but will not last forever (cf. Isa. 10:25; 15:1; Ps. 30:5; 103:9). It is not clear in what way the wrath will be executed, perhaps by means of a whirlwind (cf. Isa. 29:6; 30:30). Thereafter, however, "my people"—that is, the saved remnant—will live in peace and be restored in the new age to come.

The LORD will "punish the inhabitants of the earth for their iniquity." The prophet uses language that reminds us of Mic. 1:3.

This punishment represents the vengeance of God because the earth has been defiled by the blood of murder (cf. Isa. 24:5), and the blood of the righteous which has been shed upon the earth will be disclosed and cry for vengeance (cf. the blood of Abel, Gen. 4:10, 11; and Ezek. 24:7). The earth will no longer hide the victims of ruthless murder.

DELIVERANCE AND RENEWAL OF ISRAEL

27:1-13

LEVIATHAN WILL BE SLAIN (27:1)

If Isa. 24:21 proclaims God's punishment against the host of heaven and the kings of the earth, this verse proclaims God's punishment against the powers ruling the seas; these powers are symbolic of the "deep" mentioned at Gen. 1:2. The figure of Leviathan is derived from the ancient Canaanite mythology of Baal who defeated Yam, the god of the sea. Afterwards Yam became identified with Leviathan, who at times was also called Rahab (cf. Isa. 30:7; 51:9-10; Ps. 89:10; Job 26:12-13), whom Yahweh had crushed and slain. Nevertheless the dragon was still a danger to human beings (cf. Job 3:8; 26:13). In this verse Leviathan is described as "the fleeing serpent," "the twisting serpent," "the dragon that is in the sea." According to some interpreters these descriptions signified the great rivers flowing across Assyria (the Tigris), Babylonia (the Euphrates), and Egypt (the Nile; Ps. 74:13-15); the Nile is also at times identified with the sea (Isa. 18:2; 19:5). In a broader sense these descriptions point to all those earthly powers which oppose God and his people. No earthly power was considered able to withstand Leviathan. Only Yahweh, the mighty LORD, with his great and strong sword could overcome all the earthly powers. Note the anthropomorphic language used here.

However, here the "dragon" is death. Consequently, to "kill death" is to bring to life. The dragon has the unique advantage of not existing. Thus it admirably symbolizes the paradox of evil, which is a powerful and positive force in the realm of human life. Yet in itself the dragon is pure negation or nonbeing. In the NT Rev. 17:8 expresses this paradox in a powerful picture.

159

ISRAEL AS THE PLEASANT VINEYARD (27:2-6)

After the outpouring of God's wrath is over and the total destruction of all opposing powers has been accomplished, a sweet song
is heard. It is the song of the "pleasant vineyard," expressing the
intimate relationship that will obtain between God and Israel.
This song ends with a shout of praise for the future glory of
Israel, or "Jacob." As such it shows some similarities but also dis-
similarities with the Song of the Vineyard in Isa. 5:1-7. In ch. 5
the vineyard does not yield good grapes and is therefore rejected.
But here the pleasant vineyard yields an abundance of sweet
grapes.

27:2   What is meant by "the pleasant vineyard"? The Hebrew
text (MT) reads "a vineyard of wine," which means a fertile and
productive vineyard, producing an abundance of sweet grapes.
Other ancient versions (LXX, Vulgate, Syriac, Targum) employ a
slightly different word, meaning "pleasant." In fact, however, there
is no contradiction in meaning. The pleasant vineyard is obviously fertile and well kept, and therefore yields an abundance of good
grapes.

27:3-4   The LORD himself is the divine "keeper" of the vineyard.
He loves his vineyard; he is its diligent guardian, and he protects
it against thieves and robbers, thorns and briers. The "thorns and
briers" might be taken in a figurative sense as referring to internal
disturbers among the people themselves. They will immediately be
removed and burnt up. This would then be the final purification.

27:5   If there are indeed thorns and briers in the vineyard, the
LORD will deal with them gracefully before removing them. The
way of repentance and salvation is still open for those disturbers
among the people. They can still flee to God and "lay hold" of
his gracious help. This reminds us of the altar at the temple as a
place of refuge for sinners (cf. 1 Kgs. 1:50). Repentance means
seeking the LORD and making peace with him. This is the good
news for sinful mankind, namely that God prefers to forgive and
make peace with people rather than to condemn and punish. The
prophet, being moved by the good news, repeats the sentence

once again. The repetition reflects the amazing truth of the message.

27:6 Jacob had been the sinful ancestor of the people of God. God had wrestled with Jacob "all night"; then when morning dawned God had given him the new name of Israel (Gen. 32:24-30). Israel was thus that people who had first resisted grace, had then struggled to obtain God's blessing, and had finally received it. This song thus ends with God's promise that Israel will "take root" in him, "put forth shoots," and then "fill the whole world with fruit" (cf. John 15:1-2). Isaiah 27:6 thus depicts the future role and function of the new Israel for the salvation of mankind and as a blessing for the world (cf. Gen. 12:2). Here it is quite clear that the "vineyard" is Israel, the people of God.

THE LORD LOVES HIS PEOPLE BUT PUNISHES HIS ENEMIES (27:7-11)

This pericope starts with a rhetorical question to which the answer is obviously in the negative (Isa. 27:7). The LORD has loved and kept his people in a wonderful way (vv. 2-6), although they are virtually no better than their slain enemies (26:21; 27:1). If Israel had indeed laid hold on this gracious love, they can only thank and praise the LORD for enabling them to do so. Based on this acknowledgment Israel had consequently raised the song of the pleasant vineyard (vv. 2-6).

The first word of v. 8 raises some problems. Hebrew *sa'seah* means "measure." The RSV thus follows the traditional translation, "measure by measure." But modern textual research suggests another reading (followed by the new Indonesian translation) using the Hebrew verb *sn'* and translating "by driving (her) out." The traditional reading following the MT text, however, still makes sense. The love and care of God for his people (v. 7) does not exclude punishment and suffering (cf. 26:16; Rev. 3:19). But this chastisement is meant for the good of the people and never arbitrarily goes beyond measure. Yahweh chastises in just measure (cf. Jer. 2:19; 30:11; 46:28). As such God's chastisement had fallen repeatedly upon Israel, culminating in the Exile. The Exile had been felt as a severe punishment but not unto death. Even in the Exile

161

the LORD had shown his loving-kindness and faithfulness; he had punished "in just measure" as it pleased him (cf. 40:2).

The LORD sent his people into exile as if with a "fierce blast" (cf. Jer. 18:17a; Job 27:20-21). It is called *his* fierce blast, denoting that it was God's act and personal intention for his people. The "east wind" mentioned here is the scorching sirocco wind, blowing from the eastern desert. It creates storms at sea and fatal dryness on land (cf. Ps. 48:7; Ezek. 27:26; Hos. 13:15). Nevertheless this sirocco wind has its own season, namely, autumn. This terrible wind is thus also controlled by the LORD in just measure!

27:9   The Exile had turned out to be a blessing in disguise for Israel. It had led Israel to a new spiritual understanding and to repentance. At the appointed time the LORD had shown again his merciful righteousness and had allowed Judah to return to Jerusalem (cf. Isa. 40:2). The Exile was also meant as an expiation for Israel. Their repentance now resulted in the removal of their sins and the gift of a new sanctified life. This was to be lived out in a concrete and radical manner: it was to be a life full of the fruits of repentance. Israel would have to crush all idol worship. Not only was one's personal life to be so expiated, but the whole land as well. This was to be the way back to "the pleasant vineyard," and all to the glory of the LORD. (See G. A. F. Knight, *The New Israel*, in the *International Theological Commentary* series.)

27:10-11   These two verses seem to stand on their own. Again the destruction of "the fortified city" comes to the fore. This might serve as a background in contrast to 27:12-13, which declare the restoration of the unity of Israel.

The basic questions are: what city is this fortified city, and what people is meant by "a people without discernment"? Those two questions are closely related to each other. Concerning the city many suggestions have been made, such as Jerusalem, Babel, and Samaria. In line with our interpretation of 25:12 and 26:5 we may adopt a symbolic meaning here, that is, an anonymous city representing the "world-city" which opposes God and is finally destroyed forever. Thus it might be equated with the "inhabitants of the earth" (24:6).

The destroyed city is now (in 27:11) depicted as a withered tree,

whose boughs are dry and finally break off. Women come to collect all these dry boughs to be consumed in their home fires, so
nothing of them is left.

A "people without discernment" means a people without any
"knowledge" of God; they are the ungodly who oppose God and
his people. For such a people God has no compassion.

ISRAEL COMES HOME (27:12-13)

The closing verses of this long series of apocalyptic-eschatological
prophecies in chs. 24–27 reflect the climax of the hope of Israel. In
both the Old and New Testament, apocalyptic employs the picture
of "harvest home" for the last judgment.

27:12   The LORD is pictured as the One who threshes out grain
from the chaff. The "grain" illustrates the scattered Israelites in dispersion in Egypt, Assyria, and Babylonia. One by one they will be
gathered together into their home country. The "Euphrates" signifies Mesopotamia, that is, Assyria and Babylonia. By "the Brook
of Egypt" is meant the Wadi el-'Arish, at the southern end of the
Palestinian border.

27:13   A further description of the way God's plan will become
visible is given here. A "great trumpet" will be blown to call and
gather together all Israelites who are in dispersion. In the Bible a
trumpet is often used for the call to common worship (cf. Ps. 81:3;
Joel 2:15). Similarly, in eschatological times a trumpet will be used
to call the nations (cf. Joel 2:1; Rev. 1:10; 8–9; 10:7) to judgment.

Northern Israel had been carried into exile in Assyria; the nation never returned from there as a whole (cf. 2 Kgs. 17:6). At the
time of the prophet Jeremiah many Jews fled to Egypt and remained there, living in Jewish colonies (cf. Jer. 42). There is no
mention of Babylonia here, possibly because there had by now
been an official return from the Babylonian Exile. "Assyria" and
"Egypt" can therefore be taken as representing all Jewish colonies
still in dispersion. These people all will come home to Jerusalem to
worship the LORD (cf. Isa. 19:19-25). Their unity is not based on
any nationalistic or political interest, but on their common worship of Yahweh. They will return to Zion together with the nations,

because Zion will then be the center of the world (cf. 2:2-3; Mic. 4:1-3; Matt. 24:31).

At the end only Yahweh will be victorious and so will be glorified by all the world's inhabitants. The kingdom of the LORD, as the kingdom of peace, will be established on the foundations of love, faithfulness, and righteousness. Ever since, this has been the living hope and the good news for Israel and for the nations throughout history.

PART IV

A COLLECTION OF WOE PROPHECIES: JUDGMENT AND CONSOLATION

Isaiah 28:1–33:24

ORACLES AGAINST THE
LEADERS AT JERUSALEM
28:1-29

This chapter is the first in a collection of "woe prophecies" (Isa. 28:1; 29:15; 30:1; 31:1; 33:1) raised against the leaders of Samaria and, especially, of Judah who had leaned upon Egyptian help. It has been generally agreed that most of these prophecies originate from the time of the prophet Isaiah.

In its present form the text seems to be confused in its chronological order as well as in its line of thought. Most probably this has been caused by post-Isaian redactors who have inserted a variety of diverse materials from an earlier period (e.g., 28:1-4, from before the fall of the northern kingdom in 722 B.C.) as well as from a later period. Generally these materials proclaim a double message of judgment (woe prophecies) and of comfort and hope.

THE DRUNKEN LEADERS OF SAMARIA (28:1-4)

This is the only prophecy in the book of Isaiah uttered by the prophet Isaiah against Samaria. It may display some influence of the prophet Amos, his predecessor (cf. Amos 6:1). Samaria had been sharply criticized because of its pride and extravagance, its banquets and its drunkenness, prior to its downfall in 722 B.C. Based on this shocking historical fact of Samaria's end the prophet now reminds Judah of God's terrible judgment that might eventually also befall Judah and Jerusalem. Judah is therefore summoned to repent from similar sins and reconfirm its trust in Yahweh.

28:1   In a figurative way the city of Samaria is called "the proud crown." This might be derived from the geographical setting of the city. It was built on a hill and was surrounded by high fortified walls. The wealth of Ephraim was stored there (Amos 3:15). It was

167

the one place where the highest authorities and the royal crown felt completely secure (cf. Amos 6:1).

But in an ironical fashion this "proud crown" is associated with Samaria's drunkenness. Such is surely a shameful reputation for the inhabitants of Samaria to possess, living lavishly as they were, yet in moral and spiritual decay (cf. Amos 6:6-7). They had been "overcome with wine," indicating complete drunkenness.

All this pomp and "glory" would soon be taken away, like "the fading flower of its glorious beauty." This beauty was like a wreath "on the head of the rich valley," that is, the city of Samaria with its drunkards.

28:2-3   The Assyrian king and his army are pictured here as "one who is mighty and strong; like a storm of hail, a destroying tempest," like "a storm of mighty and overflowing waters." The Assyrian army consisted of many subjugated nations and was therefore numerous and irresistible like mighty overflowing waters (cf. Isa. 17:12-13). The LORD in his sovereignty employed such a nation to carry out his plans; so Assyria would be God's agent to punish Samaria.

28:4   There would be no more opportunity for Samaria to escape its downfall. The enemy's army was forming up and was ready to attack at the first opportunity. Samaria would be like a "ripe fig" before harvest time. Such a fig was too conspicuous and tempting just to look at. As soon as anyone saw it he would pluck the fig and "eat it up." The illustration means that God's judgment would not be postponed any longer.

A CROWN OF GLORY (28:5-6)

Though the picture of a crown (28:3) is continued, the content of the message is quite other. In fact, the picture is now in reverse. Therefore these verses are to be distinguished from the preceding vv. 1-4. "In that day" points to an eschatological moment. It is the LORD of hosts *(YHWH tsebaot)* who will be a crown of everlasting glory for the remnant of his people. The glory and beauty of the remnant will not be determined by human pride, wealth, or by a mighty army, but will be based on spiritual values such as righteousness, justice, security, peace, and human welfare (cf. 26:3; 1:27-28; Amos 5:4, in contrast to Amos 5:12-13). The "spirit of justice" possesses the dynamic meaning of fighting against all kinds of injustice or attacks by one's enemies. Therefore it is closely connected with a "strength" that makes people like mighty heroes able to turn back the battle that has reached to the gate (cf. Zech. 12:7-9).

So it is the LORD himself who will be the beautiful "crown of glory" and who will reign at Zion (cf. Isa. 24:23). This eschatological perspective is sharply contrasted with the actual situation in Jerusalem as described in the following verses.

THE DRUNKEN LEADERS OF JERUSALEM (28:7-13)

Now the prophet directs his prophecies against "Jerusalem" (Judah), since Jerusalem considered itself to be the remnant that was to be saved (cf. 7:4-7).

We are reminded of certain present-day Christian sects who consider themselves to be the only group in Christendom that will be saved. Such self-centered believers have not understood what Isaiah declares in this section—that the people of God is elected, not to be saved but to save. For Israel has been called to share in God's plan for the redemption of all God's creatures, both mankind and the natural world. But in fact Jerusalem was no better than Samaria. This was evident from the behavior of the leaders, the priests, and the false prophets in Jerusalem.

28:7-8   The leaders who exercised judgment, the priests who led the ritual ceremonies, the prophets who proclaimed God's word to the people all now "reel" and "stagger" with wine and strong drink. The priests ignore the statute on drink addressed to them at Lev. 10:9; the prophets have become totally "confused" and err in their visions and in their teaching of the law. In describing such drunkenness and total spiritual confusion, Isa. 28:8 remarks that "all tables are full of vomit" and "no place is without filthiness." All the people have become deluded and are like those blind persons who are led by the blind and who inevitably fall into the ditch.

28:9-10   The prophet Isaiah is ridiculed. It is most likely that this mockery comes from those leaders who have been strongly criticized by the prophet, namely, the priests and the false prophets.

The priests were authorized to teach the law; the prophets received visions from which they spoke for God. These now mock him, saying that his teaching and admonishment are meaningless and not worth listening to! Maybe babes would listen to him, but they would never understand a word. Or it may be that the priests and prophets are asking, "Does he consider us as infants 'weaned from the milk'?" They say, "For it is precept upon precept . . . line upon line . . ." (v. 10). This literal translation of the Hebrew text might be interpreted as denoting the meaningless, boring, and superficial teaching of Isaiah. Some interpreters, however, think we are not meant to translate the Hebrew words *tsaw latsaw . . . qaw laqaw,* considering them instead to be mere gibberish (Otto Kaiser, *Isaiah 13–39,* 245). The NEB translates more freely: "It is all harsh cries and raucous shouts." The RSV translation "here a little, there a little" is rather obscure in meaning.

To many unbelievers today the prophetic word of God sounds rather naive. It sounds like childlike chatter, it is illogical, and it belongs to an out-of-date tradition. Such a challenge should humble the Christian believer, forcing him to ask himself, "Is this not due to presenting the gospel—the good news—in the wrong way, if it sounds no longer 'new' or 'good'?" Jesus came "not to be served but to serve, and to give his life as a ransom for many" (Mark 10:45). The Christian must ask if he really witnesses to this central message of the gospel in his daily life and work. If he does not, then the world can say of the gospel what these religious leaders here said of Isaiah's preaching.

28:11-13   The prophet replies. The LORD has been patient and merciful towards the people of Judah, because he considers them to be a tired and weary people (Isa. 28:12). But now the prophet proclaims a clear message, urging the people to repent and to receive peace in the LORD (cf. Matt. 11:28-29). But instead they look forward to receiving support from Egypt and to enjoying themselves with banquets and wine, even as they oppress the poor (cf. Jer. 7).

Now the LORD will execute his judgment through "men of strange lips" who speak an alien tongue (cf. 1 Cor. 14:21), that is, the Assyrians. Then the people will be forced to listen to their oppressors, although they will not be able to understand them. In

170

an ironical way the prophet repeats their obscure expression uttered in Isa. 28:10, but now the roles are reversed. The people must now obey continuously all the alien's precepts and rules. They will feel tempted to disobey and flee away, but the consequences would be even worse. They would fall backward, bruised and broken, like an animal that has been snared and captured (cf. 24:18). Such then will be the fall of Jerusalem and of its leaders.

THE TERRIBLE COVENANT WITH DEATH (28:14-22)

28:14-15 Now the prophet turns to the scoffers in particular. They seem to be very influential in Jerusalem. They seem also to have influenced the ambiguous policy of King Hezekiah towards Assyria. All of this the prophet now sharply criticizes. It is not clear, however, whether the scoffers or the prophet himself uttered the words of mockery quoted in 28:15. More likely the prophet has spoken them to characterize the attitude of his opponents (cf. Otto Kaiser, *Isaiah 13–39,* 251).

According to Canaanite mythology, death was personified as Mot, the god of the realm of death. Mot was engaged in a continuous struggle with Baal, the god of life and fertility. So the "covenant with Death (Mot)" and the "agreement with Sheol (the realm of death)" underscore the leaders' unfaithfulness towards the covenant with Yahweh. As such they feared neither death nor the overwhelming scourge of the Assyrians. Yahweh, the Rock of refuge and salvation (cf. 17:10; 25:4), was replaced by "lies" and "falsehood"!

The "overwhelming scourge" that "passes through"—that is, the mighty armies of the Assyrians—is pictured as a flood of water sweeping over the whole country (cf. 8:8; 10:22). In the OT death (or Mot) is closely related to flood and torrent (Ps. 124:4) or to "the deep" (Ps. 42:7). Again the refuge of lies and falsehood might refer to sheer ambiguous political pretenses towards Assyria.

28:16 In opposition to all this, Isaiah points to a far more solid and reliable stronghold of refuge, namely, to Zion, the city of God (cf. Isa. 25:4; Ps. 18:1-2). The LORD himself, the divine Builder, will lay its sure and unshakable foundation and will safeguard it against all hurricanes and floods. This reflects the faithfulness and

171

righteousness of God to his Covenant of Grace throughout the ages. The sure and solid foundation is guaranteed by a carefully selected precious and tested cornerstone. Considering its vital function, it is understandable that this picture was later applied in the NT to Jesus Christ (Matt. 21:42; cf. Ps. 118:22). As such this verse has messianic significance, for it may be seen to refer to the Davidic dynasty which was built on the everlasting covenant. From this Davidic descent the Messiah would come to build the kingdom.

Again the prophet emphasizes the vital importance of faith and trust in the LORD: "He who believes will not be in haste" (or "dismayed" NIV). This famous expression is quoted in Rom. 9:33; 10:11; 1 Pet. 2:6 (following LXX "put to shame"). These NT quotations produce a combination of two texts, Isa. 8:14 and 28:16. The words "in him" found in the NT references do not occur in 28:16. Both Paul and Peter use the quotation to illumine the significance of the "stone" that is mentioned in the previous line (v. 16), concluding thereby that the Isaian quotations refer to Christ.

We today possess Bibles with both the Old and New Testaments bound as one, so compact that they may be slipped into a pocket. But in Paul's day the OT was written upon many large scrolls, so large that they could be preserved only in the temple or in a local synagogue. For this reason the early Church apparently produced in a small vellum volume, much like a modern book, a collection of those OT texts which they believed spoke of Christ. Such a single small "book" Paul could well have secured in his baggage during his itinerant preaching. We note how in the NT many quotations from the Hebrew OT are not reproduced with word for word accuracy. This may have had several causes. First, the translation from the original Hebrew into the Greek of the LXX was already at hand, and it did not always agree with the Hebrew. Second, because they could not carry with them the whole OT as we can do, when the early missionaries wished to quote the Scriptures they had to rely very much on their memory. Third, the quotations they employed may in fact have been "secondhand," coming from this "portable" collection of texts rather than direct from the Hebrew text of the OT from which all modern translations derive.

28:17   In sharp contrast with the leaders' refuge of lies and falsehood, this edifice at Zion is built accurately according to the measuring line used by the builder, which here symbolizes justice and righteousness. The plummet guarantees that all walls stand up right in their correct position. This symbolizes a pure and right relationship with God. "Justice" and "righteousness" are inseparable values penetrating all aspects of life in the kingdom, providing peace, protection, and security for all people. On the contrary, how fragile is the refuge of lies and falsehood. It is like a house built on sand (cf. Matt. 7:26-27) and will be swept away by the waters of God's judgment.

28:18-19   Not only will the shelter be swept away, but also the whole covenant and agreement with Sheol will be annulled. The people will be completely beaten down by the waves of the scourge "morning by morning . . . , by day and by night."

The scoffers will no longer scoff at the word of God, and the word will no longer sound like "harsh cries and raucous shouts." At that time they will understand and realize the truth of the Word, but unfortunately it will be a message of "sheer terror" for the scoffers at Jerusalem.

28:20-21   The LORD'S offer to give rest to the weary (Isa. 28:12) has been rejected. Therefore there will be no rest any more for the sinners. Verse 20 seems to quote a popular saying. People will be dismayed because they will be deprived of the most basic human needs just at the moment when they are most needed. If we apply the saying to vv. 15-16, then we could say that the "bed of lies" will not give rest and the "pillow of falsehood" will fail to give protection.

The prophet reminds the people of Jerusalem of two ancient historical events. First, according to 2 Sam. 5:18-25 King David defeated the Philistines twice, at Perazim and at Geba (2 Sam. 5:25) or Gibeon (1 Chr. 14:16). The point of interest in both of these stories is the saving intervention of the LORD: "The LORD has broken through my enemies before me, like a bursting flood" (2 Sam. 5:20; cf. 1 Chr. 14:11). This picture of the bursting flood is in parallel with the picture of the overwhelming waters in Isa. 28:2, 15, 17.

The second event is still more ancient. It refers to the defeat of the Canaanite kings at Gibeon when they fled before Israel. The

LORD "threw down great stones from heaven upon them" (Josh. 10:11). This is also parallel to the "storm of hail" in Isa. 28:2.

However strange it might sound, such a punishment could befall Judah also. God's righteousness and holiness will not tolerate the derision of the leaders of Jerusalem. Yahweh is the jealous God (Josh. 24:19; Nah. 1:2)!

God's Strange Work

We are dealing with a God who acts in ways quite other than our human philosophies can grasp. With his own eternal purpose in view God made covenant with a people whom he had chosen in love to be his partner and agent to accomplish the salvation of all mankind. But there were those in Israel who scoffed at being bound to God in the bonds of the Covenant. This group went so far as to make counter-covenant, not with the "living" God but with the "dead" god, Mot, the god of death!

For centuries the LORD had sought to educate his chosen people to let him use them in this task. But some would not allow him to employ them in such an effort (cf. Ps. 95:8, 11). From his first chapter onwards, Isaiah had revealed the anger of the LORD against the kind of disloyalty such in Israel had shown. At Isa. 10:5-6 we saw how the God of love had to do love's "strange work" of calling upon the Assyrian army to come and bring the people of God to their senses. Now, however, years later things have come to a head. Isaiah had heard that the LORD of hosts is actually enunciating "a decree of destruction . . . upon the whole land." In consequence, from this moment on the destruction of Jerusalem and of Judah has become inevitable, and the exile of God's people to Babylon must necessarily follow. Yet God's "alien" work—alien to our conception of how love should act—will be of a double nature. (1) God will take upon his own shoulders the task he has allotted to Israel of being the Servant, for God will now be *in* Israel as they suffer the pain of the Exile through which the world might be saved (see G. A. F. Knight's commentary on Isa. 53 in *Servant Theology*). (2) God will bring new life to Israel actually out of death. He will "resurrect" them as his "new" people, forgiven and loved as ever, but now at last seeking to be loyal to God's plans within the bonds of the Covenant (see G. A. F. Knight, *The New*

Israel). We should note that this strange deed of God, the pattern of which is revealed in the book of Isaiah as a whole, is followed once again in the NT's understanding of this "strange deed." It took form when "God was in Christ" in the cross and resurrection of Jesus. God's strange work again becomes visible in the case of believers today. For as Paul puts it, it is only "if anyone is in Christ," crucified and resurrected, that "he is a new creation . . . . All this is from God . . ." (2 Cor. 5:17-18).

28:22   The situation becomes most critical. The prophet now turns to the scoffers in a pastoral capacity. Every mockery they utter will tighten the Egyptian "bond" of slavery, because that bond is not just a political but a religious issue as well. Therefore stop scoffing! The "decree of destruction" is at hand! This is the last call to repentance!

EVERYTHING IN GOD'S OWN TIME (28:23-29)

This closing pericope seems to be a later addition, giving a further description of God's amazing work (cf. Isa. 28:21). God's wisdom is described here in a figurative way using pictures derived from agricultural life.

28:23   The call to "hear" is often used in the Wisdom Literature (e.g., Prov. 4:1; 5:1; 7:24; Job 34:2) and occasionally in the book of Psalms (Ps. 49:1) as well as in the Prophets (Hos. 5:1). Our prophet strongly emphasizes and repeats this call by using four synonymous verbs. This emphasis arises from the fact that the scoffers have been mocking continuously at his prophetic message.

28:24-26   The parable of a farmer preparing the soil is introduced by a rhetorical question, which obviously requires a negative answer. The hard and stony ground must be plowed, opened up, and harrowed before the seed can be sown. Each action has its own appropriate time and manner. Likewise through various blessings and punishments God is preparing human hearts to be receptive to the seed of the Word (cf. Matt. 13:1-23).

The act of sowing requires knowledge and skill because of the variety of seeds; each seed requires its own specific treatment and appropriate place. All must be planned beforehand and then worked out accurately, diligently, and neatly. As such the parable gives a picture of an attractive and well-cared-for garden with various plants, colors, and all in perfect arrangement.

Likewise the kingdom is like a beautiful garden of God, in which a great variety of nations, faiths, and cultures reflect the glory of the LORD. Salvation is not the specific privilege of Israel. In fact, it is promised and prepared for all nations, even to Egypt and Assyria (Gen. 12:3; Isa. 19:19-25), through pruning and fruit bearing, through punishment and blessing.

God's mandate has been given to mankind, that is, to dominate and cultivate the earth (Gen. 1:27-29). He teaches humanity how to till the ground and to preserve the garden in the right way. Therefore people must humble themselves before God and praise him. The leaders of Jerusalem have to realize their foolishness and stop scoffing.

28:27-29 Even the most common ordering of human life, no matter how simple and obvious it may look, comes from the all-wise God. To deviate from it can be disastrous for mankind, and the "dill," "cummin," and "grain" might be crushed forever. All such skill and wisdom in husbandry comes from the LORD of hosts, not from Baal, the fertility god, nor from any deified science (Isa. 28:29). This closing verse contains a message at which the parable is aiming. It is primarily directed to the foolish leaders at Jerusalem, urging them to repent. God's counsel is wonderful and his wisdom is excellent, and he acts accordingly in a variety of ways and always at the right moment. Blessed is the person who can see and understand God's mighty works and counsel in nature, in history, and in personal life. Look attentively at the signs of the times!

PUNISHMENT AND CONSOLATION

29:1-24

This message is directed to Jerusalem (Judah) and is closely related to Isa. 28:7-22. The historical situation seems to be similar. It includes a later addition to the basic Isaian text.

JUDGMENT AND RELEASE FOR BESIEGED JERUSALEM (29:1-8)

29:1-2   The prophecy of woe is now addressed to "Ariel." The meaning of the name (literally, "the lion of God") is in itself obscure. As a place name the Hebrew word occurs five times in the OT (Ezek. 43:15, 16; Isa. 29:1, 2, 7). In Ezek. 43 and Isa. 29:2b it is translated as "altar hearth," the place on which burnt offerings are placed to be consumed by fire. However, in v. 1 it refers specifically to "the city where David encamped (NIV 'settled')," that is, Jerusalem or simply, as it was called more frequently, "the city of David." It has been suggested that the "altar hearth" (Ariel) is the most revered holy spot in the temple accessible to visitors. The prophet, who might have been attending the temple cult when he uttered this prophecy, then applied this name to the whole city of Jerusalem (Jan Ridderbos, *De profeet Jesaja*, 1). But nowhere else in the OT in this epithet given to Jerusalem.

In an ironical manner the prophet criticizes the city even as it was in the act of celebrating. The main celebrations were the New Year in our October, the Passover in spring, and the Feast of Tabernacles in autumn. These feasts were all completely legitimate; but the manner in which they were celebrated had become too ostentatious and formalistic, thus depriving them of their spiritual meaning. The prophetic warning on this matter has evidently been ignored and ridiculed. And this had happened year after year.

However, there is no reason why we should not connect Isaiah's thinking here, through his use of pictorial theology, with what he has to say at 33:14. There we read: "Who among us can dwell with the devouring fire? Who among us can dwell with everlasting burnings?" Ever since the exodus from Egypt prophetic minds had recognized that "our God is a consuming fire." We see this truth at Lev. 10:2; Deut. 4:12, 24; 32:22; Isa. 10:16, and throughout the rest of the book of Isaiah. In particular it is Zion that is to experience the blazing heat of the passionate, saving love of God, because Zion is that one spot on earth where God as Immanuel ("God *with* us") chooses to be uniquely present (cf. Amos 3:2; Ps. 76:1-2).

The LORD will "distress" Jerusalem through the Assyrian siege, causing mourning and lamentation. "And she shall be to me like an Ariel" (Isa. 29:2; "altar hearth" NIV). As the place where burnt offerings were consumed by fire, the altar hearth revealed the wrath of God towards human sin. But at the same time it was also the place where God showed his redeeming mercy. After the punishment Jerusalem would be purified once again (cf. 31:9b).

29:3-4 How terrible is the consuming heat of the altar fire. Jerusalem was to be burnt completely without any chance of escape. Contrary to its previous haughty attitude (cf. 28:7-15) the city would be brought low even to the dust. Its mockery would be silenced, and only its feeble mourning whispers arising from the dust would be heard instead. These would sound like ghostly murmurings from the depth of the earth.

29:5-8 God's punishment, however, does not last forever. This new pericope shows another side of the scene. Although the multitude of enemies is as countless as fine dust, eventually they will be driven away. They are not only numerous, but also ruthless and cruel; nevertheless they will be like "passing chaff."

The LORD will liberate Jerusalem in a sudden and wonderful way. The almighty LORD will "visit" them (the enemies) in an instant. The LORD'S visitation here has a double function, that is, of punishing and destroying the ruthless enemies but simultaneously of liberating his people.

The LORD will "visit" as in the days of old, in a mighty theophany, shaking the earth and releasing the terrible forces in nature (29:6). This image may well be influenced by the Sinai tradition. Compared with all those mighty forces, the earthquakes and "devouring fire" from heaven, the multitude of enemies are just like "passing chaff" indeed!

This event will be experienced as a passing "dream": for Jerusalem as a nightmare but for the city's enemies as a pleasant dream. When Jerusalem should awake early one morning, it will rejoice and find itself released from the terrible nightmare (i.e., the Assyrian siege); but in reverse the city's enemies will wake up in terror from their pleasant dream. They will flee in confusion and leave Ariel alone.

The last sentence of v. 8 seems to be a later additional conclusion following the apocalyptic tradition in proclaiming the final glory of Zion (cf. 28:16). The LORD is the great and wonderful Helper, but a terrible consuming fire as well!

DOOM FOR THOSE WHO ARE BLIND AND FOOLISH (29:9-16)

The negative reaction of the people against the prophet shows the blindness and the foolishness of their inner spiritual life.

29:9-10   The people's pretensions will be turned into reality. The people had rejected the teaching of the prophet with mockery. They had pretended to be stupefied, blind, and drunken. They did not give ear even to the wonderful message in the preceding verses (vv. 1-8). This stubbornness eventually resulted in God's punishment when God visited them. "The LORD is slow to anger . . . and the LORD will by no means clear the guilty" (Nah. 1:3). Therefore the time would come when they would be really amazed and stupefied, blind and drunken—both physically and spiritually. Their spiritual leaders, the prophets and seers, would grope in darkness or blindness. "A spirit of deep sleep," one of total unconsciousness or "stupor," would be poured upon them. In this respect the prophet would experience existentially what had been prophesied concerning Israel at the time of his call (Isa. 6:9-10). This prophecy now gives an answer to the secret of Israel's stubbornness and punishment. But on the other hand it also shows how great is the LORD's mercy and grace towards his people.

29:11-12   These verses written in prose seem to be a later addition, giving a further explanation of the people's spiritual blindness. A sealed book (or scroll) cannot be opened for reading (cf. 8:16). Moreover even if the book were opened, its meaning would not be understood by anyone. Consequently the book remained a "closed" book for the people as a whole, because they were all in darkness and in deep sleep.

Again and again Israel has been reproached because of its spiritual darkness or blindness. In the OT this is recorded, for example, in Deut. 29:4; Ps. 82:5; Isa. 1:3; 9:2; 27:11; 42:18-20; 44:18; Jer. 5:21. In the NT also such a reproach is often heard (e.g., Matt. 13:13-19; 15:15; 23:19–24:6; 2 Cor. 3:14-15). Even the disciples were rebuked by Jesus for the same reason (Luke 24:25-27).

29:13-14   It is noteworthy that in these verses Hebrew *adonay* ("Lord") is used instead of the name Yahweh as in the preceding pericope. Originally these two verses seem to have stood each on their own (cf. Isa. 1:10-15), yet together they fit well in this present context.

Due to spiritual blindness the people had deceived themselves and had hidden behind a facade of external worship, formalism, and traditionalism. Their worship, paired with pompous ostentation, was really in vain, because "their hearts are far from me," says the LORD (29:13). The human heart is the center of life and the storehouse of all feelings and thoughts. But God knows the secrets of the heart (Ps. 44:21). The sacrifice acceptable to God is a clean heart, a broken spirit, a broken and a contrite heart (Ps. 51:10, 17; Matt. 15:8-9). But on the contrary their worship was merely formal, "made up only of rules taught by men" (Isa. 29:13 NIV). What a dramatic misunderstanding and self-deception!

In fact people did not know the meaning of fellowship with God. They were deaf and blind to God; yet they claimed to be quite sensitive, and keen on human wisdom and eager for the praise of mankind.

Once again the LORD would take the initiative. His light would shine in the darkness, and the darkness would not overcome it (cf. John 1:5). Marvelous things would happen at the time of deliverance, just as they happened in Egypt in ancient times. But now they would be delivered from mankind's vain wisdom, haughtiness, and blindness. God would make foolish the wisdom of the world (1 Cor. 1:20ff.). This marvelous good news is continued later in Isa. 29:17-24.

29:15-16   Once again the prophet shows the utter foolishness of mankind in pretending to be hidden from God's sight. In fact they could not hide their counsel and deeds in darkness. They derided the all-knowing God (cf. Ps. 14:1; 53:1; 39:1-6), but the LORD "will bring to light the things now hidden in darkness" (cf. 1 Cor. 4:5).

In an ironical way the prophet shows up mankind's foolishness, in that they "turn things upside down" (Isa. 29:16). The people had rebelled against the almighty and creator God! Mankind is described as being just like clay, in itself worthless, formless, and weak (cf. Job 10:9; 33:6). But God is like the skillful and creative potter who is able to transform the clay into precious, useful, and attractive utensils. How can the clay exalt itself against the potter (Isa. 45:9; Rom. 9:21; cf. Jer. 18:6)? This is indeed the root of mankind's sin, their pride and foolishness, in either wishing to be like God or in ignoring God in all his ways.

JUDAH WILL BE REDEEMED AND PURIFIED AGAIN (29:17-24)

This pericope describes a glorious hope and provides in eschatological perspective how God will transform both nature and the hearts of mankind.

29:17-18   God will indeed turn things upside down. The poor and the weak will be exalted, and the haughty will be brought low.

In a poetic way the prophet announces the wonderful and marvelous acts of God through the transformation of nature (Isa. 29:17-18). Obviously his words cannot be interpreted literally. These wonderful acts of God will be done in "a very little while." They will not follow at the end of a long process but will happen in a short while through the intervention of God's spirit (cf. 32:15-16). This expression reflects the eschatological hope that eternity is ever breaking through into time.

This universal transformation is to be essentially a wonderful act

181

of liberation (cf. 6:10; 28:13; 29:9-10; 42:18-19; 43:8). The people who were in deep sleep will be awakened by the Spirit which is poured "from on high" (32:15), so that they will be able to hear and see again. The book containing the word of God will no longer be sealed. The people will be liberated not only from deafness and blindness, but also from gloom and darkness as well. "In that day" mankind will have fellowship again with God; they will praise God because they will now hear God's voice and see God's mighty acts of salvation.

29:19   The "meek" and the "poor" are those who put their trust in the LORD, who wait for him and fear him (cf. 14:30a; 11:4a; Matt. 5:3, 5). To them justice and glory will be given, so that they "obtain fresh joy" and "exult" in the LORD, the Holy One of Israel. As such the LORD is declared as the glorious and transcendent God in heaven, but still near in the midst of mankind. He is still Immanuel (8:8), acting in and "interfering" in the world. His holiness reveals his blessing and loving-kindness, but at the same time also it reveals his wrath and punishment against sin, as we see now in the following verses.

29:20-21   God's wrath will be revealed against the "ruthless," the "scoffer," and those "who watch to do evil." They are the human source for all kinds of sufferings and oppression among mankind. The "ruthless" are those who depend on their exalted position and wealth to do evil and to act with cruelty without any fear of God (cf. 13:11; 25:3; 29:5). The "scoffers" are those who despise the word of God and his commandments (cf. 28:14; Ps. 1:1; Prov. 21:24).

All such evildoers will be cut off and put to nought. Isaiah 29:21 gives an example of injustice and evil at the place where one would expect the best administration of justice, namely, at the city gate, the place of the official court (cf. Deut. 21:19; 22:15; Josh. 20:4). Cases which are brought to the court at the gate are usually minor civil ones. Criminal cases were dealt with outside the gate (cf. Deut. 17:5; Acts 7:58). The judges were expected to honor justice and exercise it impartially (cf. Deut. 17:8-20).

But here dishonest judges are acting arbitrarily. People are caught and sentenced only "by a word," without any further legal process. What will happen to those who have the courage and wit to defend themselves and claim justice and reprove injustice? The judges concerned will not hesitate to "lay a snare" for them. And if this snare fails, then they use "an empty plea" to "turn aside" the accused person even when he is virtually "in the right." In so doing righteousness is turned into falsehood! No respect and trust can be expected any longer from a court of law when justice is violated in such a brutal way.

29:22-24   These closing verses convey a great message of salvation and glory for the house of Jacob, which even then was suffering, ashamed, and frightened. Such a situation might point to the exilic period in Babylonia.

The redemption of Abraham might refer back to his initial calling (Gen. 12) and to the promise of universal blessing which made him the patriarch of the new covenant people, on through Jacob down to the people of Judah. God's acts of redemption never cease. They will therefore soon be experienced by the descendants of Jacob (Isa. 29:23).

There will then be general repentance, and people will praise and sanctify "the Holy One of Jacob." Moreover there will be inner renewal and transformation of heart (v. 24). All spiritual darkness and murmurings against the LORD will vanish, and there will be a new understanding and willingness instead to accept instruction (cf. v. 18). In view of the scoffing attitude of the leaders of Jerusalem (cf. vv. 9-16), this act of redemption will be like a new creation.

God is still acting in history towards the ultimate redemption and renewal of all things (Rev. 21:5), through the coming and the works of Jesus, the Messiah (cf. Matt. 11:4-6). In this eschatological perspective therefore we have to see the realization of the kingdom of God in this world.

JERUSALEM REPRIMANDED, YET COMFORTED

30:1-33

As part of the series of woe prophecies (Isa. 28–33), this chapter has the same historical background as described above. Judah, in facing the Assyrian threat, had sought help from Egypt and had neglected the prophetic message of Isaiah. That attitude is now strongly criticized by Isaiah.

JUDAH CRITICIZED FOR LEANING UPON EGYPT (30:1-5)

30:1   The people of Judah are called "the rebellious children" (cf. 1:2). Judah had turned their backs on Yahweh, and in devising their own plans and stratagems had ignored God's plan *('etsah)* for them; in fact, they had "hidden it deep" (cf. 29:15). All this was done "not of my spirit," and in so doing Judah had just "added sin to sin." Judah followed their own way, one that led to destruction. For this reason Judah would come to "shame and disgrace" (30:5).

30:2-3   Contrasting the traditional faith which considered Yahweh as the Rock of refuge and a safe stronghold (e.g., Ps. 90:1; 27:1; 18:1-2), Judah now sets out "to go down to Egypt" to seek refuge and shelter. In ancient times Egypt was frequently subjected to foreign powers: the Hyksos, Ethiopia, Assyria, Babylonia. In Moses' time, however, the power of the Pharaoh had been paralyzed by Yahweh, the Holy One of Israel.

30:4-5   At the time of Hezekiah, Egypt was under the Ethiopian dominion of King Shabaka, who founded the 25th Dynasty of Egypt. Contrary to what has been told us in ch. 18, this time it is messengers from Judah who went to Egypt to secure help and protection. The city of Zoan was located on the delta of the Nile, up in the northern region where one of the Egyptian kings was still in power, defying the Ethiopian dominion. Hanes, called Heliopolis in later times, was located farther south on the Nile. Making serious efforts to seek help and protection, the messengers cruised the country from north to south. Nevertheless all these efforts were to be in vain (30:3). "Shame and disgrace" was the result of their foolishness.

THE BEASTS OF THE NEGEB (30:6-7)

This oracle seems to be a later addition to the preceding five verses.

Concerning the meaning of the word "oracle," see the interpretation at 13:1. The titles given to oracles are usually taken from keywords found in the oracle in question. But this is not quite so evident in 30:6. The animals which are relevant to the message are "asses" and "camels." It has been suggested that this oracle had appeared originally in a longer version (Otto Kaiser, *Isaiah 13–39,* 288).

On the way to Egypt the messengers (v. 4) had to pass through the Negeb, the desert south of Judah. In Deut. 8:15 it is called "the great and terrible wilderness, with its fiery serpents and scorpions." It was so identified, not only because of the wild beasts in it but also because of the robbers who lay in wait to attack and plunder passing travelers. The "flying serpent" was a mythological animal denoting evil and demonic power threatening human life (cf. Isa. 14:29).

In an ironical way this oracle describes the foolish and frantic efforts of the Judeans to seek refuge in Egypt. They carried all their treasures through that terrible "land of trouble and anguish." They were prepared even to risk their lives and to face all manner of troubles connected with the transportation of their wealth and treasures. Presumably all this wealth was meant to bribe the Pharaoh in order to gain his help and protection.

Why did they not take the shorter and more usual route which followed the highway along the coast? There may have been two reasons: (1) the highway may have been occupied by the Assyrian army and (2) the mission had to be carried out secretly.

Egypt is called "Rahab who sits still" (30:7). According to Canaanite mythology Rahab (also known as Leviathan) was the sea-dragon who defied the creator at the time of creation. As such

185

Rahab dominated the seas and was considered to be a divine power. Although hidden in the sea, the sea-dragon continued to threaten human life. Elsewhere in the OT Rahab (or Leviathan) is declared to have been totally defeated and destroyed by Yahweh (cf. 27:1; Ps. 74:14; Job 26:12; Ps. 89:9). In our present usage (cf. Ps. 87:4; 89:10; Isa. 51:9) the name means then that Egypt is like a paralyzed Rahab doing nothing (NIV "Rahab, the Do-Nothing"), just sitting still, powerless, although it does still appear to be potent. Another interpretation considers this phrase as a severe warning against Egypt. For the time being Rahab "is sitting still," nonactive and nonaggressive towards Judah. But nevertheless Egypt is still like Rahab, who could rise at any time and become a danger to Judah again. Beware of Egypt! Therefore those who relied on Egypt would be "deeply dismayed" (cf. 36:6).

THE CONSEQUENCES OF JUDAH'S REBELLION (30:8-17)

This pericope describes the terrible situation of Judah resulting from their rebellion against the LORD. Some interpreters suggest that the "book" here was "opened" only decades later when Israel was in exile. It was opened in a symbolical sense by Deutero-Isaiah, who thereby carried on the meaning of Isaiah's name, "The Lord is Savior," into the period when God's people were at their lowest ebb (cf. 8:1, 16-18; 29:11).

30:8-9 The rebellious people despised the word of God. Isaiah 30:8 contains two different instructions: (1) to "write on a tablet" and (2) to "inscribe in a book." The first seems to refer to the last sentence of v. 7 ("Rahab who sits still"), which was meant as a permanent warning. The second seems to refer to the prophetic message that follows as well as to other oracles in this connection. As such v. 8 can serve as a link between vv. 7 and 9.

Verse 9 gives the reason for these instructions. At the very outset of the prophet's calling (6:9-10), God had foretold him of the "rebellious" nature of the people. The truth of it had been experienced throughout Isaiah's prophetic ministry (cf. 1:2-6; 29:9, 14). Yet the Judeans were still called "lying sons" (cf. 28:15) and were still reluctant to hear "the instruction of the LORD" (cf. 28:9-13).

The word "teaching" comes from the same Hebrew root as does

186

"Torah," the name of the first five books of the OT. This latter word is incorrectly rendered in English if we translate it by "law," such as "the law of Moses." In its root form the verb *yarah* means "to throw," even "to shoot (an arrow)." In its transitive (hiphil) form also the verb still means "to shoot," but now it can be used of "shooting" an idea from one mind into another; so it comes to mean "to teach" or "to give instruction." But the person who receives the instruction receives at the same time a revelation of what is in the mind of his teacher. So instead of "law" we might translate the word "Torah" to mean both "the instruction of the LORD" and "the revelation of the mind of God."

30:10-11   The prophet now describes the inner attitude of these "lying sons" who would not pay attention to the LORD'S instruction. There is a negative interaction between the erring leaders (cf. 28:7) and the "rebellious people" who liked to tell their leaders what to do. The people did not need visions, because these visions contained only terrible prophecies. They did not ban all the prophetic words; rather they welcomed only "smooth words," those words they liked to hear. In fact they liked to change the prophetic words into a "song of fools" (Eccl. 7:5), adapting them to their own taste. Unfortunately, this kind of attitude is still apparent nowadays in many congregations; many pastors have to struggle hard to maintain faithful, biblical preaching.

Moreover, the rebellious people went one step further. They actually led the prophets astray from going the right way ("turn aside from the path"), luring them instead to follow the people's erring ways. The people totally rejected the prophets' preaching concerning "the Holy One of Israel" because it was meant to recall them to the claims of holiness in their life that they liked to avoid. That was why the prophet Isaiah was rejected; his preaching was centered on the holiness of God which he had experienced so intensely at the moment of his calling (Isa. 6).

30:12-14   As a true and faithful prophet Isaiah proclaimed only the word of God, whether people liked it or not. The word of doom resulted from their rebellious attitude (cf. 8:6; 30:9), from their oppression of the poor, and because of their perversity (28:15; 29:15, 21).

The picture of the high bulging wall, cracked and "about to collapse," shows a long process of decay. On the other hand, the violent smashing of a potter's vessel shows a sudden collapse and total break caused by ruthless enemies.

30:15-17 Essentially the prophetic message was one of hope and salvation. At this critical moment there was no other source of salvation for Judah than the LORD himself. His ways of salvation were like "the waters of Shiloah that flow gently" (8:6). What then did the LORD demand from Judah? Repentance, resting "in quietness and in trust." Repentance here means "returning" to the terms of the covenant of God (cf. 28:15), along with due obedience and with respect for the word of God. "Rest" means to stop all vain efforts at rebellion. "Quietness" and "trust" meant the people were to put a halt to their haughty mockery and instead to humble themselves before the LORD and wait patiently for his redeeming act (cf. 30:18; 28:16). Here again the Holy One of Israel has raised his gracious voice, but the people have misunderstood it and have chosen their own way. This was evident from Judah's reliance on the "swift steeds" and chariots of Egypt (cf. Exod. 14:17; 15:1; 2 Chr. 12:3; Jer. 46:4, 9), even though according to the law an Israelite king was prohibited from doing so (Deut. 17:16). Judah, however, felt more secure with the swift horses of Egypt, for these would enable them to reach Egypt quickly. But this calculation would fail them because they underestimated the terrible power of the Assyrian armies. Judah would have no chance at all to escape (Amos 2:14, 15; Ps. 20:7-8). The Assyrian armies were so much stronger than the army of Judah that it was a case of a thousand to one! The Judean army would flee at the threat of only five Assyrian soldiers! Still a small remnant would be left, but Judah would be miserable and helpless, bereft of their former glory like a "flagstaff" or a "signal" left lonely on a hilltop.

THE PROMISE OF SALVATION TO ZION (30:18-26)

30:18 God's righteousness always shows a double aspect, both of judgment and of grace—but each at its own appropriate time! "Therefore" (note the emphasis) the LORD waits (NIV "longs") in eagerness to show his grace and mercy. This eagerness is also expressed by the verb "he exalts himself" or "he rises" (NIV), ready to execute his act of compassion and blessing.

30:19-22   The people in Zion will weep no more. Zion, which is part of the city of Jerusalem, is the dwelling place of the LORD. It is symbolized by the presence of the sanctuary, and as such was the center of Israel's worship throughout the ages. It is often described as the "safe refuge" for all believers (cf. Isa. 28:16; 8:18; 11:9). It is inseparably connected with Jerusalem, the city of David, "the faithful city . . . full of justice" and "righteousness" (1:21).

The LORD will hear the cries of his people because they eat "the bread of adversity" and drink "the water of affliction" (30:20). He will show his grace; ". . . your Teacher will not hide himself . . . but your eyes shall see your Teacher." Who is "your Teacher"? Obviously the LORD himself. But Hebrew *moreyka* could also be understood as a plural form meaning "teachers" (NIV); in this sense it means those prophets who will teach them about the word of God (as a contrast to 28:9, 10). Yet it may be a plural to conform with the word for God *(elohim)* and with the name *adonai,* the plural rendering to be read for *YHWH* in the Hebrew text.

These teachers will teach the "revealed" way; the people will hear the instruction and will not deviate to either right or left (30:21). This is the way of holiness where "silver-covered graven images" and "gold-plated molten images" will no longer be tolerated (v. 22). These should be thrown away as "unclean things" (NIV "like a menstrual cloth").

30:23-25   Besides spiritual blessings (vv. 20-22), the people will also enjoy national blessings for general prosperity and peace that will benefit both humans and animals. The blessing of rain and fertility is always of first importance. In the past Israel had been tempted by the Canaanite worship of Baal, who was believed to be the giver and source of fertility (cf. Hos. 2:2). Now cattle will graze in "large pastures." Even the oxen and asses that till the ground will receive the best food prepared for them, "salted provender" that has been carefully winnowed.

Besides the incidental blessings of rain at appropriate times, there will be a permanent water supply. The wells will not dry up, and down the slopes of lofty mountains and high hills there will be "brooks running with water." (Isaiah 30:25b seems to have slipped in from its original place following v. 28.)

30:26   A total transformation and renewal will be realized on this day of the LORD, when he will make all things new (cf. Rev. 21:5). All darkness, the symbol of evil, will vanish, and there will only be radiant light. For the LORD himself will be the everlasting light (Rev. 21:23; Ps. 27:1).

All the authors of the long book of Isaiah, over a couple of centuries, seem to have had before them the very ancient poem we know of as the Song of Moses (Deut. 32). Its theological depth is amazing. In a manner that many today find difficult to grasp, Deut. 32:39 declares:

> See now that I, even I, am he (cf. Isa. 43:10),
>   and there is no god beside me;
> I kill and I make alive;
>   I wound and I heal;
>   and there is none that can deliver out of my hand.

In conformity with this statement, Isaiah can dare to say as an interpretation of God's "strange work" (28:21): "The LORD ... heals the wounds inflicted by his blow" (30:26).

THE LORD COMES IN HIS TERRIBLE INDIGNATION (30:27-33)

30:27   The "name" of the LORD means simply the LORD himself (cf. Exod. 23:20-21). He "comes from far," meaning from heaven, yet actually from Mt. Sinai where he had revealed himself to Moses (Exod. 19:20). His "tongue" refers to his uttered word. The picture of "rising smoke" and "devouring fire" reminds us of the Sinai tradition (Exod. 19:18) and other occasions of theophany (e.g., Ps. 18:8ff.): "The appearance of the glory of the LORD was like a devouring fire on the top of the mountain" (Exod. 24:17).

30:28   Three pictures are given to depict the anger of the LORD. First, "his breath (or 'spirit') is like an overflowing stream that reaches up to the neck"—but no further (cf. Isa. 8:7-8; 17:12;

28:2). Second, it is like a sifting of the nations with "the sieve of destruction," as the chaff of the nations (probably Assyria) will be burnt up (cf. Amos 9:9). Third, peoples are depicted as wild horses, with a bridle that God places "on the jaws," so that he himself actually leads them to destruction. Thus they will not be able to escape from "the devouring fire" of God.

30:29 This message of terrible judgment upon the nations is interrupted by the prophet's description of the coming joyful liberation of Israel. It is not clear what is meant here by a "holy feast." There are various interpretations; some suggest the Passover, others the New Year festival or the Feast of Tabernacles. Probably no one particular feast is in view. The reference is to the common festive mood on the night of any feast. There will be "gladness of heart" as when pilgrims set out to go to Zion, with songs of praise and with the music of lyre, harp, and cymbals (2 Sam. 6:5; Ps. 24). Thus, even as God's burning anger is manifested against the nations (Isa. 30:27-28), Yahweh the God of Israel will remain the "Rock of Israel" (cf. Ps. 18:2, 31, 46; 31:2, 3; 62:6).

30:30-32 These verses continue the description of God's wrath, now making direct reference to Assyria. God's "majestic voice" will be heard (cf. Ps. 19:1-4), and his punishing arm will be seen in "devouring fire," "cloudburst," "tempest," and "hailstones."

The Assyrians, now mentioned explicitly, will be "terror-stricken"; they had never realized how terrible the God of Israel can be. The reference may be to the wonderful release of Jerusalem from the Assyrian siege in 701 B.C. (2 Kgs. 19:1-37; 2 Chr. 32:20-23).

In proportion as Assyria suffers the "staff of punishment," Israel will rejoice in the worship of their LORD; for he himself will fight against them with his "brandished arm." This declaration might be a later addition referring to the great battles preceding Assyria's collapse in 612.

30:33 Finally Assyria will be totally destroyed and thrown into "a burning place" (*tophet*; cf. NIV). This Hebrew word is another name for the valley of Hinnom, where children were sacrificed to the god Moloch (Melech), a name which means "king" (cf. 1 Kgs. 11:7; 2 Kgs. 16:3; 17:31). The following phrase, "yea, for the king (*melech*)," is an ironical play upon words, now referring to the Assyrian king himself. He himself will be offered as a burnt offering to the god Molech! This burning place had been prepared long before. A deep and wide pit had been dug in the ground and filled up with an abundance of firewood. The LORD will then kindle the fire himself through his breath, which is like "a stream of brimstone (NIV 'sulphur')"; for sulphur keeps a fire constantly blazing.

The terrible fate of Assyria at "Tophet" thus denotes both God's punishment and his wrath. Presumably basing their idea on these verses, some Christians in Indonesia refuse to accept the cremation of a human corpse, for cremation is considered a curse from God.

YAHWEH THE ONLY
REDEEMER OF ISRAEL
31:1-9

This shortest chapter in the series of woe prophecies provides a strong admonition for Judah. Judah must not rely on Egypt or Assyria because these nations, however mighty they may seem to be, will be destroyed eventually. Yahweh is the only Helper and Redeemer of Israel. This chapter is closely related to the preceding ch. 30 and reflects the same historical background.

WOE TO THOSE WHO RELY ON EGYPT! (31:1-3)

31:1 Judah's effort to withstand the Assyrian threat is considered from the political viewpoint, and quite understandably. Egypt has offered Judah horses and chariots and has even sent messengers to Judah (Isa. 18:2). So it was reasonable for Judah to send its messengers also down to Egypt to secure their help (30:4, 6).

Judah's fault and foolishness were revealed in their attitude towards Yahweh. Judah exerted all their political efforts "without asking for my counsel" (30:2); that is, they ignored, refused, and derided the word of God (cf. 30:9-11). At the end of 31:1 we read that they "do not look to the Holy One of Israel."

On the contrary, Judah put their trust in the "horses" and "chariots" of Egypt, which were considered safer and more reliable than Yahweh. Apparently Judah was ignoring the lesson from the Exodus tradition where the mighty hand of the LORD destroyed all the horses and chariots of Pharaoh (Exod. 14:23-28). It is in this connection therefore that Yahweh is called "the Holy One of Israel," for he had proved his holiness by destroying all that was unclean as well as all his enemies right throughout history (cf. Deut. 17:16; Ps. 52:7).

31:2 The Holy One is the all-wise God. He knows exactly what are the inner and hidden motivations of Judah; he cannot be deceived by the follies of mankind (Isa. 29:15). His acts are in accordance with his words of mercy, and yet of punishment as well. His wisdom is rooted in justice and righteousness; so punishment will surely be enforced on "the evildoers" and "the helpers of those who work iniquity." Who are those workers of iniquity? They are the unfaithful people of Jerusalem themselves (cf. 1:4; 28:14-15; 30:12). The protection of Egypt will be turned to "your shame" and to "your humiliation" (30:3).

31:3 The Egyptians are just people with human feelings and weaknesses—"and not God; their horses are just flesh, and not spirit." The OT frequently points to human frailty and limitations (e.g., Job 7:17; 8:9; 28:12-13; Eccl. 3:20; Ps. 8:4; 144:3-4).

Horses too as a symbol of strength, endurance, and speed are just "flesh" and not "spirit." Flesh denotes weakness, temporariness, and vanity. By contrast spirit denotes power and life, because with the spirit *(ruah)* the Creator has given life to creation. Only God, the Creator, is spirit (cf. John 4:24).

From this pericope it is clear that faith should be the basis of all human life (cf. Isa. 30:15). Faith does not exclude human reason or human efforts, but these must not be absolutized at the expense of faith and spiritual values. As part of the creation they should be subservient to the glory of the Creator: *sola fide—sola gratia—soli Deo gloria!* The equivalent today could be the trust in God's purposes shown by those who seek to ban all nuclear weapons. This faith is exemplified in chs. 36 and 37.

THE LORD WILL PROTECT AND DELIVER JERUSALEM (31:4-5)

We note first here how the prophet personalizes his message: "The LORD said to *me*." Then, to follow the prophet's argument, we must ask, Who is represented here as a "lion," and who are meant by "a band of shepherds" (31:4)? One interpretation suggests Assyria as the "lion," while the Egyptians are the "band of shepherds" (John Mauchline, *Isaiah 1–39*). Thus at the critical moment when Egypt could not rescue Judah from the Assyrian grip, the LORD of hosts came down to help.

Another interpretation, one which is more likely, considers the lion to be the LORD himself defending and protecting his "prey," Jerusalem, while the band of shepherds are the Assyrians who try to capture that prey. This picture would then illustrate the safe protection of the LORD, who will come down upon Mt. Zion to fight against his enemies. Thus two parallel pictures seem to be used in vv. 4 and 5. Both of them illustrate the LORD'S protection and loving care. Note the various verbs used in v. 5 to describe the LORD'S concern for Jerusalem, namely, to "protect," "deliver," "spare," and "rescue." While in the previous pericope (vv. 1-3) God is called "the Holy One of Israel," here he is called "the LORD of hosts."

A CALL FOR REPENTANCE AND THE DEFEAT OF ASSYRIA (31:6-9)

31:6-7   These verses in prose have been inserted into the poetic section (31:1-5, 8-9). They contain a call for repentance within the eschatological prospect of the vindication of God's kingdom and the vanity of all idols. These idols, as works of people's own hands, will prove to be worthless and ineffective (cf. 17:7-8; 2:20; 27:9). Then there will be a general repentance by the remnant of Israel (cf. 25:9), and all opposing powers will be nullified. This will then be the final outcome of all history! These two verses might be considered as a conclusion to the whole prophetic section following 31:8-9.

31:8-9   These two verses, as a continuation of vv. 1-5, describe the deliverance carried out by the LORD himself. Assyria will be completely defeated "by a sword, not of man." Their "rock" (v. 9), meaning the Assyrian king, and "his officers" abandon the royal standard and flee away in panic. This miraculous final blow from the LORD most likely points to the Assyrian defeat at Jerusalem (2 Kgs. 19; Isa. 36–37).

The expression "whose fire is in Zion, and whose furnace is in Jerusalem" denotes the reality, to which Isaiah has referred now a number of times, that "our God is a consuming fire." The fire that burned on the altar in the temple was thus meant to remind Israel that the love of God is "hotter" than the heart of mankind can conceive. The heat of God's love is intense. It rescues the perishing. It protects his own people (Exod. 13:21-22). It melts and refines the metal in human nature until the dross is separated from the pure gold.

To this final outcome Judah must pay serious attention!

A KINGDOM OF RIGHTEOUSNESS AND JUSTICE

32:1-20

A JUST GOVERNMENT AND A NOBLE PEOPLE (32:1-8)

After the downfall of Assyria (Isa. 31), the symbol of the defeat of all unjust powers, the LORD will establish a just government free from all lies and falsehood (28:15). Judging from its form and contents, this pericope is similar to a "wisdom teaching" on the coming age of justice. Some interpreters consider it to be a messianic prophecy, although no description is given of the king's personality.

32:1-5   These verses describe a just government that provides sure protection and real justice. Throughout history Israel had been longing for a king who would truly reign in righteousness, but this expectation had never been fully realized. The king and the priest together represent the government, both the legislative and the executive authorities. So righteousness and justice based on obedience to God will be fully realized at the messianic age (cf. 9:7; 11:1-5). This prophecy conveys a message for all believers at all times, encouraging them to promote and strive for a just government in the world.

Till now it has been God who has been known as the Rock of refuge (cf. 2 Sam. 22:2-3). He has lovingly provided for the weary traveler in the desert a cool shadow from the blazing heat of the noonday sun. Now it will be the privilege of the government officials of the people of God to be to others what God has been to them. They in their turn will now be a "rock" of refuge to the pilgrims who travel across the deserts of life to the City of God.

This new life creates a total change, materially and spiritually, such as has never been known before (Isa. 32:3-4). People will be released from their foolishness and falsehood (cf. 28:15). Their "eyes" and "ears" will function as they should, sensitive to God's truth and justice (cf. 6:9, 10); they will no longer deride God's word (cf. 28:14). As a result they will possess profound knowledge and their mind will be so balanced as to make right judgments. Those who are handicapped with a "stammering tongue" will speak fluently and clearly. This might refer to those drunken citizens mentioned at 28:7 or even to the wizards who used to "chirp and mutter" (8:19).

In a corrupt society the "fool" and the "knave" (32:5) are usually very successful in achieving personal benefits and high positions through their falsity. To win people's hearts they pretend to be generous, noble, and friendly. But in the new society where good judgment and freedom of speech prevail, they will be unmasked and never again be honored.

32:6-8 The wickedness of the fool will be revealed. The fool's heart and mind, his speech and folly, his cruel and oppressive practices towards the poor and the hungry all will reveal his ungodliness and broken relationship with the LORD. Likewise "the knaveries of the knave" will be revealed. At present, through his lies and wickedness, the knave succeeds in diverting the just plea of the needy and the poor (v. 7). How different are the mind and the devices of the noble (v. 8)!

A MESSAGE FOR THE WOMEN OF JERUSALEM (32:9-14)

This pericope seems to be unrelated to the one that precedes. In a way it can be taken as a continuation of the woe prophecies in chs. 28–31, yet it is directed at the women and the city of Jerusalem shortly before its destruction (32:14). It shows no clear relationship either with the following pericope (vv. 15-20), except as a contrast in background. On the other hand, it shows some similarity with Amos' prophecy against the women of Samaria (Amos 4:1-2).

The prophetic message is primarily directed at the elite women who lived luxuriously and leisurely in their capital city. The strong language employed indicates that they are completely submerged in their style of living. The call is the more urgent because within a short time (Isa. 32:10) destruction and suffering will surely come.

198

The women will then "shudder," and no wine will be available to bring relief to their dejection of spirit. On the contrary, their suffering will increase and the situation will only become worse. Now they are called to "tremble" and put on mourning clothes ("sackcloth"), girding these upon their loins (cf. 2 Sam. 3:31; Isa. 15:3). They will beat upon their breasts in utter despair, because the "pleasant fields" and the fruitful "soil," their luxurious houses, and the "joyful city" will all be stripped of their former glory (32:11-13).

Verse 14 mentions three centers of joyful city life most favored by the women at Jerusalem. These are the "palace," the "hill" (called Ophel), and the "watchtower." At the palace (NIV "fortress") the elite used to hold their rich banquets and store their precious treasures. The hill of Ophel, located at the southern end of Jerusalem, was the place where the temple stood. The watchtower looked after the security of the city and was therefore of vital importance for its safety. All these places of pleasure and security are to be deserted and become wasteland forever, good only for "wild asses" and "flocks" of goats.

But this sinister picture is not the end of the prophecy. The disastrous situation will be followed by wonderful blessings above all human expectation. The LORD will remember the city and will pour down upon it his gracious blessings, as we read in the following verses.

RENEWAL THROUGH THE SPIRIT (32:15-20)

Once nature has been utterly destroyed and mankind left in anguish and despair, the prophet turns to God's wonderful re-creation that will bring salvation and prosperity, justice and righteousness through his gift of the Spirit. The Spirit will be "poured upon us from on high." These verses provide new hope of future glory, and are a testimony to the LORD'S vindication and final victory. Within this context of universal renewal, the message of destruction given in 32:19 seems to be rather misplaced. It evokes the impression of being a later insertion, so that it might be advisable to read it after v. 14.

32:15-16   Evidently the LORD'S judgment will not last "for ever" as proclaimed in v. 14. God's creation cannot have been made in vain only to be turned back into chaos again. The LORD is ever faithful and will not forsake the work of his hands.

Throughout the Scriptures, Old and New Testament alike, God is seen to work in this "strange" way (28:21). We do not meet with a gentle evolution of his plan for the world or a progressive revelation of his nature to mankind. As the Song of Moses (Deut. 32) had put it, five hundred years before Isaiah's day, God works through crisis and death—and then renewal and resurrection. He brings "life and immortality to light" only after he has *totally* destroyed the old and the evil (2 Tim. 1:10). Such is what Isaiah's successors will describe in Isa. 40–66, even as they themselves live through those terrible days of the "death" of the people of God. But by living in them, they will make the unbelievable discovery that they are not alone in it, even as they suffer God's "alien work." Immanuel will be with them (cf. 43:2), just as he had promised to Moses so long before (Exod. 3:12). And in doing so the God who had brought the punishment upon Israel that they were then undergoing was suffering *with* his people the effects of his own judgment upon them.

God's merciful and renewing intervention will be expressed by the outpouring of the Spirit "from on high." This action is not described in an abstract manner. Rather, the Spirit is shown to be a dynamic force operating concretely and effectively both in human life and in nature. In describing the coming of the Spirit, the verb "to pour" suggests the idea of water or of some other liquid. It will soak the wilderness and the dry land and turn them into fruitful and fertile fields.

In the OT the outpouring of the Spirit is mentioned in several places (e.g., Isa. 44:3; 61:1; Ezek. 39:29; Joel 2:28; Zech. 12:10). In these passages the Spirit is primarily described as a dynamic and creative force. It is the spirit of new life, even of eternal life and of total salvation. The NT too teaches that no one can enter the kingdom of God unless he or she has been born of water and the Spirit (John 3:5). In other instances, however, the Spirit is pictured in terms of fire or of a mighty wind (Acts 2:3; John 3:8).

It is interesting to note that the outpouring of the Spirit also revives nature. The dry wilderness becomes fertile and productive, a blessing enjoyed by both animals and human beings. In this new re-creation mankind and nature together enjoy peace and well-being *(shalom)*, justice and righteousness (Isa. 32:16). The fertility of the field will be so much improved that it will be like a "forest" similar to the forests of Lebanon (cf. 29:17), so well known in those days. So fertility, justice, and righteousness are closely related to each other. The verbs "dwell" and "abide" suggest that justice and righteousness are permanent inhabitants of the fertile land. Even in the wilderness there will be justice and righteousness. This is amazing, because the wilderness is known as a most insecure place, plagued by robbers and wild beasts. The point of this renewal is not the abolition of all wilderness, but the presence of justice and righteousness even in such an area.

In the beginning of creation God created light and order by uttering his Word—not out of nothing, but out of *tohu* (Gen. 1:2), desolation, a reality that the prophets never ceased to recognize. They saw this *tohu* represented before their eyes in the mystery of the desolation of the wilderness of Judea. That "desert" could be reached in only a few hours walk from the ordered life of the city of Jerusalem. So Isaiah here proclaims the faith that God actually uses evil to create the good, while allowing evil to continue to exist.

32:17-18   "Peace," "quietness," and "trust" are the important factors which constitute a harmonious well-being for life. They reflect a right relationship between God, mankind, and nature. We envisage a situation where there is no more enmity, hatred, violence, fear, distress, or distrust, no more drought, famine, sickness, or even death. Obviously this is not the result of human efforts, but can come about only in the power of the Spirit of God. So Isaiah speaks of a true secure dwelling place and a quiet resting place for "my people." These are the covenant people who live from God's love and mercy, and in quiet obedience to him. In fact, this state of harmonious well-being transcends our imagination and human philosophies on social and national welfare. It transcends any secular ideology on the best possible social system or the composition of the welfare state of the world today.

This eschatological reality opens a new vision and offers a challenge to all believers who have received the Spirit to be God's co-workers for renewal, transformation, justice, and righteousness in this world's "wilderness."

32:19 For what purpose has this verse been inserted in this pericope? This pericope (Isa. 32:15-20) seems in some way to be a close parallel to 29:17-21, though it might be related to 29:20. Moreover this verse should not be interpreted literally; it emphasizes once again that all haughtiness, falsehood, pride, and trust in material things will "come to nought" (29:20). As such it provides a contrasting background to the following closing verse.

32:20 This verse may be taken as a natural consequence of 32:18. Using the second person plural form ("you"), it can be understood to be in the form of a blessing on those who are noble (v. 8) or who dwell in the secure "resting places" (v. 18). These are now described as farmers, sowing seed and shepherding cattle in peace and abundance. Even at this eschatological moment daily labor and work are to continue, because creative work is an aspect of human happiness!

And so we see that "eternity" is not something which begins only once time is at an end. Eternity, for the prophets, impinges upon our human life at all times and in all places. Eternity is the dwelling place of the Most High, the living God, who is both Alpha and Omega, the beginning and the end. But he is also the God of every "now" in the life and experience of his people even as they live in this world of space and time (33:10).

THE TRIUMPH OF GOD'S KINGDOM

33:1-24

This last chapter in the series of woe prophecies (Isa. 28–33) does not seem to be well structured. Its contents are rather complex and reveal heterogeneous factors.

In view of its form and contents, the chapter seems to contain a liturgical prophecy, perhaps for use at a cult ceremony in the temple, such as that of commemorating Judah's deliverance from a cruel enemy. It simultaneously proclaims the triumph of God's kingdom (see John Mauchline, *Isaiah 1–39*). Accordingly ch. 33 heralds on the one hand the enemy's destruction and Judah's deliverance and triumph, and on the other hand it offers a prayer of complaint. Moreover, the question and answer in vv. 14-16 presuppose a dialogue.

To whom then is this woe prophecy addressed? No particular nation is mentioned, nor is any clear historical context given. We read only of a general qualification of the enemy in vv. 1, 8, 19. But the judgment is also directed at "the sinners in Zion" (v. 14). The message of woe then shifts to a message of hope and assurance of deliverance. As such it most likely reflects the hope cherished during the exilic period.

YAHWEH IS OUR HELP AND REFUGE! (33:1-6)

33:1   The enemy is pictured as a "destroyer" and a traitor. As such nobody has been able to oppose him. He is continuously destroying and deceiving other people. It would seem that he is "the old deceiver" (serpent) from the garden of Eden, the author of all lies and falsehood himself, the destroyer from the very beginning, and so is the eternal principle of the powers of evil.

However, the destroyer's dominion will not last forever. For a while he is allowed to act freely, but eventually he too will be destroyed and deceived. This will happen at God's appointed time when the LORD will arise and "lift himself up" (v. 10). How true this is in history can be seen, for example, from the fate of Sennacherib (37:38) and that of the king of Babylon (ch. 13).

33:2-4 These verses comprise a prayer of supplication. Living with the hard realities of human life, with all its anguish and pain, the believer needs the aid of constant prayer. Then "in quietness and in trust" (30:15) he can wait for God's help and protection.

In 33:2 the NIV translates "Be our strength every morning." The "morning" is in some respects decisive for the day. In OT thought morningtime is considered critical and full of danger. Armies used to attack in early morning when the city was still quietly asleep. The LORD too struck the Assyrian army outside the walls of Jerusalem in the early morning (cf. 28:19; Ps. 46:5; see also 2 Kgs. 6:14-15).

The "arm" of the LORD (RSV) is the symbol of God's might and strength when it is "bared," for so God enters into space and time (cf. Ps. 89:10, 13; Isa. 30:30-32; 51:9; 53:1-2) and is active in his people's history. Such a prayer is based on the conviction that God, the Almighty, has dominion over all nations and their history. If God arises and stretches out his hand to act, who can stand before him?

33:3 The "thunderous voice" (rather than RSV "noise") announces God's rebuke upon the nations (cf. 17:13; 29:6). At Sinai the LORD had revealed himself in thunder. Here the thunderous voice is related to "the lifting up of thyself" and the flight of the nations now scattered (cf. Ps. 2:5). This had been demonstrated in Israel's history when God made his redeeming intervention against Egypt, Assyria, and Babylonia.

33:4 In a lively way the prophet describes the situation after the enemy has had to flee suddenly. People pounce on the spoil like "caterpillars" or as "locusts" devour the grain. Collecting the spoil after an enemy army has retreated in haste creates great joy because everybody can get a share. It is the LORD'S justice which chases the rich enemy away empty-handed and which allows the oppressed people to collect the spoil.

33:5-6   In contrast to the enemy's confusion and the excitement of the people, these verses describe the serenity and the glory of the LORD and the stability of Zion, now secure, just, and righteous. Those who put their trust in the LORD will not be dismayed. Yahweh the God of Israel is completely different from all other gods. He is "exalted, for he dwells on high"; yet he chooses to dwell at Zion in particular and fill it with his justice and righteousness. It pleases him to make Zion the city of God, the center of his kingdom of peace (cf. Isa. 2). He will then maintain a peaceful and stable society forever. Its real treasure consists of "abundance of salvation, wisdom, and knowledge" and "the fear of the LORD." All these are clearly interrelated. This wisdom is based on the fear of the LORD, and therefore leads to knowledge of faith. It is remarkable how such spiritual values and qualifications are so highly appreciated. Therefore "seek first his kingdom and his righteousness . . ." (Matt. 6:33).

MOURNING, WEEPING, AND LANGUISHING (33:7-9)

Such sorrow and distress as are described here fit into the situation of Judah at the end of the 8th cent. B.C. under the reign of Hezekiah. At that time Assyria had destroyed the greater part of the land and had called upon the city of Jerusalem itself to surrender.

The meaning of the Hebrew noun *er'ellam* is unclear. Many interpreters have suggested it comes from the root word *ari'el* (plural *ari'elim*) that is used in Isa. 29:1. Literally *ari'el* means "lion of God"; as such *ari'elim* could then mean "the valiant ones" (RSV) or "the brave ones" (NIV). As we have seen at 29:1 it might lead us to translate "those purified by God's love."

How loudly they cry in the streets! The city is besieged by the enemy, and there is only hunger and confusion among the inhabitants. They walk the streets crying pitifully. Envoys are sent to the enemy to seek peace, but the enemy is not to be trusted in making treaties (cf. 2 Kgs. 18:14-17) and so "the envoys of peace weep bitterly."

Isaiah 33:8 gives a further description of the confusion in the country: nobody feels secure, especially on the highways where marauders move around freely or lie in wait. No wayfaring people dare to travel there.

It is not only human beings but the whole countryside that

suffers. The famous forest of the Lebanon with its mighty cedars, the pride of the country, now languishes. The plains of Sharon, famed for their roses and wild flowers, now look like a desert. Bashan and Carmel with their fertile meadows are now like trees deprived of their leaves, dry and barren. In short, the whole of life has been ravaged and there are no other resources available to save the situation. There is no way out of this spiritual, moral, social, and economic crisis!

THE LORD WILL ARISE AND PUNISH (33:10-14a)

The LORD has shown his forbearance towards the enemy and the wicked. But there is indeed a limit to his patience. Now (mentioned three times here) God will indeed "arise" and "be exalted." The LORD will act as a judge who will pass final judgment, as declared in 33:1.

The enemies, as described in v. 1a, are now pictured as a pregnant woman (v. 11). When the day of deliverance approaches great hopes are cherished for the newborn baby and for the mother. During the process of "pregnancy" the enemy becomes increasingly evil and cruel. When the moment of the delivery comes it appears that what has been conceived has been merely "chaff" and what is now brought forth is merely "stubble," that is, what is vain and worthless. All that has been cherished and achieved by the enemy is just vanity, and vanity destroys himself (cf. 5:24).

". . . You will be destroyed" (33:1c) is explained here as self-destruction by "your breath," which is "a fire that will consume you" (v. 11). This is in contrast to the burning passionate fire of God's love (cf. 29:6; 33:14).

In 33:12 the fate of the peoples is also pictured in a tragic fashion; they "will be as if burned to lime." This suggests that the enemy's corpse is left unburied. People then rejoice at his death, which will be "like thorns cut down, that are burned in the fire."

33:13-14a Such is the prophetic message of the Church in this modern age, too, a message that must be proclaimed even by employing the mass media. To those who are both far away and those nearby, whether they are poor or wealthy, strong or weak, this same call must ring loudly throughout the world: ". . . Acknowledge my might!"

When they hear the call, the "sinners" at Zion are afraid and "godless people" tremble. Evidently there are still such people present in Zion, so these greatly need to hear this call. The prophet warns them not to misunderstand God's justice and righteousness and the salvation of Zion. As citizens of Jerusalem they are now admonished not to consider themselves safe automatically or to be self-complacent. For they have in fact rejected the word of God and ignored the prophets (cf. 28:7ff.); they have put their trust in their own policies and resources or looked for help from neighboring countries. They have in fact forsaken the LORD.

WHO CAN DWELL ALONG WITH THE LORD? (33:14b-16)

This rhetorical question is raised by "the sinners in Zion" and put to the Holy One of Israel. Here God is symbolized as an everlasting burning fire (cf. Deut. 4:24; 9:3; Ps. 50:3; Exod. 19:18; 1 Kgs. 19:12). The "sinners'" question is rather an expression of their guilt and fear, because it is clear that no sinner can stand or dwell before such a burning fire!

It was Moses who first experienced the "fire" of the LORD at Sinai (Exod. 3:1-6), his burning ardor and fierce, passionate zeal for the execution and completion of his plan for the redemption of the world. Or was it Abraham (cf. Gen. 15:17)? Modern mankind, with a castrated and indulgent awareness of the meaning of ardor, cannot understand this biblical view of God as "passion" unless they interpret it when they behold the "passion" of Christ—the "zeal" or furious love of which John 2:17 speaks. Jesus' disciples, as they watched the Lord's total commitment to the will of God, could quote Ps. 69:9 about him: "Zeal *(qin'ah)* for thy house has consumed me (or 'eaten me up')"; John uses the Greek term *ho zelos,* found in the LXX rendering of the Psalm, and so our word "zeal."

Thus, in reality, Isa. 33:15-16 gives a comforting answer to the sinners in Zion. That answer reveals God's grace and his promise of life even when he is present in his wrath. Certain moral requirements are set forth for the "righteous" people, those who have been "put right" by God himself. The participial forms of the Hebrew

verbs and the plural forms of the nouns used at the beginning of
v. 15 suggest continuity of behavior. In all matters and at all times
God's "forgiven sinners" must do no less than despise and reject
"the gain of oppressions" and the taking of bribes. The "righteous"
must have nothing to do with "bloodshed" and all forms of evil;
they must not even hear of evil or see it, because they must avoid
any temptation that might come from dallying with evil. This verse
says much the same thing as that clause in the Lord's Prayer which
is best but inadequately rendered: "In the time of trial may we be
tested without being tempted" (cf. George B. Caird, *The Language
and Imagery of the Bible* [Philadelphia: Westminster, and London:
Duckworth, 1980], 60, n.).

The dwelling place of the righteous will be on a sure high place,
a mighty "fortress of rocks." No enemy will be able to capture it.
Even if enemies should encamp around the foot of the hill, the
"righteous" will not fear, because water and bread—which signify
the basic needs for life—will never be wanting.

Zion in its Glory and Righteousness (33:17-24)

If vv. 15-16 deal with the question of who can stand before the
LORD, then these verses show what God's forgiven people will see
and experience when the power of the enemy has been abolished.
A completely new situation will arise at Zion, and so this pericope
points to the coming of an eschatological messianic era. As such it
can be considered as the closing verses of the whole chapter, providing as it does hope and comfort for the "righteous" people.

33:17-19   Who is "the king in his beauty"? Referring back to vv.
10-13, it is unlikely that a human being or a Judean king is meant.
This king seems to be the LORD himself who reveals himself
through the temple cult and finally when he bares his "arm" (33:2).
The royal "beauty" is related to the "land that stretches afar." His
will be a dominion whose boundaries can never be surveyed. The
"righteous" will only be able to wonder and be amazed. All this
beauty will be too astonishing to be taken in all at once. The people
will still be able to remember the former terror, connected with the
heavy tribute enforced upon Judah (cf. 2 Kgs. 18:14ff.). They cannot easily forget the cruel tax collectors who counted and weighed

out piles of silver and gold. Besides them there were the officers who "counted the towers"; the number of these fortified strongholds had then been limited and controlled. But all these memories are now just like a terrible nightmare in the past.

The enemies, described in Isa. 33:19 as "insolent people" of "obscure speech," will be no more. None of them will be found among the righteous. They will not even be able to hide themselves because of their strange speech. As noted at 28:11, these arrogant ones might be identified as the Assyrians who laid such a heavy tribute on Judah and who finally besieged Jerusalem. However, owing to the LORD'S intervention they failed to capture the city (cf. 2 Kgs. 19:35-36). Obviously these arrogant people were punished, not because of their alien speech but because of their sins and oppression against Judah. All human language can be sanctified to the glory of God; this was later made clear at the day of Pentecost (Acts 2).

33:20-21 Zion, identified with the New Jerusalem, is considered to be the center of the "land that stretches afar" (Isa. 33:17), where the glory of God will be revealed. As such Zion is called "the city of our appointed feasts," that is, the center of Israel's cult worship and festivals, visited by all peoples from afar. At these cult feasts the LORD will reveal his glory.

In addition, Jerusalem is pictured as "an immovable tent" or hut which will stand forever. In contrast to the wanderings in the desert in former days where their ancestors led a nomadic life, Zion (Jerusalem) will become the people's permanent and unshakable abode, their inheritance forever. In the days of the prophet Jeremiah, however, this conviction had been misunderstood in a secular sense. Consequently, Jeremiah had reproached Jerusalem and had announced the fall of the city (cf. Jer. 7:12-14, 26-29). Indeed, the adoration of a "holy city" could evoke serious misunderstanding in people's minds and in some cases even a fanaticism that neglected the real spiritual values and significance of the city. The fall of Jerusalem proved that the presence and glory of Yahweh could not be bound to any city in a material sense.

In Isa. 33:21 the glory of God is described in yet another way. His glory is like "a place of broad rivers and streams." Considering Israel's nomadic background, such a place of many waters enriches the previous picture of "a land that stretches afar" (v. 17). The broad rivers and the abundant streams refer to the many wells in the dry regions to the east of Palestine. Now they will never dry up throughout the year. One characteristic of these broad rivers and streams is that, unlike the river Nile, no galleys with arms or mighty battleships will sail them. Such ships were used by foreign peoples for both war and commerce. If we apply this "place" to Jerusalem (Zion), then this picture is most appropriate. Jerusalem has never been a commercial center, nor could enemies reach and attack it by sea (cf. vv. 5, 20). On the other hand, Zion will become the center of worship. In a spiritual sense it will possess many springs that will provide plenty of water ("rivers" and "streams") which it will send forth to the surrounding lands, and thus it will become a great blessing to the whole region. Such a conception is reflected again in the prophecy of the prophet Ezekiel (Ezek. 47).

33:22 All this wonderful situation (Isa. 33:18-21) is not one created by human hands, but is the work of the LORD himself. This work can be comprehended by faith alone. Therefore this verse contains a confession and an act of praise to the LORD as Judge and Ruler (NIV "lawgiver"). He is the divine source and maintainer of all true justice and righteousness. He is "our king" and our Savior!

33:23a The connection between these few words and both the preceding and the following verses is rather obscure. Nor is it clear who is being addressed here, Judah or the enemy (Assyria). It is hard to imagine Judah in this context being shipwrecked. It would be more appropriate to apply this picture to Assyria. Here Assyria then is like a mighty warship, used to conquer the nations and carry home abundance of spoil. But when this mighty ship enters the "holy waters" of Zion (cf. v. 21), in the land where the LORD himself is the Ruler, it gets shipwrecked and becomes helpless. There will then be an abundance of spoil left as a "gift" to Jerusalem. This seems to be the link to the following vv. 23b-24.

33:23b-24 The abundance of "spoil" left by the enemy is taken freely by the people. There is a link here also with v. 4 above. Because of this abundance, people need not make any special effort to snatch at or fight for their prey. A just and fair distribution will be made among all the people, including even the weak and the disabled. This is an appropriate understanding of these lines if we consider this abundance of spoil as being a gracious gift from the LORD who is King and Judge (v. 22).

Here we see an important message for today's world. Justice and the fair distribution of goods can be achieved only when people acknowledge wealth to be basically a gracious gift from God, to be used in faithful stewardship towards our fellow mankind. Nobody will then be neglected in such a "social welfare" state, not even the lame, the sick, and weak old people.

Verse 24 declares that welfare should be accompanied by a state of holistic well-being—physical, mental, spiritual, and social. The ultimate key for this ideal situation is the gracious love of God himself who will forgive all of mankind's iniquities. Consequently there will be reconciliation between mankind and God. Such alone will guarantee everlasting well-being and peace among the inhabitants of Zion.

However, this reconciliation obliges us to full obedience and to "diligently harken to the voice of the LORD your God, and do that which is right in his eyes . . ." (Exod. 15:26). Rebellion against the LORD (Isa. 1:5) makes people totally "sick" (33:24). Only the grace of the LORD can heal them, because "I am the LORD, your healer" (Exod. 15:26). It is such a ministry that the Church is called upon to render everywhere in its world mission today. All various services in this "holistic healing ministry" should be integrated and coordinated, making them witness to the core of the gospel message: "Jesus has come to save the world!" (John 12:47; Mark 10:45).

In the light of the coming of the kingdom we see how Jesus revealed himself, not only as the Healer from physical suffering but also as the One who "gives his life as a ransom for many" (cf. Mark 10:45; Luke 4:8-21).

PART V
UNIVERSAL JUDGMENT
AND RENEWAL

Isaiah 34:1–35:10

THE WRATH OF JUDGMENT
34:1-17

Isaiah 34 and 35 are closely related and form one unit. Chapter 34 proclaims a total and universal judgment, while ch. 35 proclaims consolation and universal renewal to follow. Nevertheless, a particular nation is mentioned in ch. 34, namely Edom. This reminds us of the judgment against Babylon in ch. 13, where Babylon too was regarded as a personification of world power. The judgment upon Edom here is only representative of universal judgment; Edom has been selected because its sin was uniquely evil.

Considering the universal and eschatological features of the prophecy, a postexilic date for it is most likely.

THE LORD'S JUDGMENT AGAINST THE NATIONS (34:1-4)

These opening verses present a most sinister picture of the nations and of the whole earth. The "peoples" are considered to be one entity in union with the "nations," the "world," the "earth," and all that comes out of it. God's wrath then will be poured down upon all of these. In this connection people, as ethical beings, bear a tremendous responsibility towards the whole of nature and of the world of nations. This picture also reveals God as the universal LORD of all (cf. Ps. 24:1; Isa. 41:1; 43:8-9; 45:20; Mic. 1:2).

There is presumably a projection of the "holy war tradition" in this eschatological prophecy, in which all enemies will be destroyed at the final war (cf. Exod. 15:3; Ps. 24:8; Zech. 9:13). The nations will not only be given over to slaughter but their corpses will lie unburied, and the terrible stench of these dead bodies will fill the air. This was considered to be the most disgraceful fate that could befall any human being. In a poetic way and according to the literal meaning of the Hebrew text, the streams flowing down the mountains will be filled, not with water but with blood. Nature will be destroyed in consequence. The whole universe will be affected (Isa. 34:4). All the host of heaven (i.e., the stars, sun, moon, and all the other astral bodies; cf. 40:26; Zeph. 1:5; Jer. 19:13; 2 Kgs. 21:5) will become pale, wither, and finally fall down like "leaves falling from the fig tree" in autumn. The skies will then be "rolled up like a scroll." Such then is a picture of the end of world history.

In view of the ancient fertility cults and of astral worship, this prophecy proclaims the triumph of the LORD Almighty at all times.

However, this judgment does not mean that total collapse of the universe which God has created (Ps. 33:6). Rather, it points to the universal renewal in which the glory of the LORD will rise forever and all nations will come to "the brightness of his rising," and so will behold his justice and his righteousness (cf. Ps. 33:5). Accordingly it is a picture of what would inevitably happen to this earth should God not have a loving purpose for it.

JUDGMENT UPON EDOM (34:5-7)

The wrath of God is now concentrated on Edom. All the terrible disasters described in Isa. 34:1-4 could be brought about by the sword of the LORD, which "has drunk its fill in the heavens." It is as if the heavens, like a sponge, can contain no more of the fullness of God's wrath. Consequently it must spill over onto the earth, and in particular light upon Edom.

There are Christians today who take it as axiomatic that God's judgment rests particularly upon "the poor heathen," the masses of the peoples of the earth who have made no response to the call of the gospel. But such a view is simply not biblical. God's judgment, in the view of Amos for one, rests first of all upon his chosen people, the people he has "known"—with whom he has made covenant—in order that they might be a blessing to humanity (Gen. 12:2-3). Amos' words to the descendants of Jacob are:

You only have I known*
    of all the families of the earth;

* *yd'*, a verb used of deep intimacy, such as exists between husband and wife, and so describes the covenant relationship.

216

therefore I will punish you
for all your iniquities. (Amos 3:2)

Jacob and Esau were twins. Both were "children of Abraham," Israel's ancestor, whom God had chosen in the first place. At Gen. 36:1 we read: "These are the descendants of Esau (that is, Edom). Esau took his wives from the Canaanites." And at Gen. 36:8: "So Esau dwelt in the hill country of Seir; Esau is Edom." Gen. 36:43 again emphasizes the relationship between Esau and Edom: "These are the chiefs of Edom (that is, Esau, the father of Edom)." Yet Esau, the firstborn of the twins, had "despised" his heritage and his calling (Gen. 25:34) and so had thrown it away, selling it to his younger brother Jacob for a mere "mess of pottage" (Gen. 25:29-34). In doing so Esau thereby revealed the contempt in which he held God's Covenant of Love.

Thus when the people of Israel entered Canaan they avoided every contact with Edom (Num. 21:4; Deut. 2:4-5; 23:7). During the early Israelite monarchy Edom continuously annoyed Israel until Solomon succeeded in subjugating it for a time (1 Sam. 14:47; 2 Sam. 8:13; 1 Kgs. 11:14-22; cf. 1 Kgs. 9:26-28). King Amaziah of Judah then attacked Edom and killed ten thousand of the people (2 Kgs. 14:7; 2 Chr. 25:11-12). Afterwards Edom took its revenge and attacked Judah, just at a time of great crisis when the southern kingdom was opposing the Syro-Ephraimite War (734-733 B.C.). Judah then suffered badly from the Edomites (2 Chr. 28:17). After the fall of Judah (Jerusalem), Edom rejoiced and cursed Jerusalem (Ps. 137:7) and violated Judah (Obad. 10-12). Consequently the OT frequently prophesies judgment upon Edom. Afterwards the history of Edom becomes obscure. Finally Edom was subjugated by the Arabs and assimilated into the Arabian tribes.

Isaiah pictures the LORD who executes judgment as a slaughterer of the animals needed for the various sacrifices. These animals evidently represent the inhabitants of Edom. That is why the "sword" and the "soil" of Edom are soaked with blood and fat. The slaughter will be executed at Bozrah, the capital of Edom, which as such represents the whole country.

EDOM'S TOTAL DESTRUCTION (34:8)

Isaiah 34:8 gives grounds for both the preceding and the following pictures of destruction. As our prophet has shown before, in accordance with Gen. 1:2-3 and with Jer. 4:23-28, God brings good out of evil; that includes salvation out of, not nothing, but chaos. This word, *tohu,* which occurs at Isa. 34:11, includes the arrogance of Esau. That is why the "day of vengeance" upon Edom becomes "a year of recompense for the cause of Zion."

But to accomplish the total salvation of Jacob (Israel, the people of God), Esau (Edom) must first be "put to the ban" *(hrm),* that is, be totally annihilated, even as Joshua sent up the whole city of Jericho in smoke to Yahweh as required of him by the LORD himself (Josh. 6:2, 17). For such alone in God's sight is "justice" or "judgment" *(mishpat,* Isa. 34:5). Our prophet is not talking of any scales of justice, that is, of a kind of tit-for-tat. His emphasis is upon God's chosen *means* of salvation.

THE FRIGHTFUL AFTERMATH OF EDOM'S DESTRUCTION (34:9-15)

This picture of Edom after its destruction is in some ways similar to that of the destruction of Sodom and Gomorrah in prehistoric times. The two most fundamental elements needed for human life, water and soil, are to be turned into pitch and burning sulphur. It is not clear how this is to happen, probably through the eruption of volcanoes. Sulphur, smoke, and unquenchable fire will cover the land. After this catastrophe the land will lie desolate for many generations.

The measuring "line" and "plummet" (v. 11) used by a builder point to God's accurate planning and design. Measured by this line and plummet, the LORD will find only "confusion" and "chaos" in Edom.

A detached word, *horeyha,* meaning "her nobles," actually begins v. 12 in the Hebrew. It should probably be the subject of the following verb, so that we might read: "Her nobles will name her [for both land and city are feminine in Hebrew] 'the Negation of a Kingdom,'" in other words, as the reverse of the kingdom of God. Furthermore, all of Edom's government officials will be nonpersons. This, of course, is because Esau is an aspect of the *tohu* out of which God builds the kingdom of God.

Verses 13-15 describe the inhabitants of this negation of God's ordered world, often illustrated for the prophets by the wilderness that lay at Jerusalem's very door. In that wilderness only thorny shrubs could grow, so that the wilderness of Judea was the abode only of the "hyena" with its horrible cry, like that of a ghostly "satyr"; and there the "night hag" was accustomed to alight, as from her witch's broomstick! This wilderness of Judea, this *tohu,* was the very place out of which the positive message of both John the Baptist and of Jesus was born.

The "night hag" has a name here, *Lilith,* a feminine noun built from the word for "night." Lilith is a very ancient name going back through Babylonian times to ancient Sumer. Thus it reveals the general Near Eastern fear of such nightly horrors. Israel however had been released from all fear of the dark (Ps. 139:11-12). They had long since learned both that Lilith was one of God's creatures (Gen. 1:21) and that God had full control of the darkness (Gen. 1:4).

This terrible picture of the fate of Edom thus emphasizes implacably what both Judaism and Christianity have been very hesitant in appreciating. All those persons who have been chosen by God to be members of his covenant community, with the purpose of saving the world (Isa. 49:6), yet who despise God's grace and turn their back upon him are the persons *most* under judgment from among all mankind (cf. Heb. 10:26-31). And yet, while they may actually repudiate God, God will never repudiate them. In and through his justifiable punishment the promise of the Covenant remains, and God uses their apostasy to his own glory and for the salvation of the world.

34:16-17   These closing verses once again emphasize the fulfillment of all that has been prophesied until now. It is most interesting to note that the books of the OT which were in existence by the time of the Exile are referred to here as "the book of the LORD."

The people of Judah are summoned then to consult this "book of the LORD"; it contains God's proclamation of judgment upon Edom, found in the books of Jeremiah, Lamentation, Ezekiel, Joel, Amos, and Obadiah. The judgment upon Edom has indeed been proclaimed several times in the past. It has been partly fulfilled, but the complete fulfillment is still to come. Thus we have here the prophetic warning. Its ultimate meaning can be seen only in terms of the cross of Christ.

Once again in Isa. 34:17 the prophet emphasizes that all the creatures mentioned in the preceding verses (vv. 13-15) will indeed occupy the whole land of Edom while no human being will abide there. These creatures will continue to abide there "from generation to generation."

Verse 16b can be taken as the closing verse of the whole chapter. The Word which has been spoken through "the mouth of the LORD" and now to be found in the Bible, the "book of the LORD," will not be withdrawn nor will it have been uttered in vain (cf. 55:10-11; 40:9). The Word works through the Spirit, which upholds it and puts it into effect. Here the Spirit is said to have full command over all God's creatures and over even all evil forces: "his Spirit has gathered them." For through the Spirit the Word becomes "sharper than any two-edged sword" (Heb. 4:12). We are reminded of this in the frequent phrase "God is Spirit" (John 4:24; cf. Isa. 11:2; 31:3; 32:15; John 3:5; Acts 2:2-3). Throughout the OT Spirit is seen to be Almighty God acting in *power*.

THE GLORY OF SALVATION
35:1-10

This chapter has been well placed. The last word of the preceding prophetic message pointed to the bright future of Zion and to the joy of salvation among the redeemed people and also in nature. This prophecy now gives the impression of reflecting the spirit of Deutero-Isaiah (cf. Isa. 40:3-4; 55:12-13). On the other hand, considering the strong apocalyptic features found here, some interpreters suggest even a postexilic dating to conform to 25:6-8 and 32:15-20.

THE DESERT SHALL REJOICE (35:1-2)

The poem commences with a picture that is very different from the preceding one (cf. 33:7-9; 34:1-4). Suddenly shouts of joy are heard arising from the desert and from that dry, desolate place that was the abode of hyenas and of witches flying by night. The time of grace has come, bringing new life to the wilderness—to the chaos of evil—from which God had originally created order and light (Gen. 1:1-3). The "dry land" and desolate places are transformed into a beautiful fertile garden, the garden of Eden restored. The desert has now become attractive because it receives "the glory of Lebanon" and "the majesty of Carmel and Sharon." The hills of Lebanon are covered with forests where the tall and famous cedars grow abundantly. The mountainous area of Carmel is famous for its fertility and agriculture; indeed, Carmel is synonymous with fertile soil. South of Carmel along the Mediterranean coast lies the plain of Sharon, known for its beautiful roses—or perhaps crocuses (Cant. 2:1)?

Who is meant by "they" who "shall see the glory of the LORD"? At first sight it might mean the desert itself, which has now been transformed and is rejoicing. Yet it seems more likely that the re-deemed people in Zion is meant here. "They" might even be "the remnant of Israel" still in exile who have now suffered long and yearned for deliverance (cf. Isa. 35:10; 40:27).

This passage is saying, then, that in the day of final judgment, when all God's enemies have been destroyed, his creation will be glorified and the relation between God, mankind, and nature will be restored according to God's initial purpose. So the passage promises the total renewal and re-creation of all things (cf. Rom. 8:20-23; Rev. 21:5; and note the use of *apokatastasis* in Acts 3:21).

COMFORT FOR THE WEARIED AND HOPELESS (35:3-4)

The prophet addresses his suffering people and those who are fear-ful of heart (cf. Heb. 12:12). These words of comfort sound sim-ilar to the opening verses of Isa. 40 which were addressed to the people of God in exile. But of course they sound forth to all genera-tions of God's people as they pursue their pilgrimage towards the New Jerusalem.

The vengeance of God is related to the many arguments against his enemies that we have already heard (cf. 33:10-11; 34:8-9). "The recompense of God" (NIV "divine retribution") could be un-derstood as having a meaning parallel with "vengeance"; but it could also be related to the salvation of those people who have suffered so long; thus the NIV translation, ". . . with divine ret-ribution he will come to save you," may be more correct than that of the RSV.

What is required from the people is that they prepare the way of the LORD's coming (cf. 40:3-4), show strong faith, and have a courageous heart (cf. 28:16). Personal effort to avenge or liberate oneself from one's enemies will be in vain: "Vengeance is mine, and recompense . . ." (Deut. 32:35). The deliverance and the salvation of the people are part of "the cause of Zion" (Isa. 34:8) which is in the LORD's hands. People should leave all doubts behind them because the LORD is "your God" and at the same time they are "my people" (cf. 30:11). It is a living personal relationship that is spoken of here.

THE JOY OF THE NEW LIFE (35:5-7)

People and nature will enjoy the new abundant life of salvation. Physically handicapped people, such as the blind and the deaf, the lame and the mute, will be relieved from their infirmities. This is of great importance because it means that the restoration and re-habilitation of human beings will enable them to function normally again in accordance with God's initial plan for them. That is why Jesus performed his wonderful healing ministry for both the physically and the mentally handicapped. However, this physical healing has a deeper meaning as well; it announces that "the year of grace has come" (cf. Luke 4:19). Therefore this physical healing is not an end in itself, but functions as a sign pointing to the total and everlasting deliverance from the powers of sin that shackle all humankind.

Those who have been healed are not just able to see, hear, speak, and walk physically. Rather, all these organic functions that they have regained are now dedicated to the glory of the LORD, in holiness and truth. As such human beings are renewed and sanctified to be in the image of the holy God.

Isaiah 35:6b-7 describes the radical transformation of nature. The desert will be changed into a land of many waters breaking forth from springs in the wilderness, and these will form a pool that will never dry up. This will transform the desert into a flourishing orchard (vv. 1-2). These springs of water can of course be taken as symbols of the water of life and of salvation (cf. Ezek. 47; John 4:10-15). Isaiah 35:7b reminds us of the fertile land around the Jordan or the river Nile; the NIV translation reads, "in the haunts where jackals once lay, grass and reeds and papyrus will grow."

THE HOLY WAY (35:8-10)

In this new land, which was once a wilderness or desert, there will be a highway, called the "Holy Way" (or "Way of Holiness"). This is the highway followed by pilgrims on their way to Zion (35:10). Only those who are clean (according to the Torah) are allowed to walk in it. When they reach Zion all peoples will gather together to worship and praise the LORD (cf. Ps. 2), ". . . and fools shall not err therein" (Isa. 35:8). "Fools" are those who neglect the LORD

and his worship (cf. 19:11; Ps. 14:1); they are the godless who are
arrogant and self-complacent. Such people will not "err" from the
highway. To err is to take the wrong road through folly or way-
wardness.

No one who walks in that way need fear any threat from the
wild beasts that used to terrorize the desert road. These may represent the attack of evil even in the human heart (cf. Mark 1:13).

Isaiah 35:9b-10a suggests a further qualification of those who
are allowed to walk in the way of holiness. They are called the "redeemed" or the "ransomed of the LORD." Considering the close
relationship of this chapter to 40:1-11, we can conclude that the
people referred to are the people of God returning from the Babylonian Exile. The LORD himself will pay the ransom that will liberate this people from Babylonia, just as he had done before in ancient times at the deliverance from Egypt. It is worth noting here
that these people are not now accounted as either "clean" or "unclean"; they are merely called "the redeemed" and "the ransomed."
Thus it is not mankind's faithful and careful observance of the law
which is considered to be decisive, but it is the grace of the LORD
(sola gratia) who has redeemed and ransomed his people. As such
this message is one with the gospel in the NT.

It is to be noted that in this prophecy it is "Zion" that is mentioned and not "Jerusalem." Jerusalem was the capital city of the
kingdom of Judah and the seat of the temple. But at the time of this
prophecy Jerusalem had collapsed and the temple was in ruins.
Jerusalem then became the symbol of the national cult and of a mere
secular hope. On the other hand, the use of the word "Zion" points
to the heart of the new creation, the kingdom of God, to which all
people will go to worship the LORD. Zion has a particular eschatological and messianic significance. Therefore the Holy Way must
not be identified with the ancient caravan highway that connected
Egypt with Mesopotamia through Palestine. Rather, it is to be understood in a spiritual sense, just as is the "cry" at 40:3-4.

Most probably chs. 34 and 35, which bear apocalyptic features,
are a later addition to the Isaian prophecies recorded throughout
chs. 1–39. If this is so, then chs. 34–35 can be regarded as the closing chapters of the whole collection of chs. 1–33 before the Isaian
collection is continued again in chs. 36–39, which provide a historical witness to the prophecies' veracity. Chapters 34–35 can

therefore be considered as a unity. They offer an apocalyptic interpretation of the historical events to be described in chs. 36–39.
That is, on the one hand they interpret the judgment of God and
the destruction of his enemies; and on the other hand they show
the salvation of God's redeemed people, along with the renewal at
Zion both of nature and of human life in joy and gladness.

Finally, we observe that this prophetic message of Isaiah brings
us close to the gospel in the NT. In connection with the Holy Way
Jesus said, "I am the way, and the truth, and the life; no one comes
to the Father, but by me" (John 14:6). For in Christ there is a total
renewal, in fact a "new creation" (2 Cor. 5:17).

PART VI

EPILOGUE: A HISTORICAL NARRATIVE CONCERNING HEZEKIAH'S FAITH

Isaiah 36:1–39:8

These last chapters of First Isaiah serve as an epilogue, but simultaneously form a link to Second Isaiah (Isa. 40–55). This is especially so with the last chapter (ch. 39).

Most interpreters share the opinion that these chapters originally stood apart, being compiled after Isaiah's day. They were then added to chs. 1–35 before the book continues with ch. 40. The following reasons are worth considering (see O. Kaiser, *Isaiah 1-39*, 367-68).

1. These chapters contain historical notes concerning Isaiah's activities during Judah's national crisis at the time of the Assyrian threat in 701 B.C. They are virtually similar to 2 Kgs. 18:13, 17–19:37 and 2 Chr. 32:9-26. Considering the fact that this historical record is more complete and in line with the contents of 2 Kings, it can be assumed that the book of Isaiah in this respect actually quotes 2 Kings.

2. This historical record also mentions the Babylonian attack and the Exile (Isa. 39:6-7).

3. Some parts of this record show certain inconsistencies. The faithfulness of Hezekiah when he praises the LORD (38:9-20) is not in line with his reluctant attitude to God at 39:8. Nor is it in accordance with the portrayal of Hezekiah's faith given in previous chapters in this book (e.g., chs. 29, 30, 31). There the leaders at Jerusalem (obviously including Hezekiah) are sharply criticized for their political attitude and reliance on Egypt.

If chs. 36–39 indeed function as a bridge to the book of Deutero-Isaiah, then a postexilic dating is very likely. However, the Isaian mind is still recognizable in these chapters. They can be divided into two parts, chs. 36–37, dealing with Sennacherib's attack upon Jerusalem, and chs. 38–39, concerning the healing of Hezekiah and the visit of the messengers from Babylonia.

FACING THE ASSYRIAN THREAT: HEZEKIAH'S FAITH TESTED

36:1-22

In accordance with other historical narratives in the OT, Isa. 36–37, based as it is on 2 Kgs. 18–19, also reflects its prophetic nature. It offers no theological reflection on what happened around the close of the 8th cent. B.C. at Judah and Jerusalem. Holding strongly to faith in the LORD meant one would not be put to shame (Isa. 28:16); on the contrary, it resulted in a wonderful deliverance from the mighty enemy (Assyria). Contrary to the attitude of King Ahaz, who rejected the prophet's warnings, Hezekiah shows in these chapters a much more positive and trusting attitude (cf. ch. 7).

In the light of recent historical research, the historical data in the biblical narrative do raise critical questions. The main problem concerns whether the historical events as described in ch. 36 and continued in ch. 37 actually happened in 701 or at some later date. Further, it is unclear whether there were two different events (i.e., Hezekiah's going to Lachish to offer submission to Sennacherib and the sending of the Rabshakeh) or only one. For a lengthy discussion of the issues, see John Bright, *A History of Israel*, 269-309; Brevard S. Childs, *Isaiah and the Assyrian Crisis*.

SENNACHERIB'S ENVOY TO JERUSALEM (36:1-3)

36:1 The opening verse presents a general picture of the situation and position of Judah in the fourteenth year of King Hezekiah, which means according to most interpreters 701 B.C. At that time Judah was completely powerless against Assyria. This was because all the fortified cities had been taken by Sennacherib, except Jerusalem and Lachish (37:8). But for Jerusalem and Hezekiah there was no possibility at all of deliverance. As the Assyrian source describes it, Hezekiah was shut up "like a bird in a cage." Indeed the crisis had reached its climax.

Again the prophet gave the same warning as had been given to Ahaz previously, namely, to remain faithful to the LORD, for God would deliver Jerusalem from the Assyrians. Unlike Ahaz, Hezekiah humbled himself before the LORD.

36:2   At the time of this verse Sennacherib had his headquarters at Lachish. It is not clear whether this city had by now been taken or was still being besieged by the Assyrians (cf. 37:8). It does seem that the fortified cities located in the plain of the Shephelah had in fact been taken. Eastward this plain becomes hilly as it gives entrance into the land of Judah. Lachish was located at the border area, and as such was of strategic importance for the defense of Judah and Jerusalem.

From Lachish Sennacherib sent his envoy, the Rabshakeh (NIV "field commander") to Jerusalem to persuade Hezekiah to surrender unconditionally. For this purpose the Rabshakeh came with "a great army" to put pressure on Hezekiah. According to 2 Kgs. 18:17 the Rabshakeh was accompanied by two other officers, the Tartan and the Rabaris. Also, before the Rabshakeh was sent to Jerusalem Hezekiah had sent a messenger to Sennacherib at Lachish to apologize for being unfaithful to Assyria and to confess he was prepared to bear the consequences on condition that Jerusalem should not be attacked (cf. 2 Kgs. 18:14-16). As a result Hezekiah had to pay a very heavy tribute. This part of the story has been omitted from Isa. 36, perhaps because it would have distorted the image of Hezekiah as a faithful and pious king.

The Rabshakeh and his mighty army took up their position at the most vital and strategic spot, the aqueduct from the upper pool on the road to the Fuller's Field. Precisely at that place the prophet Isaiah had been confronted by King Ahaz some twenty years before (ch. 7). Concerning the importance of this particular place, see the Commentary at 7:3.

By occupying this vital position with a great army virtually assures that Jerusalem was already under enemy control. Therefore the Rabshakeh had been sent to persuade Hezekiah to capitulate.

36:3   Hezekiah then sent three messengers to meet Sennacherib's envoy. These were Eliakim, the palace administrator; Shebna, the

231

secretary; and Joah, the recorder. Concerning Eliakim and Shebna, see the interpretation at 22:15-25. The functions of Shebna here as "secretary" (Heb. *sopher*; NEB "adjutant-general") and that of Joah as "recorder" (*mazkir*; NEB "secretary of state") are rather obscure. On the basis of the root meaning of the Hebrew terms, it appears that Shebna was Eliakim's personal secretary. Joah's task as "remembrancer" was to record important historical events and to register the state's treasures in the national archives. Referring back to 22:15-25, it seems that the position and function of Shebna had been degraded since then and made subordinate to Eliakim. It is interesting to note that the name of Shebna's father is never mentioned, either in ch. 22 or here.

HEZEKIAH RIDICULED BY SENNACHERIB (36:4-10)

In this pericope we hear crude and haughty words from the Rabshakeh meant to ridicule Hezekiah and persuade him to surrender immediately and unconditionally. This is an example of ancient diplomatic discourse!

36:4 The haughtiness of the Rabshakeh is expressed immediately at the opening of the address. Out of reverence and awe, Sennacherib's name is not mentioned; rather, he is called by his predicate "the great king, the king of Assyria." In contrast Hezekiah is mentioned without any royal predicate at all. The Rabshakeh starts his discourse with a mocking and rhetorical question, in which Hezekiah is ridiculed for being foolish enough to put his trust in vain things. According to the Rabshakeh those vain things are the alliances with the Philistines and Egypt and holding to faith in Yahweh, who according to the prophetic message will surely protect Jerusalem. The vanity of all these actions is elaborated in the following verses.

36:5-6 The Rabshakeh explains further that the allied forces or even Yahweh himself will not be able to act meaningfully in the war against Assyria. These allies can only talk and give promises, but "mere words" (NIV "empty words") do not provide a strategy nor produce power in war.

"On whom do you now rely, that you have rebelled against me?" The Rabshakeh talks as if he were the king himself!

Egypt, on whom Hezekiah relies, is described as a "broken reed of a staff," one that will "pierce the hand" of anyone who leans on it (36:6). Although Egyptian troops under Tirhakah might come to the city's aid (37:9), this would be meaningless for Jerusalem. Such is the persuasion of the Rabshakeh.

36:7 It seems that the Rabshakeh was well informed about the religious reform of Hezekiah. Hezekiah had diligently purified the religious practices of Jerusalem using quite drastic actions. In line with his anti-Assyrian attitude, he had tried to abolish all Assyrian cultic influences. Assyrian influence had actually penetrated the temple cult, as was reflected at the "high places and altars" found everywhere in Judah (see Commentary at 6:2). The worship of these gods was against the Israelite law (Deut. 12:11-14). For this reason Hezekiah removed all of the cult places and so centralized worship at Jerusalem. This evoked many reactions from the rural people, who felt strongly attached to their own traditional places of worship (cf. 2 Kgs. 18:4). According to popular belief, such a clean sweep would create natural disasters. Moreover, it would evoke the anger of the Assyrians, who would interpret it as a rebellion against Assyria.

Being aware of all these reactions, the Rabshakeh here mocks Hezekiah's faith and at the same time seeks to win the hearts of his dissatisfied people. He sharply criticizes Hezekiah by saying that Hezekiah has committed a grave sin in removing all these high places and altars; this foolish act would bring about a terrible vengeance from the gods. Hezekiah's trust in Yahweh, the God of Israel, would also be in vain because it has already proved to be worthless against the Assyrian power. Such then is the trend of the Rabshakeh's mockery, directed not only at Hezekiah but also at Yahweh himself!

36:8-9 The Rabshakeh knew that Hezekiah expected help from Egypt, consisting of horses and chariots (cf. Isa. 30:6; 31:1, 2) to oppose the Assyrian attack. But presumably this expected help had not been realized.

The Rabshakeh felt quite sure that should the Egyptian help actually come about, Judah's military power could never counterbalance that of Assyria. Therefore the Rabshakeh now cynically offers Hezekiah an attractive "wager" (36:8). He will give him two thousand horses on condition that Hezekiah "set riders upon them." The loss of that many horses would not mean much for the Assyrian power! But to provide two thousand riders is far beyond the power of Hezekiah.

The mockery is continued in v. 9. Even with the help of Egypt, Judah's army would not be able to repulse "a single captain among the least of my master's servants"; far less might it oppose the whole mighty army of the great king of Assyria!

36:10 The Rabshakeh now raises an interesting theological issue. To intimidate Hezekiah and the people of Judah, he now boasts that Yahweh had previously been on the side of Assyria. It was Yahweh, he declared, who had commanded the king of Assyria to attack and destroy Jerusalem. It is as if the Rabshakeh is aware of Isaiah's statement at 10:5-6.

Here the Rabshakeh functions as a false prophet, by challenging the holiness of Yahweh. It is a disgusting type of diplomacy. He misrepresents divine truth merely for the sake of political and personal gain. He pretends to honor the God of Israel and does not deny the word of Yahweh. Rather, his deceit is in his proclamation that Yahweh has turned away from Judah and has left Judah to take the side of Assyria! It is possible that the Rabshakeh knew something of the prophetic judgment upon Jerusalem, so that he now considered himself to be the executor of that divine judgment. It is clear that the Rabshakeh's aim was to break down all resistance and so be able to demand immediate and total surrender.

In this way the Rabshakeh sought to win the hearts and the confidence of both the people and of the soldiers, particularly those who were "sitting on the wall" (36:12) listening to his diplomatic speech. Indeed, there were groups of people who were not in favor of Hezekiah's drastic reformation (cf. Ernest L. Ehrlich, *A Concise History of Israel*, 60). So the tension grew and the situation became ever more precarious, due to the cunning and tricky diplomacy of the Rabshakeh.

So we have a classical example of that kind of cunning diplomacy in which political interest makes use of false religious arguments in order to mislead the people. How great a temptation to employ this kind of diplomatic chicanery exists in today's world!

THE RABSHEKAH INCITES THE PEOPLE (36:11-20)

Although the Rabshakeh used crude and insolent means, he seems to have been a skillful diplomat who understood human psychology. He employed the language of Judah, that is, the popular Hebrew language. Intentionally he did not use the Aramaic language which was the current diplomatic language of the period.

Hezekiah's messengers became worried, because the people who were sitting on the wall listening to the speech could understand what was said and were becoming agitated. But that was precisely the Rabshakeh's intention. Those who were "sitting on the wall" were primarily the guards, but as well there were ordinary people who were curious to watch this diplomatic confrontation. That is why the messengers of Hezekiah requested the Rabshakeh not to speak in Hebrew. Naturally the latter refused and continued to shout even louder. It was of course part of his job to speak directly to the people and to incite them to rebel against Hezekiah and to surrender to the Assyrians.

The Rabshakeh now gives a further description of the fate of the people if Jerusalem were to be besieged. Those who would suffer most were the poor who would be doomed to "eat their own dung and drink their own urine" (36:12). However, this was an exaggerated picture, because in fact within the city of Jerusalem were several pools and aqueducts connected with subterranean springs (cf. 8:6; 2 Kgs. 20:20). It is clear, however, that such a picture was given in order to intimidate and incite the common people against Hezekiah, who refused to surrender. Moreover, the Rabshakeh alleged, the messengers of Hezekiah themselves would share the same fate. In this way the leaders and the authorities of Jerusalem were also being incited to oppose Hezekiah.

36:13 Step by step the Rabshakeh becomes ever bolder and more brutal. He continues to speak to the people "in a loud voice in the language of Judah." The request and the presence of the messengers of Hezekiah and even the royal position of Hezekiah himself are now totally ignored. The Rabshakeh speaks here as if he were the great king of Assyria himself addressing a subject people.

36:14-15   The Rabshakeh's inducement is meant primarily to undermine the authority of Hezekiah. Once again Hezekiah is called by his personal name without any royal predicate, in contrast to the predicate given to "the great king, the king of Assyria." It seems that the Rabshakeh no longer recognizes Hezekiah as king of Judah. Rather, he pictures Hezekiah now as a deceiver giving false promises and hopes to the people, because "he will not be able to deliver you" (Isa. 36:14). Indeed this last remark in itself is quite true, because the LORD himself would be the true deliverer (e.g., 29:1-8; 30:15; 31:4). Such a faith is considered by the Rabshakeh as a mere deception. In this instance therefore the Rabshakeh is merely confirming the attitude of the erring leaders of Jerusalem who had before this rejected and despised Isaiah's prophecies (cf. 28:15; 29:15).

In this chapter Hezekiah is described as a faithful king. The Rabshakeh is shown to be a cunning diplomat, agitator, and a skillful swindler who worked upon the people's emotions, and declared merely partial truths. He even turned the prophetic words of God to his own purposes and benefit. As such he is a representation of the great Deceiver of all times.

36:16-17   The Rabshakeh now makes a most attractive promise, but on the absolute condition that Judah must make peace with the king of Assyria immediately and that simultaneously the people must betray Hezekiah. He promises a time of security, welfare, and peace, in which everyone would enjoy the fruits of his own labor. There would be an abundance of water in every home, rich harvests of fruits, grains, and all other crops. Just compare this vision with the terrible and miserable situation of a besieged city (cf. 36:12; 33:7-9)!

However, the Rabshakeh goes on to announce something more. He will leave for awhile and go to defeat the Egyptian army under Tirhakah. Thereafter he will come back "to take you away" (36:17) from Judah "to a land like your own land . . . ," meaning of course a land of exile. But even this land of exile is described as being extremely attractive.

36:18-20   Finally the Rabshakeh insists that Judah should learn from history. Evidently none of the gods of the nations was able to protect its people or deliver them from the hands of the Assyrians. He alleges that Yahweh, the God of Israel, is no different from any other god of the nations now subject to the Assyrian power. He asks the people to look at the many examples in history, particularly during the period of the Syro-Ephraimite War in 734-733 B.C. With respect to the cities Arpad in northern Syria and Hamath in central Syria on the river Orontes, see the Commentary at 10:9. The city of Sepharvaim is mentioned at 2 Kgs. 17:24. It was one of the cities in Syria whose inhabitants were removed to Samaria after the downfall of the northern kingdom in 722. Finally the fall of Samaria is mentioned because it concerns the neighboring country to Judah, a sister nation worshipping the same Yahweh! Thus Jerusalem would not be an exception to the rule. There was no other choice before Jerusalem but to surrender unconditionally.

At the close of his speech, however, the Rabshakeh reveals that in despising Yahweh he is under the LORD himself. For he implies that the god of Assyria is *the* almighty God and that Sennacherib is his servant!

THE RABSHAKEH'S SPEECH FINDS NO RESPONSE (36:21-22)

To such a bold and reckless inducement no response comes either from the people or from the messengers of Hezekiah. In fact Hezekiah has commanded them to say nothing. That is the most appropriate attitude that could be adopted in such a situation. This attitude also testifies that the people still remain faithful to Hezekiah and to Yahweh.

The messengers of Hezekiah finally return in deep sorrow because of the words of the Rabshakeh.

THE VINDICATION OF FAITH
37:1-38

HEZEKIAH CONSULTS THE PROPHET (37:1-7)

This pericope continues the previous chapter, and is also parallel to 2 Kgs. 19. Hezekiah now sends messengers to the prophet Isaiah and asks for his counsel in the present predicament. Hezekiah is described here as a faithful and pious king. He has humbled himself before the LORD and waited for his help. This attitude seems to contradict the sharp criticism and admonition of the prophet towards the leaders in Jerusalem who despised and rejected the prophetic message and preferred to lean upon Egypt (cf. Isa. 28, 29).

37:1-2 The report that was submitted by the messengers (36:2) evidently deeply impressed King Hezekiah, who rent his clothes and covered himself with sackcloth as an expression of deep sorrow and remorse (cf. Mic. 1:8; Jer. 4:8). This deep sorrow was the result of the blasphemy uttered by the Rabshakeh and of the present predicament. A sense of deep remorse came upon the king because he realized the nation was suffering from the bitter fruits of the policy adopted by his father, Ahaz, and from the unpalatable consequences of neglecting the prophetic message. Now Hezekiah fully realized that their only hope of deliverance was in Yahweh, who had spoken through the prophets.

Accordingly he went on to the temple and at the same time sent messengers to the prophet Isaiah. It is not clear here for what purpose Hezekiah went to the temple, whether for prayer or to give an offering. Isaiah 37:14-15 show it was primarily for prayer.

The embassy sent to Isaiah consisted of Eliakim, Shebna, and the senior priests (v. 2). They represented the state and the temple cult. This visit was an honor for Isaiah, who was at long last recognized as a prophet of the LORD. It is interesting to note that Joah, the secretary of state, is not mentioned here.

Theologically speaking, these two steps taken by Hezekiah were meaningful. While the king went to the temple to seek God's presence, his envoys went to the prophet to seek God's word. The king, as head of state, the senior priest, representing the clergy, and the prophet now worked together, looking for God's word and help.

37:3-4, 5 Considering the logical order of verses, v. 5 might preferably be read before vv. 3-4.

The envoys recite the message of Hezekiah, saying: "Thus says Hezekiah . . . ." These opening words seem to be a repetition of Hezekiah's own words, speaking of himself by this personal name alone. It seems that Hezekiah wanted to humble himself before Isaiah, the prophet of God.

The predicament in which the king and his people found themselves placed is described in various ways, such as "distress," "rebuke," and "disgrace." These are related to the Assyrian attack, to Hezekiah's own guilty feelings and remorse at being unfaithful and in depending on the help of Egypt, as well as to the crude blasphemy of the Rabshakeh. This unbearable situation is further described as being like a woman in travail and in despair since the moment of giving birth has come but she has no strength left to bring forth. Hezekiah means that immediate help and saving intervention are urgently needed.

It is rather strange that in v. 4 the messengers refer to "the LORD *your* God" and not to "the LORD *our* God." It seems that they humbly feel that Isaiah, as a prophet of God, has a close and living relationship with God while, on the contrary, they themselves feel unworthy before the presence of God. Therefore they ask Isaiah to pray "for the remnant that is left" (see Commentary at 10:20-27a; 1:9).

They also hope for the LORD's rebuke against the king of Assyria and his envoys, who had mocked "the living God" (cf. 36:18-20). Yahweh is called "the living God," because he is utterly other than the gods of the nations who are "dead" (cf. 40:18-20). The living God of Israel has made a covenant with his people. This covenant God is "the Holy One of Israel" (37:23), who interferes in all aspects of Israel's life. He will not permit his holiness to be

239

besmirched because he is "a jealous God" (Exod. 20:5). Such a God has now heard all the mockery and blasphemy spoken by the king of Assyria and the Rabshakeh!

37:6-7 The prophet now conveys the word of God to comfort Hezekiah. He emphasizes that the LORD has heard all the blasphemy that "reviled me (the LORD)." Hezekiah therefore need not be afraid because these slanders did not have any impact or validity. They were spoken by "the *servants* of the king of Assyria." Hebrew *na'ar* used here means literally "youngster"; in other words, being immature, they like to boast.

On the other hand, the prophet foretells what would happen with Assyria and Sennacherib himself. The LORD would chase the Assyrians away and deliver Jerusalem in a wonderful way. There is talk here of an angel of the LORD. The LORD himself "will put a spirit in him." It would be a spirit of unrest that would disturb and vex Sennacherib and make him confused and afraid, because of the slanders and blasphemies he had uttered against the Holy One of Israel. The Assyrian king would tremble at merely hearing "a rumor." The contents of the rumor are not clear. It might be bad news about a rebellion and treason at Nineveh within the royal family itself (cf. Isa. 37:38). Such a rumor would compel him to leave the battlefield immediately and flee home. Actually, when Sennacherib did arrive home his sons slew him with the sword (vv. 37-38).

The realization of this prophecy seems to have happened during one of Sennacherib's military campaigns, probably against Tirhakah or Babylonia in 689/8 B.C. or later. According to Assyriologists, Sennacherib was assassinated ca. 681. To what extent this historical event was connected with the deliverance of Jerusalem is not clear.

SENNACHERIB AGAIN URGES HEZEKIAH TO SURRENDER (37:8-13)

The record of the consultation with the prophet Isaiah is now interrupted by that concerning the return of the Rabshakeh to his master Sennacherib. It is not clear whether the great army (36:2) also withdrew with him or still remained encamped before the gates of Jerusalem.

In the meantime Sennacherib had left Lachish to move further northward to capture Libnah, a fortified city on the plain of the Shephelah, ca. 20 km. (12 mi.) north of Lachish. This means that Sennacherib was moving ever closer to Jerusalem. The distance from Libnah to Jerusalem was about 25 km. (15 mi.).

According to 2 Kings and Isa. 37:9 the appearance of Tirhakah was one of the reasons for Sennacherib's withdrawal from Jerusalem and his return to Assyria (v. 37). The redactor seems to doubt such a conclusion when he offers a theological explanation for it, inserting the story about the angel of the LORD at the end of the chapter (v. 36; 2 Kgs. 19:35).

The mention of Tirhakah, a great pharaoh of the 25th Dynasty of Egypt, in this context also creates some difficulties. Tirhakah is thought to have been born in 710 B.C. and to have succeeded Shabataka as pharaoh in 690. Thus in 701 he would have been too young to be commander of the Egyptian army. Presumably the narrator mixed up this campaign with another (unknown) military campaign by Egypt to oppose the Assyrian power in the south. Because he was the most famous pharaoh of the 25th Dynasty, Tirhakah's name may have been employed uncritically in this narrative.

At any rate, the intention of the narrator seems to have been to take this historical event as a reason for Sennacherib's once again applying pressure to persuade Hezekiah to surrender. Apparently Sennacherib would have liked to avoid facing two fronts, one in the north fighting against Jerusalem and one in the south against Egypt. He may have estimated that a war to capture Jerusalem would take a long time, based on his previous experience against Samaria in 722.

According to the order of this narrative in Isa. 37:8-13, the Rabshakeh's second expedition took place not long after his first. This is rather hard to understand, because no answer from Hezekiah has as yet been heard since the first expedition. The names of the envoys at the second mission are not mentioned. The message to be conveyed is almost the same as the previous one. The question arises therefore whether there was only one or actually two expeditions. The present record, however, is too short to give any clarity on this issue.

What the narrator intended to point to was the theological understanding of this event. The haughtiness and blasphemies of the

241

Assyrian king were merely the external expression of his inner weakness and of his hidden fear of Yahweh, the God of Israel, who was worshipped at the temple in Jerusalem. By contrast Hezekiah is described as a pious king "waiting for the LORD." The prophet Isaiah put his finger on the central issue, that faith in Yahweh is never in vain because salvation comes from Yahweh only—though it may not come as we expect it to come, or even in our lifetime.

37:10 This verse seems in some ways to be inconsistent with v. 14. Although the present message shows similarities with the previous one (36:4-10, 18-20), there are some differences. The attitude of Sennacherib here towards Hezekiah is more lenient, and he addresses Hezekiah as "king of Judah." The crude mockery and attitude of the Rabshakeh apparently was not approved by Sennacherib; consequently the Rabshakeh was not sent back. This time Sennacherib does not wish to despise Hezekiah or the Egyptian power, yet his efforts are mainly concentrated on shaking Hezekiah's faith in Yahweh. He alleges that Hezekiah has been deceived by Yahweh, who speaks through his prophet Isaiah and declares that Yahweh is in no way different from the other gods of the nations. Basing his argument on this deception of Sennacherib, Hezekiah believes that Jerusalem will not be given into the hand of the king of Assyria.

Sennacherib presumably knew that the real strength of Judah lay in its faith in Yahweh. But Yahweh and Judah, according to his persuasion, were in no way different from any other god and nation which had been subjugated.

37:11-13 Hezekiah is called upon to consider the facts in the history of Assyria. People and nations had been subjugated by Assyria since the days of Sennacherib's forefathers. This was, according to Sennacherib, a clear proof that all "the gods of the nations" were powerless over against the Assyrian might. The various cities and countries which had been conquered in the past were presumably located in Mesopotamia, Assyria, and Syria (cf. 36:19).

Sennacherib's persuasive argument might be more refined than the Rabshakeh's, but it is essentially the same. Faith is called a spiritual deception! This kind of mockery gives grief to the faithful (cf.

Ps. 41:7-12). It can still be heard in modern times in many forms of secular ideologies. Where faith and religious truth are ignored or despised, then only violence and falsehood flourish, with the result that the world is brought to ruin.

HEZEKIAH'S PRAYER (37:14-20)

This prayer contains a theological reflection on Yahweh, the God of Israel. At the same time it also contains a confession of faith as a positive response to the mockery and challenge of Sennacherib.

37:14-15 Hezekiah had now received Sennacherib's letter containing the royal message uttered by the messengers. According to the narrative order in this chapter, his immediate reaction was to go to the house of the LORD a second time, even though the prophet's answer had already been given (Isa. 37:6-7). Presumably the narrator's intention was rather to point out once again the pious attitude Hezekiah assumed in the presence of the LORD. It is likely that he "spread" out the letter on the altar "before the LORD" as a symbol of submission to the Holy One of Israel.

37:16 Hezekiah begins his prayer with words of adoration and praise to the glorious and almighty LORD "of all the kingdoms on earth." This was just the point of Sennacherib's mockery. This emphasis is expressed by the predicate used: "LORD of hosts (*YHWH Tsebaoth*)," "who art enthroned above the cherubim" (cf. 1 Sam. 4:4; 2 Sam. 6:2; 2 Kgs. 19:15; Ps. 80:1; 99:1). In the OT the role of the cherubim is connected with the holiness and glory of God. Cherubim were placed at the garden of Eden to guard the way to the tree of life (Gen. 3:24). They were pictured in the form of strange creatures having wings, sitting at both ends of the mercy seat (Exod. 25:18-22), guarding and protecting the ark of the testimony. But in other instances the cherubim were pictured as the base on which the throne of God was placed, so that we sometimes read of "the God of Israel sitting on the cherubim" (cf. Ezek. 10). So the LORD spoke to Moses "from above the mercy seat, from between the two cherubim" (Exod. 25:22). Their wings expressed their mobility, ever ready to execute the LORD'S command. Their mobility also expressed the mobility of God himself, for he is the

God of all the nations upon earth. God cannot share his glory with any other being. This reflects a monotheistic view of the divine, and as such contradicts the polytheistic view of the Assyrians. Finally Hezekiah's conviction culminated in his confession that Yahweh is the creator of heaven and earth. How small and powerless was Assyria indeed before such a LORD!

37:17-20 This anthropomorphic expression shows the intensity and the urgency of Hezekiah's supplication. Yahweh is the loving God who can hear, see, and intervene in all matters in Israel's life. That is why Hezekiah spreads out the letter before the LORD and reads it in deep grief and sorrow at the mockery of Sennacherib against the living God of Israel.

On the one hand it is true that all the nations and their lands have been "laid waste," together with their gods who have proved to be powerless (Isa. 37:18). But on the other hand Hezekiah strongly protests Sennacherib's presumption to equate all those gods with Yahweh. The reason for this is because all those divinities are just the work of human hands and are made of wood or stone; so they can be destroyed at any time. These gods are "dead"; they are "no gods" at all (v. 19).

Finally Hezekiah's supplication is just this simple request, "save us from his hand" (v. 20). He does not ask God to punish or destroy Sennacherib because of his mockery. Vengeance belongs to the jealous God. But the salvation of Judah from Sennacherib's hand will lead the nations to know Yahweh, the God of Israel, as the only true God. It will be a living testimony to the glory of Yahweh, who is able to bring good out of evil, salvation out of despair and unfaith.

Hezekiah's prayer shows then that he was indeed a faithful and theocratic king who sought Yahweh's glory among the nations on earth. As such he was a type of a messianic king.

YAHWEH'S ANSWER THROUGH THE PROPHET (37:21-29)

The prophet now sends messengers to convey the answer of Yahweh to Hezekiah. The answer is written in poetic form. It should be understood in relation to vv. 5-7, 37-38, where the prophet has prophesied concerning Sennacherib's retreat with fear and confusion (v. 7).

Now the reverse is to happen: Assyria will be despised in turn by Jerusalem. Jerusalem is called here "the virgin daughter" (v. 22; cf. 1:8) who had successfully withstood the crude and cruel enemy who had tried to violate her. After the enemy had failed and had fled in confusion, "the virgin daughter of Zion" would despise and mock at him, wagging her head behind his back to express her contempt for him (cf. Ps. 22:7). Sennacherib, the subjector of nations and peoples (Isa. 36:18-19; 37:10), had now fled away, terrified and despised by a virgin! This is a picture full of shameful irony!

In v. 23 the king of Assyria is reprimanded by the virgin daughter of Zion. Sennacherib has misunderstood the reality badly and has acted foolishly. All his crude mockery has in fact been directed at Yahweh himself, the Holy One of Israel. He has mocked with a loud voice and with "haughtily lifted . . . eyes"! Now the LORD will protect and save Jerusalem, but to Assyria he will be like a devouring fire (cf. 10:17).

37:24-25   Yahweh had surely heard all the haughty words of the king of Assyria as spoken by his servants. The prophet now reminds the king of his own words and deeds, but in reverse, to his own shame.

The king of Assyria had boasted of his "many chariots," with which he could triumph in all his battles, especially on the plains. But even the mountainous and steep parts of the country he could conquer with ease. The hill country of Lebanon, covered by mighty forests, was an example of this. Even the utmost heights of the Lebanon he could reach and conquer without any difficulty, by felling the mighty and precious cedars and cypresses. Such remote forest-covered heights were moreover considered to be the dwelling places of the gods, the protectors of the country in question.

Furthermore the king of Assyria had boasted that even drought could not hinder the progress of the Assyrian army, because even in the desert he was able to dig wells. These wells, which were hidden deep down in the dry earth or sand, could be made to serve the Assyrian armies as could the rivers of Egypt. At the Nile Delta there were many distributaries which emptied into the Mediterranean Sea. At times these rivers (like the Jordan River) could be an obstacle to the advancing armies, especially the great river Nile itself. The Nile was a symbol of the glory of Egypt and Ethiopia, from whose countries Hezekiah expected help. But to the Assyrian armies these mighty waters were just small pools which could be dried up easily by the "sole" of the Assyrian king's foot, his armies (37:25).

Such was the boast of the Assyrian king. In an ironical way the prophet pictured Sennacherib's power as if it was equal to Yahweh's, who had led his people out of Egypt and dried up the Red Sea and had given them water to drink in the desert (Exod. 17:6). By boasting of his great armies and of the multitude of his chariots and horses, the Assyrian king was pictured as if he were on a par with the almighty LORD of Hosts. Nothing whatsoever could hinder him. The poor man did not realize that he was just a tool in the hand of the LORD and that eventually he too would be destroyed (cf. Isa. 30:27-33), as explained in 37:26 (cf. 10:6).

37:26-27   What had been achieved by the Assyrian king was not just accidental or surprising to the LORD, who said: "I determined it long ago," "I planned from days of old." This was indeed the crucial point of difference between Yahweh and all the other gods of the nations. The rhetorical form of the question indicates that this revelation was not secret, but had been known to many peoples. God's revelation had been given to mankind in many ways. Even Sennacherib himself had heard of Yahweh, the God of Israel (cf. 36:15ff.). But this hearing caused misunderstanding in Sennacherib's case; he pretended to have been commissioned by Yahweh to subject all peoples beneath his feet, including Judah (36:10). But to do so Sennacherib should have first humbled himself before Yahweh and glorified him. Instead he had become haughty and boastful, and had even mocked and reviled Yahweh in blasphemous language.

From the viewpoint of the LORD'S plan to punish the nations because of their sins, peoples were powerless to withstand the Assyrian armies. They are described as "tender grass" in the fields now trodden down, withered, and dried up. Grass growing in the mud on the housetops can never grow well, because the plastered clay becomes "scorched before it grows up" (NIV).

37:28-29 The prophet now reprimands Sennacherib. As a tool he must always be under God's control. Nothing that the Assyrian king has done is hidden from God. God knows the deliberations of Sennacherib's heart and his "raging against me." Yahweh is the living God, therefore it is most foolish to try to hide oneself from God (cf. 29:15).

God "knows." The verb "to know" does not mean mere superficial and general knowledge in a rational way. It means a deep personal knowledge of a human life in a comprehensive way, externally and internally, knowledge of the person's private as well as public life (cf. Ps. 139:2ff.).

As such the LORD "knows" the "raging" of Sennacherib's behavior, which comprised mockery, insult, blasphemy, foolish words, and uncontrolled boasts. Therefore Sennacherib too would be punished. He is pictured as a wild beast that has been caught with a hook in its nose and a bit in its mouth. This means that the animal was bridled and forcefully led to the slaughterhouse, dragged back along the same path as it had come before. Concerning the fulfillment of this declaration see Isa. 37:37-38.

A SIGN FOR HEZEKIAH (37:30-32)

Unlike the previous pericope, which is written in poetic form, this one is written in prose. The previous section describes the haughtiness and foolishness of the Assyrian king, who deserved his punishment. The present pericope deals with a sign for King Hezekiah, one that points to the future glory of the so-called remnant of Judah. However, neither pericope (37:21-29, 30-32) gives an answer to Hezekiah's prayer of supplication (v. 20). The answer comes only in the next pericope, which begins in v. 33.

On account of this discontinuity in the narrative order, some interpreters have suggested that vv. 21-29 and 30-32 were later additions inserted into the narrative and adapted to the historical situation being faced by Hezekiah. This might explain why the two pericopes are written in two different literary forms.

37:30 To confirm the faith of Hezekiah and the trustworthiness of the prophetic message of deliverance and renewal for Judah, the LORD now gives a sign to Hezekiah. This sign could be observed in the workings of nature over the following years. Its form was quite normal and understandable. It revealed how long the period of suffering would last and also the time of deliverance as determined by the LORD. During the current year the people would eat "what grows of itself." There would be neither time nor opportunity to plow and sow. After that harvest the soil would lie bare. Nevertheless some grains of wheat would necessarily fall to the ground, and wheat would eventually "grow of itself." In the following year there would still be no opportunity to till the ground and to sow. This would be due to the continuing presence of those enemies who had ravaged the land and had threatened the lives of the peasant people. The peasants had therefore left the country and taken refuge in Jerusalem. Their suffering would then climax. Nevertheless the untilled ground would still bring forth something edible, although very scantily.

In the third year deliverance would come. The enemy would have been driven away, and a remnant of the people could emerge from Jerusalem to till the ground once again, sow it, and reap a harvest.

Based on this description a problem arises concerning the actual length of the time of suffering. Was it to be three years, two years, or one year? According to Assyrian sources the Assyrian armies were in Palestine for only one year. Yet, according to vv. 7-9 which precede and vv. 33-37 which follow, the deliverance of Jerusalem was to come quickly.

One interpretation suggests that the coming of the Assyrian armies happened at the end of the first year after sowing time; this means that the first year actually covered only its few remaining months. The second year would then be the year of real suffering owing to the Assyrian occupation of Judah which lasted until almost the end of the year. People would be able to eat only what "springs of the same." The entire occupation thus covered a period of almost one full year. The suffering of Jerusalem itself and its surrounding villages might then involve a shorter time (Jan Ridderbos, *De profeet Jesaja,* 1).

A figurative and eschatological interpretation suggests that the prophet was seeking to emphasize one main point, namely, that the time of suffering would not be long and the situation would improve gradually thereafter. The following two verses (vv. 31-32) also suggest an eschatological interpretation. Accordingly this sign would indicate the one eschatological reality, that is, that after a time of many struggles the "remnant" of Israel would be renewed and glorified at the end of the times (Otto Kaiser, *Isaiah 13–39,* 396-97).

Both interpretations may be true, as this sign must have involved a historical context as well as an eschatological perspective.

37:31-32 After the final deliverance people will live in peace. They are called "the surviving remnant of the house of Judah" (cf. 10:20-21). They are pictured as a big tree deeply rooted in the ground. This tree will never fall over or wither because of drought; rather, it will grow steadily and "bear fruit upward." This expression denotes that fruitful growth is due to God's grace alone (1 Cor. 3:7), not to the merit of mankind. Such fruit will glorify the LORD (Isa. 37:31).

It is by the use of just such pictorial language that the majority of the peoples of the world today do their own theologizing, a fact that the West must never forget. Consequently these peoples are able to interpret the prophecies of Isaiah in a natural manner. Those in the West can be unaware that their own predisposition is to accept as axiomatic for the interpretation of the OT the scientific Greek-philosophical view of life and faith which they unconsciously bring to the study of Isaiah. On the other hand, that is why throughout the whole of the Third World—both North and South, American Indian and Zulu alike—the Church is able to interpret to its own understanding Isaiah's pictorial theology more nearly than the sophisticated West can do.

The fruits which the "tree" bears are now further described and connected with the mission of the "surviving remnant," the new Israel. The latter will "go forth" out of Jerusalem. A band of survivors will leave Mt. Zion to bear witness to and glorify the great name of the LORD. This of course is exactly the task and the calling of the Church in the world today (cf. Matt. 28:17-20; Acts 1:8; see also the thesis of Trito-Isaiah as discussed in G. A. F. Knight, *The New Israel*).

Finally this prophecy is confirmed by the promise that "the zeal of the LORD of hosts will accomplish this." Two aspects of the LORD's nature are emphasized here, namely, the almightiness and the holiness of God (cf. Isa. 9:7; Deut. 5:9). These two aspects must never be neglected by mankind.

Sennacherib Shall Never Enter Jerusalem
(37:33-35)

As a response to Hezekiah's entreaty, the LORD gives the king an assurance concerning the deliverance of Jerusalem. Sennacherib will not set foot in Jerusalem. The city is to be delivered in a most wonderful way, without any confrontation. As for the Assyrian king himself, he will retreat hastily with his armies following the same route as that by which he had come. There will be no other way left for him to go.

The LORD will do this "for my own sake and for the sake of my servant David." Yahweh has been insulted and despised by Sennacherib, but now all the peoples on earth are to know that Yahweh is the mighty God both of Israel and of the nations. The LORD had made an eternal covenant with David (2 Sam. 7), and Hezekiah was a descendant of that David. So the deliverance of Jerusalem would be closely related to the covenant relationship between Yahweh and Israel. Yahweh is indeed the Almighty and the faithful God, and no one will ever be disappointed who puts his trust in him (cf. Isa. 28:16).

Yahweh Delivers Jerusalem and Punishes the
Assyrians (37:36-38)

These verses describe the fulfillment of Isaiah's prophecies concerning the judgment on Assyria (cf. 10:33; 19:14; 30:31; 31:8). The execution of that judgment was carried out in an unexpected and terrifying manner.

37:36 The slaughter of the Assyrian armies presumably occurred shortly after Isaiah proclaimed the LORD'S answer to Hezekiah. According to 2 Kgs. 19:35 this event happened "that night," which means in one night's time. It reminds us of the execution of the LORD'S judgment at midnight in Egypt when the firstborn sons of the Egyptians were killed (Exod. 12:29). In both cases the LORD himself acted through the angel of the LORD. This was not an ordinary created angel but a form of Yahweh's self-manifestation in particular events. At Isa. 31:8 it had been prophesied that "the Assyrian shall fall by a sword, not of man," and that this sword "shall devour him." Obviously it would be "the sword of the LORD of hosts" himself that would slay the Assyrians (cf. 34:6).

Just how the LORD slew them is not explained. The execution happened at night when everyone slept. There was no living witness of the event. The LORD's judgment was carried out in a mysterious way at an unexpected moment. Its result could be observed only "when men arose early in the morning" the next day. It might have been brought about by two coincidental events, that is, by an epidemic (2 Kgs. 19:35) and by the news which required Sennacherib's immediate presence at home (Isa. 37:7).

The place of slaughter is not mentioned either. There are various possibilities in this regard. It might have been in front of the gates of Jerusalem, or at Libnah where the Assyrian armies encamped (v. 8), at a particular spot between Libnah and Jerusalem, or even near the Egyptian border where Tirhakah and his armies appeared to fight against the Assyrian army (v. 9).

Some interpreters believe that the number of victims (185,000) is an exaggeration because the numbers enlisted in ancient armies were generally much less than this. It is hard to imagine what the miserable consequences of such a great slaughter could be. What really interested the narrator was the fact that Sennacherib withdrew with the rest of his army and returned to Nineveh with all speed (v. 37).

There are still details in this narrative which are obscure and cannot be solved satisfactorily. Yet these may not be important, as the main purpose of the narrator was to point out that Yahweh, the God of Israel, was almighty and that the godless Assyrian king would be despised and finally destroyed by Yahweh. All this happened for the sake of the LORD's holy name, "that all the kingdoms of the earth may know that thou alone art the LORD" (v. 20).

37:37-38   Inevitably Sennacherib and the rest of his army had to withdraw to Nineveh. The Assyrian king never attacked Jerusalem again. He remained in Nineveh till his death, which happened a few years after his shameful retreat. He was murdered by his own son while worshiping "in the house of Nisroch his god"! Nothing could be more tragic and ironical. According to Assyriologists Sennacherib died in 681 B.C. and was succeeded by his son Esarhaddon.

251

HEZEKIAH'S RECOVERY AND TEMPTATION
38:1–39:8

The historical narratives in these closing chapters present some chronological problems. From the preceding chapters (Isa. 36–37) it is clear that the prophet was not aiming to produce a purely historical report, but rather at giving a theological and prophetic reflection on the events recorded in chs. 36–39 (see the chronological problem discussed at 37:9).

The difficulty here concerns the reign of Hezekiah, his sickness, and the coming of the messengers of the Babylonian king Merodach-baladan to Jerusalem. The indications given in the opening verses are obscure. The pericope containing the prayer of Hezekiah after his recovery (38:9-20) seems to have been inserted by the redactor between vv. 1-8 and 21-22. The question arises therefore whether the events recorded in these last two chapters actually took place in chronological sequence after the events as told in chs. 36–37 or whether chs. 38–39 record events which took place independently.

It is generally accepted that the Assyrian king Sennacherib took the fortified cities of Judah in 701 B.C., the fourteenth year of Hezekiah's reign (715-686; Isa. 36:1; 2 Kgs. 18:13). The events as told in Isa. 38–39 would have occurred in the final fifteen years of Hezekiah's reign (cf. 2 Kgs. 18:2), within the context of the Assyrian retreat. (See John Bright, *A History of Israel*, 278; Ehrlich, *A Concise History of Israel*, 59; C. Stanley Thoburn, *The Old Testament Introduction*, 195; John Mauchline, *Isaiah 1–39*, 16.)

But according to 2 Kgs. 18:10 the fall of Samaria into the hands of King Shalmaneser of Assyria occurred in the sixth year of Hezekiah and the ninth year of King Hoshea of Israel. According to the available historical data Samaria fell in 721. Consequently the initial year of Hezekiah could be put at 727 (rather than 715 as suggested above). The arrival of the messengers of Merodach-baladan after Hezekiah's recovery from his sickness in his fourteenth year would then point to 713. If this is the same year that the Assyrians "came up" against Judah and Jerusalem (cf. Isa. 36:1), the king who "came up" would be Sargon instead of Sennacherib. This, however, seems unlikely.

Merodach-baladan was initially head of the Bit-Yakin on the east coast of the Persian Gulf (cf. Jan Ridderbos, *De profeet Jesaja,* 1, *ad loc*), one of the most important of the Chaldean clans which had long been opposed to the Assyrian domination. At the time of Sargon (722-705) Merodach-baladan persuaded the surrounding peoples, especially Syria, to revolt against Assyria. He even declared himself king of Babylon during the early years of Sargon's reign and again following the succession of Sennacherib in 705. Based on the available historical data the arrival of the envoys of Merodach-baladan in Jerusalem could be estimated to have been around 703.

One further problem remains concerning the chronology of Isa. 36–39. According to 2 Kgs. 21:1 Manasseh, Hezekiah's son and successor, reigned fifty-five years at Jerusalem. It is generally agreed that Manasseh reigned until 642, which would mean that he began his reign in 697. Ridderbos *(Jesaja I)* finds it necessary to assume a redactional error in 2 Kgs. 21:1 with respect to the years of Manasseh's reign and suggests that we read instead "forty-five years." This might be more appropriate than any textual correction of 2 Kgs. 18:13 and Isa. 36:1 (concerning the year of the Assyrian invasion or of Hezekiah's illness), for it requires a minimum of correction. This would put the beginning of Manasseh's reign then in 687.

The following conclusions are therefore offered:

1. The period of Hezekiah's reign can be estimated to be 715-686.

2. The illness and recovery of Hezekiah happened shortly before the coming of the envoys of Merodach-baladan.

3. The coming of those envoys took place in 703-702.

4. After these events Sennacherib came up against Judah and Jerusalem in 701.

5. Hezekiah's trusting attitude as described in Isa. 36–37 might be ascribed to his miraculous recovery from his sickness, which he saw as a sign of God's grace.

HEZEKIAH RECOVERS FROM HIS SICKNESS
(38:1-8, 21-22)

This is one of the most interesting stories about Hezekiah in the OT. We learn that he suffered from some incurable disease and was at the point of death. But it pleased God to prolong Hezekiah's life and affirm this promise with a miraculous sign. As such the king's sickness and recovery could be considered as a symbolic act pointing first to Sennacherib's siege of Jerusalem and then to the deliverance of the city at the end of the 8th century. After his recovery Hezekiah's life was just *sola gratia* ("all of grace"), as was the deliverance of Jerusalem from the Assyrians.

The order of verses needs some consideration (cf. 2 Kgs. 1-11). Apparently Isa. 38:21-22 continues the narrative in vv. 1-8; and v. 22 might advisably be read after v. 6. Presumably the last two verses (vv. 21-22) were a later addition based on the testimony of 2 Kgs. 20, as an affirmative supplement that the divine healing of Hezekiah was accompanied by miraculous signs.

38:1 It is not clear what disease afflicted Hezekiah or how long he had been suffering from it. Isaiah 38:21 mentions a malignant "boil" which was incurable and threatened his life. The prophet Isaiah conveys the word of God, announcing that according to natural processes there could be no hope for recovery. So Hezekiah is called to "set his house in order" before he died. This means he was to give his last will and testament to the palace administrator and the other high officials. This was to obviate any confusion in the country if he were to die.

This hard message of death can be a blessing for those who accept it in good faith. Evidently here it is of great spiritual significance for Hezekiah. Being at the point of death, he is no longer concerned with his material wealth. Instead he repents and humbles himself before the LORD, asking for God's grace and aid.

38:2-3 It is quite understandable that Hezekiah should become deeply worried at the approach of death. He turns his face to the wall, prays, and weeps bitterly. He wishes he could have lived longer, because he is aware of his many unfinished tasks and responsibilities. At this time Hezekiah is still young, about thirty-eight years of age

(2 Kgs. 18:2). His country is involved in a political crisis, and Manasseh, his son and eventual successor, is not yet born.

Hezekiah's prayer as recorded in Isa. 38:3 is rather amazing. Why does he not start with a confession of his sins? Why does he first mention his own piety, faithfulness, and righteousness? Apparently his prayer was much longer than what is written here, because in his longer prayer (v. 17) Hezekiah does indeed confess his sins. In chs. 36–38 Hezekiah is described as a pious and faithful king; apparently it is this aspect which is pointed to in this shortened prayer.

According to the general OT view, a long life means a display of God's grace and blessing, while a short life terminated by a sudden or early death is considered to be the sign of a curse from God. Hezekiah realizes that this incurable sickness is a disaster not unrelated to his sins; yet on the other hand he is no less confident that God's grace and faithfulness are far greater than the king's shortcomings and sins. Therefore in faith he struggles with God (cf. Jacob's struggle at Peniel, Gen. 32:22-32), desperately demanding a blessing from God.

38:4-6, 21-22   In the light of 2 Kgs. 20 it is likely that this event happened at the house of God. The LORD'S answer to Hezekiah's prayer seems to have been given immediately (cf. 2 Kgs. 20:4-5). To exhibit the LORD'S faithfulness to the line of David, he will not only heal Hezekiah's boil but also prolong his life by fifteen years. In addition to that the LORD promises deliverance from the Assyrians and the liberation of Jerusalem. These promises are given both for the LORD'S sake and for David's sake (2 Kgs. 20:6). The promise of liberation has little to do with the healing. However it is not without significance. It shows that the Assyrian threat is a point of serious concern for Hezekiah during his sickness, for on his sickbed he is evidently tortured by a worry and concern for his people's future. It shows also a close relationship with Isa. 37, and so we may conclude that this event of healing happened shortly before 701.

It is interesting to note the simple method of healing here. Cakes of figs were commonly used to heal boils and wounds. Their application was a well-tried traditional treatment. How efficacious this treatment was is not clear. The biblical testimony is that the healing of Hezekiah was done by the LORD himself. The miracle of Hezekiah's healing was in curing the incurable.

Hezekiah's request for a sign does not necessarily mean any unbelief. Rather, it shows Hezekiah's humble acknowledgment of his own weakness and dependence on God's grace.

In this matter the attitude of Hezekiah is in sharp contrast to that of his father Ahaz, who rejected any sign at all offered him by the LORD (cf. 7:11ff.). At that time Isaiah had insisted that the LORD give a sign whenever it should please him, one based on his own authority, whether requested or not.

38:7-8   The present sign would confirm the promise of fifteen years of life extension for Hezekiah. This sign was visualized as a miraculous phenomenon in nature. The shadow cast by the sundial would be turned back "ten steps."

The existence of sundials in ancient Babylonia and Assyria is well known. Ahaz, who was a pro-Assyrian ruler, had taken over an Assyrian sundial and brought it to Jerusalem. What this sundial exactly looked like is not totally clear. It had "steps" as time indicators, and the shadow of the sun would fall on these steps. Following the daily course of the sun the shadow would move clockwise from one step to the other. Naturally it would be impossible for the shadow to move back counterclockwise.

It is noteworthy that in the following song of praise by Hezekiah after his recovery this miracle is not even mentioned. It is not clear either what relationship there was between the "ten steps" and the promised life span of fifteen years. Some modern interpreters consider this miracle as a popular legend in the ancient tradition. But what is important to note is the spiritual significance of the sign and the theological message involved in it. The power of death and the continuation of life are under God's control. People must realize this reality and enjoy this present life with deep gratitude in obedience to the LORD. In life and in death the faithful belong to God (cf. Rom. 4:7-9).

THE SONG OF HEZEKIAH (38:9-20)

This passage can be divided as follows: Isa. 38:9, title; vv. 10-15, a lamentation; v. 16, a prayer for healing; vv. 17-20, thanksgiving for recovery.

This song of Hezekiah is not included in 2 Kgs. 20. Most probably it was a later addition from the hands of the redactor who here repeats what has been narrated in the 2 Kings account. This song expresses the pious and trusting attitude of Hezekiah on the one hand and the grace and faithfulness of the LORD on the other.

38:9 The title explains the origin and the time of writing. The phrase "a writing of Hezekiah" does not necessarily mean it was written by Hezekiah himself. The Hebrew prefix *le-* could also mean "concerning" or "for." Moreover Hezekiah had never been a composer of songs or psalms like David. However, apart from the problem of authorship this song reflects what was experienced and felt by Hezekiah during his sickness and after his recovery.

According to the text critical footnote of the MT, Hebrew *miktab* ("writing") is thought to be misplaced here. The footnote suggests a slightly different reading, *miktam,* possibly meaning "a golden poem," which would be in accordance with the beautiful poetic form of the song.

The connotation given to Hezekiah as "king of Judah" also suggests a later time, but likely to have been before the insertion of the closing verses (Isa. 38:21-22).

38:10 The Hebrew verb *amarti* ("I said") denotes a past tense, with reference to the time when Hezekiah was at the point of death (v. 10). At that time he was at "the noontide" of his life. The Hebrew word used here means simply a time of rest for the laborer at noon. Actually Hezekiah at the time was only thirty-eight years old, and so at the peak of human physical strength and mental condition. He had reached only the midpoint of the average human life span. Great achievements could still be expected from him. But exactly at that time the king fell ill and suffered from a most serious and incurable sickness, one that led him "to the gates of Sheol."

38:11 In the OT Sheol is the world of the deceased. It is described as having gates, and these were located at the bottom of the ocean. Those who entered it would never come out again. From Sheol there was no communication with the people living on earth nor with the joys of earthly life. By contrast real life is characterized by a living and loving relationship with God and one's fellow humans.

38:12-15 The expiring of a human life is pictured here in two ways. First, it is pictured as a shepherd's tent which is "plucked up and removed" to another place. A shepherd's tent is just a temporary shelter. It will be plucked up eventually and carried away, leaving the place desolate and uninhabited again. Second, it is pictured in terms of a "weaver" who has finished his work. Then the woven cloth is "cut off" from the loom, "rolled up," and carried away. Human life is like a cloth woven with various colorful motifs and rich decorative designs, woven by God himself.

The pain has penetrated Hezekiah's bones (v. 13). It tortures him night and day and keeps him awake all night. God is depicted as a "lion" that nightly breaks all the king's bones, yet leaves him alone all day. (The RSV footnotes here declare several Hebrew words "obscure.")

No wonder Hezekiah feels increasingly weaker or that his lamenting voice changes from the "clamor" of a swallow or a crane into the soft "moan" of a dove. His eyes become weary of looking upward waiting for the LORD. He feels like an oppressed slave, helpless in his suffering. Nevertheless his hope is still with God who alone could give him "security" and deliverance (v. 14; Hab. 3:17-18). Finally Hezekiah no longer knows what to say to God, because the LORD himself has told him that he had caused the sickness. The LORD "dost bring me to an end" (Isa. 38:12b, 13b), yet this is not the end of the story!

38:16 The reading preserved in the MT is not clear, and the RSV translation is not very lucid either. Apparently there is a shift of emphasis in this verse: the focus is no more on Hezekiah's suffering but rather on the grace of God. Through all his sufferings Hezekiah now feels that he has actually been led closer to God. This knowledge now revives his spirit and makes him feel alive.

Finally he can wholeheartedly return to his prayer: "Oh, restore me to health and make me live!" It is in this yielding to God that he finds his strength again. He has now overcome his sense of helplessness and self-pity. His strains and hectic struggles have now been changed into calm self-surrender to God's mercy (cf. Amos 5:4, 6)!

38:17-20   These verses express Hezekiah's thanksgiving after the promise of healing has been realized in a wonderful way. Now he can see the meaning of the great bitterness he has had to endure (Lam. 3:31-32). He says, "Lo (NIV 'Surely'), it was for my welfare" (Isa. 38:17). This welfare is understood in a physical as well as in a spiritual sense. Hezekiah now knows the close relationship that obtains between suffering and sin, between sin and death. The welfare he now enjoys is putting him in a right relationship with God because "thou hast cast all my sins behind thy back." This means forgiveness and salvation held him back from "the pit of destruction" (Sheol). Once people experience this physical-spiritual wholeness and welfare they can truly praise the LORD for all his amazing grace and bountiful blessings.

No such life is possible in Sheol, where everything comes to an end. The OT description of the circumstances of the deceased aims only at emphasizing the importance and the beauty of human life on earth. It is while alive that mankind should praise the LORD and dedicate all of life to the service and glory of God. The OT does teach that the power of God is expressed even in Sheol (e.g., Ps. 49:15; 139:8). Yet the OT reveals the practical reality that whenever body and soul become disintegrated by sin then the organic functions of the human body begin to descend into Sheol (cf. Isa. 6:5).

Hezekiah recovered from his sickness and enjoyed a new life and a new spirit, just as if he had passed through death to life. Such a life of gratitude and praise knows no limitations. It can be continued from generation to generation. It is the duty of the parents to "make known to the children" God's faithfulness. Such too is the binding tradition of Christian education within the family (cf. Deut. 6:6-7; Ps. 73:15; Isa. 46:3).

The closing verse (38:20) expresses Hezekiah's conviction and commitment to praise the LORD all the days of his life. Such is the thankful response of Hezekiah and of his people to God's saving

259

THE LORD IS SAVIOR

act. Hezekiah's reformation once more rehabilitated the temple cult with all its music and choirs to go forward according to the ancient Yahweh tradition (2 Chr. 29:30).

Hezekiah's bitterness has been turned into abundant joy and gladness! Expressed in the form of a poem, its wording assures us of God's saving love both now and in all eternity.

Chapter 39 is worded very closely to 2 Kgs. 20:12-19. As the closing chapter of the First Book of Isaiah it serves as a link to the second part of the book of Isaiah, which begins at ch. 40. If ch. 38 provides a clarifying background of the pious attitude of King Hezekiah as described in chs. 36–37, this closing chapter presents a description of Hezekiah's political attitude towards the king of Babylon. His piety does not come to the fore. On the contrary, Hezekiah is now reprimanded by the prophet Isaiah. Here Hezekiah gives the impression of being rather materialistic and egotistic. As the reformer Martin Luther so often emphasized, a forgiven sinner is still a sinner.

Thus in chs. 36–39 we are presented with two contrasting pictures of Hezekiah. This evokes the question whether or not the two parts, chs. 36–38 and ch. 39, are in fact one continuous story. It has been estimated that the visit of Merodach-baladan took place after Hezekiah recovered from his sickness. But this chapter also announces the fall of Judah and the consequent Babylonian Exile. The latter gives the impression of being a prophecy from an exilic or postexilic date, after the fall of Judah had been realized. If this assumption is right, we can then understand how there are two different pictures of Hezekiah's faith and practice. The Deuteronomic redactor of 1–2 Kings links the fall of Judah in 586 B.C. to the attitude of Hezekiah when he welcomed Merodach-baladan into Jerusalem. Apparently the redactor of First Isaiah here inserts this event from 2 Kings uncritically.

HEZEKIAH'S FAITH TESTED (39:1-2)

The visit of the envoys of Merodach-baladan to Jerusalem evokes many interpretations, as we have seen in our discussion of Isa. 38. We are given no clear time indication in 39:1. According to our prevous conclusion the envoys arrived in Jerusalem around 703

B.C. At that time Merodach-baladan had succeeded in reoccupying the throne of the Babylonian kingdom and for the time being delivered it from Assyrian domination.

Apparently the primary aim of this visit was not a courtesy call to Hezekiah after his recovery and the bringing of royal gifts from the Babylonian king. Rather, the Babylonian king's motivations were strongly political. The letters the envoys had to convey most likely contained political persuasions advising Hezekiah to join in a common revolt against Assyria. Indeed Judah had felt the Assyrian yoke to be increasingly heavy and unbearable. At that time Merodach-baladan realized his weak position in opposing the Assyrian counterattack. Around 700 the Assyrian king Sennacherib actually defeated Babylon. Merodach-baladan had to escape and never returned to Babylon.

39:2 Hezekiah felt very much honored by the visit of the envoys from Babylon. They had come from a far and great country! They carried royal gifts and personal letters and congratulations from the king of Babylon on Hezekiah's recovery. Hezekiah felt both happy and flattered. Moreover, considered from the political viewpoint, the political persuasions were no less attractive. Hezekiah had been expecting help from Egypt to join him in his stand against Assyria (cf. 30:1-7). Therefore these new proposals were welcomed by Hezekiah with great enthusiasm. As before (cf. 30:1-4) Hezekiah did not consult the prophet Isaiah for the LORD'S counsel (cf. 28:9-10). Instead he opened up the royal treasury and showed the embassy all his treasures and his precious oil, even the whole armory not only in the palace but also in the storehouses throughout the whole country. Indeed, Hezekiah was very proud of his material wealth.

If we consider the content of Hezekiah's song in ch. 38, then we would expect him to testify to the LORD'S faithfulness and wonderful blessings. But we do not hear one single word of such a testimony here.

DIALOGUE BETWEEN HEZEKIAH AND ISAIAH (39:3-4)

After the departure of the envoys the prophet Isaiah came to see Hezekiah. Undoubtedly Isaiah had heard about the visit of the envoys and the way Hezekiah had welcomed them.

In response to Isaiah's question, "What did these men say?" Hezekiah only explains that the envoys have come a long distance. Hezekiah here is not showing himself to be a faithful king. His answer merely expresses his pride and pleasure in the "show business" he has displayed to the envoys. This attitude of Hezekiah gives reason for the following prophetic utterance in vv. 5-7.

Again we are faced with the problem of time. If this display of Hezekiah's treasures happened around 703-702 B.C. then it would be difficult to link it with what we are told in 2 Kgs. 18:15-16, namely, that at that time Hezekiah "gave him (i.e., Sennacherib) all the silver that was found in the house of the LORD, and in the treasuries of the king's house." Here we meet some obscurities in the historical data which cannot be solved satisfactorily. The historical narrative in Isa. 36 does not mention the surrender of all his silver, as mentioned in 2 Kgs. 18. It is not clear whether this obscurity was due to inaccurate redactional activity or to the possible existence of different traditions about Hezekiah.

THE PROPHECY CONCERNING THE BABYLONIAN EXILE
(39:5-7)

The visit of Isaiah to Hezekiah was not intended as a personal reproach, but to announce "the word of the LORD of hosts." This name reminded Hezekiah of the almightiness of Yahweh in heaven and on earth, who reigned over all nations and over their history—meaning Assyria, Egypt, and Babylonia, as well as Judah.

There is a bit of irony in this record. Precisely at the time when Hezekiah proudly showed all his wealth and treasures to the Babylonian envoys in order to get help from Babylon, the prophet announced that eventually all those very treasures and the glory of Judah would be carried away to Babylonia and that his descendants too would be carried away as slaves to the Babylonian king. The country from which Hezekiah was then expecting help would eventually attack Judah and take his people into exile. This is the same warning Isaiah had given to Hezekiah's father Ahaz in relation to Egypt. After the downfall of Nineveh in 612 B.C. the Neo-Babylonian kingdom achieved absolute power. In 597 King Jehoiachin of Judah was carried away into exile in Babylonia. Afterwards in 587/6 Jerusalem fell into the hands of Babylonia and all the authorities, including the royal family, together with all their treasures and the holy equipment of the temple were carried off as booty.

As such, then, this message can serve as a link to Deutero-Isaiah, which stems from the end of the exilic period and deals with God's promise of deliverance from exile.

HEZEKIAH'S RESPONSE (39:8)

The response of Hezekiah to the prophetic message, as told in this verse, shows both a positive and a negative side. He says, "The word of the LORD which you have spoken is good." This answer seems rather ambiguous. Does it suggest regret and repentance? Or does it express Hezekiah's acknowledgment of a general truth, uttered to satisfy the prophet rather than to express real repentance? Most interpretations understand it in a positive way and believe it to express Hezekiah's willingness and openness towards the prophet, resulting in real repentance.

But some critical interpretations suggest that Hezekiah was in fact not very impressed by the prophetic message, in that the prophecy dealt with future matters which were not likely to happen in his time. This impression finds its support in the second part of the verse, where Hezekiah naively informs us of his self-satisfaction and reveals his egoism. His attitude towards the future of the kingdom of Judah and towards his own descendants seems to be indifferent. However, it should be noticed that these words are not *spoken* by Hezekiah himself; "for he *thought*" might be a comment of the redactor. The MT reads, "And he said, 'There *may be* peace . . .'" If we read this sentence of the MT as a wish or a prayer, then it reflects Hezekiah's faith and dependence on Yahweh. He wishes only for peace and security in the country during his lifetime. This can be realized only if Hezekiah puts his trust wholeheartedly in Yahweh, aware that the LORD is the only safe stronghold for all believers.

Thus ends the First Book of Isaiah. May all believers of all ages wholeheartedly affirm what is written in this closing verse: "The word of the LORD which you have spoken is good" and "may peace and security be in my days." There is indeed a close relationship between the Word of God and peace and security in human life. We must not forget that our long book is neither by Isaiah nor about Isaiah. It is about God, and in an ultimate sense it is by God. The name Isaiah *(Yesha'yahu)* means "The LORD is Savior." Second or Deutero-Isaiah (chs. 40–55) therefore continues, when Israel is in exile (39:6), to report on the saving acts of the LORD.

SELECTED BIBLIOGRAPHY

Bright, John. *A History of Israel,* 3rd ed. (Philadelphia: Westminster and London: SCM, 1981).

————. "Isaiah–I," in *Peake's Commentary on the Bible,* ed. H. H. Rowley and Matthew Black (New York and London: Nelson, 1952), 489-515.

Childs, Brevard S. *Isaiah and the Assyrian Crisis.* Studies in Biblical Theology, 2nd series 3 (Naperville: Allenson and London: SCM, 1967).

Ehrlich, Ernest L. *A Concise History of Israel from the Earliest Times to the Destruction of the Temple in A.D. 70.* (New York: Harper & Row and London: Darton, Longman & Todd, 1962).

Hayes, John Haralson, and Irvine, Stuart I. *Isaiah, the Eighth-century Prophet: His Times and His Preaching* (Nashville: Abingdon, 1987).

Kaiser, Otto. *Isaiah 13–39.* Old Testament Library (Philadelphia: Westminster and London: SCM, 1974).

Knight, George A. F. *The New Israel: A Commentary on the Book of Isaiah 56–66.* International Theological Commentary (Grand Rapids: Wm. B. Eerdmans and Edinburgh: Handsel, 1985).

————. *Servant Theology: A Commentary on the Book of Isaiah 40–55.* International Theological Commentary (Grand Rapids: Wm. B. Eerdmans and Edinburgh: Handsel, 1984).

Mauchline, John. *Isaiah 1–39.* Torch Bible Commentaries (London: SCM, 1962).

Millar, William R. *Isaiah 24–27 and the Origin of Apocalyptic.* Harvard Semitic Monographs 11 (Missoula: Scholars Press, 1976).

Ridderbos, Jan. *De profeet Jesaja,* 2 vols. Korte Verklaring der Heilige Schrift (1922-1926; repr. Kampen: Kok, 1952).

Scott, R. B. Y. "The Book of Isaiah Chapters 1–39: Introduction and Exegesis," in *The Interpreter's Bible,* ed. George A. Buttrick, 5 (Nashville: Abingdon, 1956), 151-381.

Thoburn, C. Stanley. *Old Testament Introduction.* The Christian Students' Library 24 (Madras: Christian Literature Society, 1961).

Vriezen, Theodorus C. "Essentials of the Theology of Isaiah," in *Israel's Prophetic Heritage: Essays in Honor of James Muilenburg,* ed. Bernhard W. Anderson and Walter Harrelson (New York: Harper & Row and London: SCM, 1962), 128-46.

Young, Edward J. *The Book of Isaiah,* 3 vols. (Grand Rapids: Wm. B. Eerdmans, 1965-1972).